GOD & NATURE

G. F. STOUT

GOD & NATURE

BY

G. F. STOUT

THE SECOND OF TWO VOLUMES
(THE FIRST BEING 'MIND & MATTER')
BASED ON THE GIFFORD LECTURES DELIVERED
IN THE UNIVERSITY OF EDINBURGH
IN 1919 AND 1921

Edited by

A. K. STOUT

With a memoir by

J. A. PASSMORE

CAMBRIDGE
AT THE UNIVERSITY PRESS
1952

PUBLISHED BY
THE SYNDICS OF THE CAMBRIDGE UNIVERSITY PRESS
London Office: Bentley House, N.W. I
American Branch: New York
Agents for Canada, India and Pakistan: Macmillan

Printed in Great Britain at the University Press, Cambridge
(Brooke Crutchley, University Printer)

CONTENTS

BOOK ONE
INTRODUCTORY

Chapter I

ETHICAL NEUTRALITY AND PRAGMATISM

Chapter II

AGNOSTICISM, LEGITIMATE AND ILLEGITIMATE

BOOK TWO

THE UNITY OF THE UNIVERSE

Chapter III

THE HEGELIAN DOCTRINE

Chapter IV

RUSSELL'S SCEPTICAL THEORY
OF KNOWLEDGE

Chapter V

UNIVERSALS, PARTICULARS AND
POSSIBILITIES

BOOK THREE

MATTER AND OUR KNOWLEDGE OF IT

Chapter VI

NEO-REALISM AND
THE BERKELEY-MILL THEORY

Chapter VII

HOW ARE PHYSICAL OBJECTS INITIALLY KNOWN?

Chapter VIII

EXTERNAL AND INTERNAL PERCEPTION

Chapter IX

CORRELATION OF EXTERNAL DATA
(*a*) CAUSAL RELATIONS

Chapter X

CORRELATION OF EXTERNAL DATA
(*b*) NON-CAUSAL PROPERTIES OF
PHYSICAL OBJECTS

Chapter XI

THE STATUS OF SENSA

BOOK FOUR

THE UNIVERSAL CORRELATION OF MIND AND MATTER

Chapter XII

THE RELATION OF THE MIND TO ITS OWN SENSA

Chapter XIII

MIND-STUFF THEORIES AND MONADISM

Chapter XIV

THE CONCEPTION OF A UNIVERSAL MIND

Chapter XV

BODY AND MIND, AND THE DEPENDENCE OF FINITE INDIVIDUALS ON A UNIVERSAL MIND

BOOK FIVE

MIND AND OUR KNOWLEDGE OF IT

Chapter XVI

OUR KNOWLEDGE OF OURSELVES, OTHER MINDS AND GOD

Chapter XVII

COGNITIVE UNITY AS IMPLYING THE UNITY OF THE UNIVERSE

Chapter XVIII

IDEALISM AND THE UNIVERSAL MIND

Chapter XIX

UNITY OF INTEREST AS IMPLYING THE UNITY OF THE UNIVERSE

Chapter XX

MENTAL CONFLICT AND MENTAL DISSOCIATION

EDITORIAL PREFACE

G. F. Stout's *Mind and Matter*, published in 1931, is described on the title-page as 'the first of two volumes based on the Gifford Lectures delivered in the University of Edinburgh in 1919 and 1921'. It was a new work, based indeed on both courses as delivered, but including no verbatim transcription from either. In the Preface the author explained that he was confining himself in this first volume 'to an examination of certain aspects of ordinary experience —those involved in the knowledge of the physical world, of the self and of minds other than our own'. He reserved 'the express treatment of more ultimate problems for a future work to be entitled *God and Nature*'.

My father never set himself to write a new book in fulfilment of this promise. Much of the ground he intended to cover had been treated in those parts of the original Lectures which he had not used in writing *Mind and Matter*, and it was understood between us that if they had not been published before his death I was to edit them for publication. (He was already past his seventy-first birthday when *Mind and Matter* was published.) When he visited St John's College, Cambridge (of which he was an Honorary Fellow) in 1938, he told friends who asked him about the promised sequel to *Mind and Matter* that he was not sure that he would himself be able to publish the Lectures, but that he had left them in a state in which they could be published.

He had gone through the Lectures with me in 1935, and it was then that he discarded the four Lectures of the First Course (II–V) which dealt with Materialism, saying, 'These are no good now'—because they were replaced by the reconsidered and fuller treatment in *Mind and Matter*. At various times between the publication of *Mind and Matter* and his sailing for Sydney with myself and my family in

1939—-but earlier in this period rather than later—he made a number of revisions in and additions to the typescript (none of them on a large scale), deleted some passages and marked others for further consideration. Although he was still writing articles and carrying on a philosophical correspondence until within a few weeks of his death in August 1944, he did not again turn his attention to the Giffords. He had a distaste for going back to what he had already written (it will be remembered that he left the preparation of new editions of the *Manual of Psychology* in other hands); and of course conditions were very unfavourable for publishing during the war—especially when the author was living at the other end of the earth from his publishers.

My material, then, for the present volume has been the two courses of Gifford Lectures (less the four chapters on Materialism in the First Course), pretty much as they were originally written. My problem has been to produce from this a volume which, while fulfilling the promise made in the Preface of *Mind and Matter*, would not unduly repeat the argument of that work and would yet be coherent and so far as possible self-contained. It has not been possible to fulfil the last two of these requirements without some relaxation of the first, and some of the ground covered in *Mind and Matter* is traversed also in the present book. This applies mainly to Book III, on 'Matter and our Knowledge of it', which corresponds in its general topic with Book IV of *Mind and Matter*. But the treatment is on the whole sufficiently different, even where basically the same theory is being developed (e.g. in the chapter on 'External and Internal Perception'), to justify the hope that those readers who are familiar with *Mind and Matter* will not feel that they are being cheated, but will agree with me that both treatments are valuable, not only in themselves, but for the light that each throws on the other.

God and Nature is of course intended as the completion of a line of inquiry started in *Mind and Matter*, and even if it had been rewritten it would have assumed some acquaintance with the general argument of that book. But in fact, with one qualification, it can 'stand on its own legs' as a self-contained work. The one important argument of *Mind and Matter* which it presupposes is the criticism and rejection of Materialism in Book II and Book IV, Chapter VII.

The following passage from the last Section ('Ultimate Problems') of *Mind and Matter*, pp. 314–15, shows how the argument against Materialism was intended to pave the way for some of the questions discussed in *God and Nature*.

It has been a main contention of the present work that this inseparable intermingling of continuity and discontinuity between experiencing individuals and other parts of nature cannot be simply accepted as an ultimate fact concerning which there is nothing more to say. . . . There is a question, and one that calls for an answer more imperatively than any other. The direction in which an answer is to be sought may be gathered from what I have already said in the present work, more especially in the argument against Materialism. Mind, as I maintain, must be fundamental in the Universe of Being and not derivative from anything that is not mind. If we discard mind-stuff theories as failing to account for individual selves, and monadism as failing to account for anything else, we are bound to posit one universal and eternal Mind developing and expressing itself in the world of finite and changeable beings which we call Nature. But at this point there are two alternatives between which we have to decide. The Universal Mind may be ascribed to Nature itself; this implies that Nature, in spite of the endless multiplicity of distinct existences which it comprehends, is a self-contained unity. Any such view seems to break down under intolerable difficulties. The alternative is to deny that Nature is the entire Universe of Being, and to recognise that it cannot exist at all or be what it is apart from a Being beyond it and distinct from it. This Being, whatever else it is, must be an eternal and universal Mind, giving to Nature, through and through, a character which is otherwise inexplicable.

Apart from the four Lectures on Materialism rejected by the author himself, I have included in this volume all but about ninety pages of the original quarto typescript. In almost all the passages that I have rejected there have been marks of some kind made by the author to indicate dissatisfaction. A large number of passages have simply been marked off with square brackets, but with nothing to indicate whether this was merely a sign that they should be omitted in lecturing, or whether they were to be revised or possibly deleted. In interpreting marks of this kind I have in general preferred the risk of including what the author would finally have left out to that of excluding what he would have retained.

Chapters i–v and xiii–xiv belong to the First Course of Lectures, the rest of the book to the Second Course; Chapters xiii and xiv originally came between the discarded Lectures on Materialism (which immediately followed the opening Lecture on Ethical Neutrality) and the Lecture on Agnosticism which has now become Chapter ii. I have moved them to the place they now occupy (making the necessary minor consequential changes) in order to bring together the arguments about a Universal Mind. I do not claim that this rearrangement is completely satisfactory, but I think that it is better than any other. The only other major transference I have made is to bring forward as Chapter xvi what was originally the last Lecture of all. I have given my reasons for doing this in a footnote at the beginning of the chapter in question.

It might seem at first sight that there was a similar case for moving Book ii ('The Unity of the Universe') nearer to the further treatment of the same subject in Book v. But, apart from the difficulty of doing this without breaking some of the threads of the argument, the motive for bringing the two treatments together loses force when it is realised that: (1) Book ii does not itself offer positive arguments for accepting the hypothesis that the Universe is a Unity, but prepares the way for them by expounding and refuting arguments which would exclude this hypothesis; and (2) the long discussion in Book iii of the nature of matter and the way in which we know it is undertaken, not primarily for its own sake, but to prepare the way for establishing the universal correlation of mind and matter, and so ultimately the unity of the universe.

Most of Book II is a detailed exposition and criticism of certain arguments supporting pluralism in Bertrand Russell's book *The Problems of Philosophy*. Since this is an early work of Lord Russell's, and his position has changed in certain respects since its publication, I wrote to him suggesting that he might like to see these and other chapters in which he is a target, and possibly write something in reply. He answered asking me to send them to him, and with his permission I quote here from the letter he wrote to me after he had read them, in which he explains why he prefers not to write about them for publication:

I have read the six chapters you sent me with great interest, and am glad to have seen them. I am sorry I do not feel I can write about them for publication. My views are not what they were, and a good deal of rather tedious explanation would be needed. I could not defend myself—so far as I still think my past self defensible—at all briefly, and I incline to think that what working time remains to me ought to be spent rather on the future than the past. But I hope you will not take this as implying any underestimate of the importance of your father's work.

In order to make it easier to find references to chapters, I have numbered the chapters consecutively from I to XXI, instead of following the practice of *Mind and Matter* and beginning each Book with a new Chapter I. In every other respect I have preserved the form of *Mind and Matter*. This has entailed my dividing the work as a whole into books (and giving them titles), and the chapters into sections, and inserting section-headings throughout. In addition, I am editorially responsible for most of the chapter-titles, some of the divisions into chapters (which do not always correspond with the original divisions into Lectures—especially in the Second Course) and much of the paragraphing.

My father sent the typescript of the Second Course of Lectures, after its delivery, to James Ward, who wrote many brief and often illuminating marginal comments on them, one or two of the less caustic of which I have quoted in footnotes. Ward had constant difficulty in deciphering my father's minute, tailing-off pencilled emendations, and did not hesitate to say so. ('Your scribbled emendations I find almost invariably illegible', 'Pencilling as usual illegible', etc.) One particular outburst, which I remember amused the culprit himself when he read it, bears witness to a growing feeling of exasperation with which as Editor I have had occasion to sympathise, even if as a son I prefer to leave it to another to express here: 'A man who doesn't dot his *ii* or cross his *tt* is bad enough, but what is one to say when he crosses his *dd*?' Long familiarity with my father's handwriting and with his modes of expression has enabled me in the end to decipher almost everything beyond reasonable doubt, and only rarely—sometimes because of inaccuracies in the typing—have I been uncertain of the author's *ipsissima verba* and had to fall back on conjecture. I have only troubled the reader with a footnote to say so when the meaning has been in doubt.

It has given me great pleasure that my friend and former colleague at Sydney, Professor John Passmore, for whom my father had a high regard, acceded to my request to contribute a memoir of him for this volume.

I wish to express my gratitude to my friend, Dr A. C. Ewing, for helping me by reading through the typescript that I had prepared from the original Lectures, and making valuable comments and suggestions, on almost all of which I have acted; to my friend and colleague, Mr John Mackie, for his skilled help and advice in the revision of the proofs; and to the Senate of the University of Sydney for making a grant to cover typing expenses.

A. K. STOUT

SYDNEY
June 1951

MEMOIR

GEORGE FREDERICK STOUT
1860–1944[1]

BY J. A. PASSMORE

'The autobiography of a man whose business is thinking' wrote Collingwood, 'should be the story of his thought'; and the biographer may well be guided by the same principle. Stout, one can feel sure, would have approved. He was a man not given to talking about his own life; the conversation in which he delighted, to the very end, was philosophical discussion, not personal anecdote. It is typical that his biography in the *Psychological Register* does not, in all respects, conform with the entry in *Who's Who;* no doubt Stout supplied both sets of information in good faith, but with that indifference to minor details which was one of his endearing, although occasionally infuriating, characteristics.

He was born in South Shields, Durham, England, on 6 January 1860; the substantial record of his life begins in 1879, when he entered St John's College, Cambridge. His record as an undergraduate was exceptionally brilliant. He obtained First Class Honours in the Classical Tripos,

[1] This Memoir is based on one contributed to the *Australasian Journal of Psychology and Philosophy* in September 1944. But it has been considerably extended, and now bears few traces of its origin. I knew Stout only in the last years of his life; my memoir should be read in conjunction with Professor Mace's in the *Proceedings of the British Academy*, vol. xxxi, and his obituary notice in the *British Journal of Psychology*, vol. xxvi, no. 2, Professor C. D. Broad's note in *Mind*, vol. liv, no. 215, Professor Wright's obituary in *Nature*, October 1944 and that of Professor Rex Knight in *The British Journal of Educational Psychology*, vol. xvi, pt. ii. I have made some use of Stout's correspondence, and much use of the help freely given to me by his son, Professor A. K. Stout.

with special distinction in Ancient Philosophy, and went on to First Class Honours in the Moral Sciences Tripos, again with special distinction, this time in Metaphysics. In 1884, St John's elected him to a Fellowship.

Two Cambridge teachers he particularly esteemed: James Ward and Henry Sidgwick. Stout always emphasised his indebtedness to Ward, even to the point of exaggeration. He wrote to Mrs Ward: 'I do not approach your husband's work as an external critic, but rather as a disciple seeking and in a large measure finding in it a basis from which to develop his own.'[1] Ward showed Stout what a philosophical psychology should be like; he set Stout the tasks on which he was mainly to concentrate, and taught him the methods he was principally to employ. But Stout's 'discipleship' was so critical and independent that the term is scarcely applicable; it would be less misleading to think of him, simply, as Ward's heir and successor in a tradition which has persisted in British philosophy since the time of Hobbes. He wrote very little on ethics, and had no public occasion to insist upon his indebtedness to Sidgwick, but he liked to draw attention in conversation to Sidgwick's qualities as a teacher and as a thinker. The moral atmosphere of liberal Utilitarianism, so congenial to his eminently unfanatical, optimistic temperament, pervades Stout's work, even though his ethics is not explicitly formulated as doctrine.

Another young philosopher, Samuel Alexander, was by now disturbing Lincoln College, Oxford, with his psychological experiments; and the two philosopher-psychologists soon conjoined as allies in defence of psychology and in opposition to Oxford apriorism. Alexander was later to abandon the epistemological approach to philosophy, to which Stout always remained faithful, but he had learnt a great deal from Stout, even if it was not precisely what Stout had wanted to teach him. In the course of expounding his conational theory of knowledge, Alexander

[1] *Studies*, p. 127.

writes:[1] 'The whole discussion is founded on Mr Stout's treatment of perception in connexion with impulse or instinctive action; one of the greatest contributions that have been made to psychology.' On this passage, we have Stout's comment: 'This statement plainly suggests that Alexander regards his own doctrine as essentially only a further development of mine, so that whereas I have stopped at a half-way house he has gone to the end. There is no hint that his view is in radical conflict with mine and that if he is fundamentally right, I am fundamentally wrong.'[2] Here in the last, but by no means the least vigorous, of his writings, we catch an echo of the lively controversies of his younger days. He admired Alexander greatly, but his admiration was not unmixed with exasperation. It is significant that when it fell to his lot to describe Alexander's philosophical achievement, Stout concentrated on his epistemology. Of his ontology, he writes: 'What he says corresponds to nothing in my experience. It is all in the air, or rather in an airless region in which I at any rate find myself suffocated.'[3]

Stout's first articles began to appear in 1888, and he wrote freely in the next few years both for the Aristotelian Society and for *Mind*. It was clear from the beginning what his main interests were to be. Body and mind, mind and consciousness, the cognition of physical reality—these were the topics on which he began to write, and on them he dwelt most happily in his Gifford Lectures over thirty years later. His views were to alter in a great many respects, but he never lost his conviction that epistemology was the key both to philosophy and to psychology. 'Psychology', so he wrote in the introduction to his *Analytic Psychology*, 'investigates the history of

[1] *Space, Time and Deity*, vol. ii, p. 119 n.
[2] 'Alexander's Theory of Mind and Knowledge', 1944 (p. 22). Page references in parentheses are to the journals in which the articles appeared. See List of Stout's Works, p. l.
[3] 'The Philosophy of Samuel Alexander', 1940 (p. 144).

individual consciousness, and this coincides with the history of the process through which the world comes to be presented in consciousness.... When, on the other hand, the nature of knowledge is considered apart from its genesis, it becomes the subject-matter, not of psychology, but of metaphysics.' And in *God and Nature*, 'We shall inquire what is logically prior in our knowledge of the material world, and examine the logical nature and conditions of the process by which we reach that view of it which is now taken for granted by common-sense and the sciences. In this way, we may hope to gain some answer to the questions what matter ultimately is, and how it is ultimately related to mind within the unity of the universe.' Through knowledge to its constituents: that is Stout's psychological method—'a plain historical account', as Locke put it. Through knowledge to its logical conditions: that is Stout's method in philosophy.

Stout quickly established his reputation as a philosopher and a psychologist; so that when, in 1891, Croom Robertson relinquished the editorship of *Mind*, Stout was asked, and consented, to succeed him. The appointment was a particularly appropriate one. *Mind* had been founded by Alexander Bain, and, as its name suggests, his special concern was to provide a medium for the publication of contributions to psychology. 'Nothing less, in fact,' Robertson had made it clear in the first number, 'is aimed at in the publication of *Mind* than to procure a decision of the question as to the scientific standing of psychology.' Stout could appreciate and give expression to this intention: at the same time, as circumstances converted *Mind* into a purely philosophical journal, he could move with it into its new sphere.

Robertson's editorial farewell was not at all optimistic about *Mind's* future prospects; Stout was to find that a successful editor must be something of a diplomat. Sensitive authors, like Münsterberg, had to be soothed, when they felt themselves to have been personally insulted by their reviewers; ultra-pernickety authors, like Lewis Carroll, had to be assured that the printers would respect their wishes; and, above all, Cambridge must be persuaded that the formation of the Mind Association was not a dark Oxford conspiracy. But by the time Stout handed over the editorship to Moore, he could feel that *Mind* had an assured position as the leading philosophical journal, and that its prestige was in no small measure the product of his own editorial skill.

St John's College re-elected Stout to his Fellowship in 1893, and in 1894 he was appointed as University Lecturer in the Moral Sciences. Rather to the surprise of his friends, and a little to the consternation of those who feared for the future of *Mind*, he left Cambridge in 1896 for Aberdeen, to take up the Anderson Lectureship in Comparative Psychology. 'Aberdeen', wrote Adamson, 'is fortunate beyond its deserts.' But Stout felt that at Cambridge he was not free to develop the teaching of psychology as he wished to develop it; the new Lectureship gave him considerable independence and was not encumbered by tradition. The atmosphere was sympathetic, for this was the University in which Bain had taught; the Lectureship was dedicated to a special field of inquiry which at that time particularly interested him. When, in that same year, he wrote the Preface to his *Analytic Psychology*, he remarked that 'My strongest psychological interest lies in certain genetic questions, and especially in those on which ethnographic evidence can be brought to bear'. The Herbartian ethnographic psychologists—Waitz, Lazarus, Steinthal—were at this time exerting a powerful influence upon him, and, for that reason, a Lectureship in Comparative Psychology had its special attractions. But Stout and Alexander had by now persuaded Oxford that there might, after all, be such a subject as Psychology; and in 1899 Stout left Aberdeen to become the first Wilde Reader in Mental Philosophy.

'I should never have expected', wrote McTaggart, 'so sensible an election for Oxford, the way they have been going on lately.' That same year Stout married Ella Ker, a marriage which, from all accounts, was not the least of his good fortune.

The Aberdeen years bore fruit in the shape of what is certainly his best-known work, *A Manual of Psychology*. In the Preface to his *Analytic Psychology* he explains that he had at first intended 'to follow the genetic order of treatment', but soon discovered that he must first undertake 'a preparatory analysis of the developed consciousness...as a clue to the nature of mental process at lower levels'. The *Analytic*, he went on to say, 'must be regarded as a fragment of a larger whole. This will explain certain omissions which might otherwise appear strange. I have passed by whatever appeared capable of more efficient treatment from a genetic point of view'.

The *Manual* must be read with this explanation in mind. 'The present work', Stout says of the *Manual*, 'contains an exposition of Psychology from a genetic point of view.' It is not, in any sense, a summary account of Stout's psychology; it is his genetic as opposed to his analytic psychology. Certain sections of the *Analytic* are, of course, represented in the *Manual*, because genetic psychology, so Stout has argued, must rest on analytic psychology. But one should not speak, as Spearman does, of Stout as 'dropping' from his 'more comprehensive' *Manual* the theory of analogy (which, incidentally, Spearman describes as 'the most valuable work hitherto done on the matter'[1]) developed in the *Analytic*; that theory finds no place in the scheme of the *Manual*, but this does not at all imply that Stout had abandoned it. Stout never ceased to regret that, in the *Manual*, he allowed himself 'to be influenced by the fashionable prejudice against introducing general philosophical discussion into a text-book on psychology—against what is called "mixing Psychology

[1] *The Nature of Intelligence and Principles of Cognition*, p. 105 n.

with Metaphysics'''.[1] (Most probably, it was Bradley's polemics to which he is here obliquely referring.) Both because he succumbed to this prejudice, and because the emphasis in the *Manual* was genetic, the *Manual* by itself is not a sufficient guide to Stout's psychology.

Still less should the *Manual* be regarded as a text-book of the ordinary sort, a guide to 'received opinion'. It is an original contribution to psychology and one which, through its unusually wide circulation for half a century as a University text, has exerted a pervasive influence upon modern psychology. To think of it as 'the traditional psychology' or as 'the sort of thing philosophers say about psychology' is to obscure Stout's contributions to psychology and to suggest, falsely, that Stout's views are 'the verdict of philosophy'.

The same must be said of Stout's contributions to Baldwin's *Dictionary of Philosophy and Psychology*. These are so numerous that it is impossible to list them separately, but his contributions to 'A' will indicate their scope: Abstract Idea, Abstraction, Accommodation, Activity, Affection, Analytic judgment, Apperception, Association, Associationism, Attention and Attitude. Each contribution has a distinctive Stoutian flavour; they exerted influence, however, not as 'Stout's view', but as dictionary definitions.

The *Analytic* and the *Manual* were now out of the way, and Stout's interests began to turn more and more to epistemology. The break was not, and could not be, a sharp one, for the main theme was still the theory of knowledge, but the emphasis now was on the logical conditions of knowledge as distinct from its psychological constituents. Inevitably, he was affected by the strongly philosophical atmosphere in which he found himself at Oxford. Bradley was an opponent whose philosophical acuteness it was impossible not to respect, although Stout was anxious to dispute his conclusions; Cook Wilson's

[1] 'Reply to Mr Joseph', 1911 (p. 3).

philosophical outlook was to influence him more positively—his theory of universals, in particular, leads
naturally to Stout's.

So we find Stout writing, in 1901, on 'The Common-
Sense Conception of a Material Thing'; in 1902, on
'Alleged Contradictions in the Concept of Relation'; in
1903 on 'Mr Bradley's Theory of Judgment' and on
'Error'. This latter article, it is worth noting, appeared in
a volume with the general title *Personal Idealism*; in that
philosophical movement Stout found a *via media* between
Absolute Idealism and what was later to be called 'New
Realism'. He could join with the Realists in asserting
that 'the truth of judgments concerning what is real is not
logically dependent on the truth of judgments concerning
"Reality" with a capital R'[1]; but, as *God and Nature* makes
particularly clear, he was not prepared to accept the realist
disjunction of knower and known, or the pluralism which
went with it.

The change in the direction of Stout's interests was
formally recognised when in 1903 he accepted the Chair
of Logic and Metaphysics at St Andrews, where he
remained until his retirement in 1936, at the age of seventy-
six. During these years he projected many books on
a variety of topics, and in some cases went so far as to sign
agreements with publishers. But the work of editing
Mind was a constant drain on his time and energy. He
was able to write a distinguished series of articles, but he
completed no extended work until, in 1919–21, Edinburgh University invited him to deliver the Gifford
Lectures. Then, for the first time, Stout had the oppor-
tunity to develop in detail the metaphysics which was
implicit in his epistemology. There is some evidence,
however, that he was not altogether satisfied with the
results. *Mind and Matter*, announced as the first volume
of the Gifford Lectures, did not appear until 1931; and
he selected for that volume those topics on which he felt

[1] *Studies*, p. 301.

most at home—the familiar topics of epistemology—
reserving his more metaphysical arguments for *God and
Nature*.

Of course, his advancing age made him reluctant to face
the task of detailed revision—not one he ever particularly
enjoyed—but the delay cannot be solely ascribed to his age.
Stout was a vigorous opponent of Russell's particularism;
the fact remains that he was himself distrustful of large-
scale metaphysical constructions. His inclination was
towards the empirical, the positive. He saw that his
epistemology committed him to a metaphysics, and that it
was part of his task to formulate that metaphysics; but he
was anxious not to leave himself open to Hume's gibe:
'We are gone into fairy land, long ere we have reached the
last steps of our theory.' His 'critical agnosticism', as he
describes it in *God and Nature*, is meant to be an insurance
against such merely fabricated speculation. As Professor
Mace puts it: 'Stout was not so much a transcendentalist
as an extrapolationist'; and there are signs of discomfort
wherever the extrapolations are themselves transcendental.

On his retirement from the St Andrews Chair, Stout
could well have rested on his laurels. The British Academy
had elected him a Fellow in 1903; he was an honorary
doctor of the Universities of Aberdeen, Durham and
St Andrews, and an honorary member of the British
Psychological Association; St John's had elected him to
an honorary Fellowship; his reputation was assured, and
he was now in his seventy-seventh year. But Stout was
not prepared to slip into a graceful decline. There was the
theory of universals adumbrated in the Gifford Lectures,
and developed in more detail in an address to the British
Academy—that had still to be explained and defended
against its critics. The younger men were reviving
phenomenalism and Stout found it necessary to show that
the new phenomenalism was no improvement on its
predecessors. It was his duty to memorialise his contemporaries, A. F. Shand and Samuel Alexander (he had

already memorialised, a few years earlier, his teacher, James Ward). He was disputing simultaneously (for his memorial articles were simply further episodes in life-long controversies) with Alexander and with Ayer. Nothing about Stout was more remarkable than his capacity for taking a lively interest in his contemporaries at a time of life when most men are content to live in the past.

In 1939 Stout's son, Alan Stout, was appointed to the Chair of Moral and Political Philosophy at the University of Sydney, and Stout went with him, to an unfamiliar continent—an adventure few men of seventy-nine could face with equanimity. But Stout settled into the strange surroundings as many younger men have failed to do. There were still the quiet enjoyments he had loved so well; chess to be played, philosophy to be discussed, the classics of literature to be once more re-read. And there were new sources of stimulation; a philosophical group, centred around Professor John Anderson, was developing new ideas, some of them much influenced by the work of Stout's old friend and antagonist, Alexander. Stout was happy, with new and yet familiar heresies to refute. The new country, too, interested him. And he delighted in the company of his grandchildren; their personal qualities, and the diversity of their interests, contributed most of all to the happiness of his last years. In them he found the qualities—directness, simplicity and liveliness of mind— which they enjoyed in him.

Until his very last weeks, he was reading and writing with his accustomed vigour, and ready for discussion with all-comers. (He liked to tell how Bain had once asked the Chairman of a philosophical meeting to protect him from Stout. 'Bain was an old man', he would say, 'but I am sure I would never ask the Chair to protect *me*.') The final illness which eventually led to his death in Sydney on 18 August 1944, came suddenly and unexpectedly, but for some time previously he had found physical exertion difficult; his mind, however, showed no signs of decay.

So much for the life of a man whom his friends would always remember for his personal qualities, his warm friendliness, his honesty and simplicity, his tolerance (he would tolerate anything except humbug), his perennial youthfulness, even were the world entirely to forget his work. But his work is that part of his life he would wish to have remembered, and something more must be said of its nature and importance, so far as the limits of this memoir permit.

Stout began his long career as a contributor to philosophy with a series of articles on Herbart and the Herbartians. Herbart is now not much read; but his influence has been extensive and diverse. We can trace it in Freud, in Bradley, in Ward, to say nothing of the school of Brentano or the proponents of an education based on 'interests'. Ward set a very high value on Herbart's work; in his *Encyclopædia Britannica* article on Herbart he says that 'for exactness and penetration of thought he is on a level with Hume and Kant'. What, exactly, Stout learnt directly from Herbart and how much he had already absorbed from Ward, it is impossible to determine. We know only so much of what Ward was teaching in the 1880's as he chose to compress into his article on 'Psychology' in the ninth edition of the *Encyclopædia*. But I think it is fair to say that Stout grasped, as Ward did not, the possibility of a dynamic theory of knowledge (for all Ward's emphasis upon attention). If we compare Ward's *Psychological Principles* with Stout's *Analytic Psychology*, we notice that apperception (with its emphasis upon our activity in knowing) is but a minor deviation from the main stream of Ward's thought—appropriately, therefore, relegated to an Appendix; in the *Analytic*, on the contrary, apperception is of central importance, and so it remained (in one form or another) throughout Stout's philosophical history. There was very little of Herbart's doctrine to which he could fully subscribe; but Herbart was a powerful influence in liberating him from the tradition of British philosophical psychology.

These articles are important for another reason. They illustrate Stout's gifts as an expositor, which were never again, in his published work, to be given quite free play. As Sir John Adams comments: 'It is indeed pleasant to find, for once, a commentator whose work is really clearer than the text he expounds.'[1] Stout had a knowledge of the history of philosophy which anyone might envy; there are passing references in his work to an extraordinary variety of philosophical and psychological literature and, now and then, a more extended consideration of a particular philosopher on a particular topic. But only in these first articles does he subdue criticism to exegesis. It was his pupils who could most fully appreciate his gifts of exposition. One of them, Professor G. E. Moore, has put the matter thus: 'To Stout also I think I owe a great deal. The lectures of his which I attended were on the history of Modern Philosophy. It seems to me that Stout has a quite exceptional gift for seizing on some particular point of importance involved in a confused philosophical controversy, and putting that point in the simplest and most conversational language.'[2] His pupils, it should be remembered, include not only those who felt his impact as undergraduates, but that array of philosophers who served under him as assistants in the University of St Andrews; there were few of them who did not communicate his influence, although he was not a man who attracted, or wished to attract, devout disciples.

Most of the early articles, the exceptions being that vigorous *jeu d'esprit*, 'The Philosophy of Mr Shadworth Hodgson', and certain, relatively minor, contributions to symposia, were absorbed into the *Analytic Psychology*, which is certainly Stout's major contribution to psychology. As Flügel says: 'It is at once an acutely penetrating and

[1] *The Herbartian Psychology*, p. 55.
[2] 'An Autobiography' in *The Philosophy of G. E. Moore* (ed. P. A. Schilpp), p. 18.

profoundly satisfying book, and it is astonishing how
many anticipations—or, at least, adumbrations—of later
twentieth-century developments are to be found in it.'[1]
But most younger psychologists find the *Analytic* foreign
to their experience both in its method and its emphasis;
for the *Analytic*, in Stout's own words, adopts 'the time-
honoured procedure of such men as Hobbes, Spinoza,
Herbart, Locke, Berkeley, Hume and Bain'. It must be
emphasised, since the fact is often overlooked, that Stout
was greatly interested in, and made extensive use of, the
contributions of experimental psychology. To Stout,
however, experimental psychology was a source of information, not a substitute for thinking. His adherence to
'the time-honoured procedure' means two things: first,
the treatment is thoroughly philosophical (the harder
questions are not shirked) and, secondly, the central
theme is the nature of knowledge. The curious tradition
that the analysis of human character was a task for the
moral theorist, not for the psychologist, still survived; and
it is significant that when, in the *Groundwork of Psychology*,
Stout felt that a chapter on the sentiments was needed, he
asked A. F. Shand to write it for him. That, he thought,
was not his field—somewhat surprisingly, when one recalls
his literary enthusiasms.

Yet such is 'the cunning of history' that Stout was to
be a principal agent in turning the emphasis of psychologists away from the analysis of cognition and towards the
analysis of character. Stout wrote: 'The laws of mental
grouping which we have laid down in the preceding
chapters cannot be considered by themselves except by
a convenient abstraction; they are merely modes in which
conscious striving seeks satisfaction. To regard them as
containing by themselves the explanation of the grouping
and sequence of presentations is like the attempt to explain
the course of a vessel merely by reference to the arrangement of the sails, without taking into account the existence

[1] *A Hundred Years of Psychology*, p. 152.

and direction of the wind. Such laws as those of association are only modes in which mental striving tends to
realise itself.'[1] This sentence sounds the death-knell of
British 'philosophical psychology' (at least, of the tradition which has persisted since the time of Locke: Hobbes
had already maintained that 'the discourse of the mind
is nothing but seeking'); for that was, precisely, 'the
attempt to explain the course of a vessel by reference to the
arrangement of the sails'. Stout might be indignant when
Alexander ascribed to him a thorough-going conational
theory of knowledge; that indignation he would need to
direct also against McDougall, who points out that 'the
germ of my conception (the theory of sentiments) was
contained in and derived by me from Professor Stout's
chapter on "Emotions" in his *Manual of Psychology*' but
who also protests against Stout's continued emphasis upon
cognition.[2] The implications of Stout's views have still
not been fully worked out; far from being antiquated,
Stout is much more revolutionary than exponents of such
'modern' doctrines as the conditioned reflex (association
in disguise) or Spearman's 'laws of cognition' (Hamilton
refurbished). It is interesting to observe that in *God and
Nature* (as early, that is, as 1919) Stout recognised the
importance of Freud's psychology; he could appreciate its
importance for the understanding of mind, as so many of
his fellow-psychologists could not, because it was consistent with his own emphasis upon conation.

In yet another important respect, Stout's *Analytic*
helped to change the course of psychology. Ward had
already criticised atomism; and Bradley had pronounced
that 'association marries only Universals'. But Stout was
the most vigorous and influential critic of associationist
psychology. There were three major confusions, so he

---

[1] *Analytic Psychology*, vol. ii, pp. 82–3.

[2] The quotation is from McDougall's *Social Psychology* (Preface to the
14th ed.). The protest can be found, for example. in McDougall's chapter
on 'Volition'.

thought, in that psychology, all of them derived from its atomism. The first was 'the exclusive emphasis on mere combination'; Stout maintained that 'every new synthesis results from the further determination of a psychical whole which in some way already pre-exists'. In the second place, the associationists displayed 'a complete failure to recognise the apprehension of a *form* of combination as a distinct psychical element'; in the third place, they had 'a strong disposition to regard mental elements as entering into new combinations, without themselves undergoing transformation in the process'. This, so Stout argued, 'never is and never can be true'.[1]

That this is a psychology closely akin to that of the *Gestalt* school needs no further illustration. Of course, there are differences. Writing to Stout, Koffka emphasises one of the most important. 'As you say in your letter, you derive the supersummative, unitary character of melodies —or any other temporal wholes—from the unity and continuity of interest.... My system demands that melodies must be wholes apart from the interest of the listener.' Stout recognised that a melody has a continuity of its own, but he rejected the metaphysics of the *Gestalt* theorists, since to him nothing short of *the* whole could be a whole, in the sense in which the *Gestalt* theorists talk about wholes; and, even then, the parts of the whole were not constituted by their relation to that whole. The *Gestalt* school 'have thrown out the baby with the bath-water. The bath-water is associationism; the baby is the use of empirical explanation in the psychology of perception.'[2] In their anxiety to reject the view that perception can be built up out of sensations, they have been led to the equally untenable conclusion that there is no such thing as sensation. Stout believed that his psychology could account for the experimental evidence which the *Gestalt* school

---

[1] *Analytic Psychology*, vol. ii, pp. 47–8.

[2] Supplementary Note on the *Gestalt* psychology in the fifth edition of the *Manual*, p. 674.

adduced, without departing to the same degree from the traditional 'analytic psychology'.[1]

In innumerable other ways, sometimes on points of detail, sometimes through its manner of approach to psychological problems, the *Analytic* (along with the *Manual* and the *Groundwork*) has left its mark on philosophy and psychology. We can trace the influence of these three books in the most diverse places: in John Wisdom's *Problems of Mind and Matter*, in Alexander's *Space, Time and Deity*, in Koffka's *Principles of Gestalt Psychology*, in McDougall's *Outline of Psychology*, in Blanshard's *The Nature of Thought*, to mention only a few examples. But we must be content to say of Stout's *Analytic* what he wrote of Ward: 'Ward has dealt with all the main problems of general Psychology; and he has thrown fresh light on every one of them. To do justice to his work it would be necessary to follow him carefully and critically in his treatment of each of these special topics. This is a task which ought certainly to be undertaken soon by some enlightened critic. I hold it to be especially needful, because I am convinced that there is much of permanent value in Ward's detailed work which has not yet been assimilated and utilised by others. But within my present limits I cannot attempt anything of the sort.'[2]

We shall turn now, so far as the distinction can be made, from Stout the psychologist to Stout the philosopher, beginning at that point where philosophy and psychology touch one another very closely—Stout's account of our knowledge of the external world. The most rewarding thing to do would be to trace the development of Stout's theory of perception from his earliest papers to those last articles which he contributed to the *Australasian*

---

[1] On the general question of Stout's attitude to *Gestalt* psychology see, besides his Supplementary Note in the 5th edition of the *Manual*, Professor Mace's Introduction to the 4th edition (reprinted in the 5th) and also Koffka's *Principles of Gestalt Psychology*, esp. pp. 432–8.

[2] *Studies*, p. 92.

Journal of Psychology and Philosophy. But one may well hesitate to undertake so difficult a task. As Professor Mace has pointed out[1], 'the greatest difficulty will be to draw the line correctly between the real changes in his views and changes merely in expression'. His views would change, but he would still express them in the same terminology; on other occasions he would alter his terminology, if he thought it misleading, without altering his views in the slightest. And there is another difficulty. In the *Manual*, he deliberately eschewed metaphysics; and, even in the *Analytic*, its role is a subdued one. Thus so acute and sympathetic a critic as Joseph[2] was led to ascribe to Stout a purely psychological account of our knowledge of the external world, as if it were a matter, simply, of the operation of psychological laws upon original sensations, themselves psychological states. At vital periods in the development of Stout's views, he has left us with only glimpses of his systematic thinking.

We shall be content, therefore, to insist upon the continuities in his thought without doing justice to the subtle modifications of detail. In the *Analytic* he wrote: 'In the process by which we take cognizance of an object two constituents are distinguishable. (1) A thought-reference to something which, as the thinker means or intends it, is not a present modification of his individual consciousness. (2) A more or less specific modification of his individual consciousness, which defines and determines the direction of thought to this or that special object: this special mode of subjective experience we may call a *presentation*.'[3] This distinction between thought and

[1] *Proc. Brit. Acad.* vol. xxxi.

[2] 'The Psychological Explanation of the Development of the Perception of External Objects', pts. i and ii, *Mind*, vol. xix, nos. 75–6.

[3] Vol. i, pp. 46–7. Once again, the influence of German speculation had been decisive; Stout shook himself free from British subjectivism with the help of Brentano. He found confirmation of his manner of interpreting Brentano in the work of Meinong and Husserl. But Professor J. N. Findlay suggests that Stout was further from Meinong than he himself

presentation, together with the insistence that they must
be distinguished only as separable phases of the one
cognitive process, was characteristic of Stout's epistemology and set for him his special problems. At one
time, indeed, he believed that there were certain sensations
which did not point to objects, but that view he had rejected by 1905, when he published his paper on 'Things and
Sensations'. As he remarks in his 'Reply to Mr Joseph'
(1911): 'my final position is that some apprehension of
external existence, however vague and rudimentary, is
indivisibly bound up with all sense-experience'.[1]

Thus there is no question, for Stout, of a transition from
a world of sensations to a world of independently existing
objects. What we know from the beginning, he wrote in
that same 'Reply', 'is matter directly apprehended as it is
in itself'. 'Only', he continued, 'I must insist that what
is existentially present both is and is thought as being
partial and fragmentary. For thought, it signifies its own
continuation and completion in a whole which transcends
and includes it.'[2] (This is the point of transition from
Stout's epistemology to his metaphysics.)

We remember something; in our mind, now, there is
a certain presentation; at the same time, what we remember is a past event, not inferred from the presentation, not
identical with it, but signified by it, known in and through
our having, now, this particular presentation. Here,
Stout argues, is the clue to the nature of our experience in
general. There are two propositions it is impossible to
deny:[3] the first, that 'the physical world has a distinct
existence independent of the process of knowing', the
second, that 'it is immediately known through experience
without being actually experienced'. The case of memory

believed. Stout's 'Some Fundamental Points in the Theory of Knowledge'
(*Studies*, p. 353) should be considered in the light of Findlay's *Meinong's
Theory of Objects* (esp. pp. 26–7).
[1] (P. 2).   [2] (P. 9).
[3] *Mind and Matter*, p. 222.

shows that these two propositions are not incompatible with one another; and every account of perception, so Stout argues, must find room for both of them. Representative perception will not do, for it does not admit that the physical world is immediately known and cannot explain how we could ever know it at all; naïve realism will not do, because it cannot account for the difference between the world as it is and the world as we experience it.

Stout was anxious to insist that the physical object and the presentation (or, as he later came to call it, the 'sensum') do not belong to 'different worlds'. The problem, then, was to give an account of the world such that it could include both presentations and physical objects as constituents without suffering any loss of unity. At one time, he thought he had found the solution to his problem in monadism (that was natural enough in a pupil of James Ward); but, as he writes in his Preface to the *Studies*, he came to hold that 'mind and matter are ultimately and essentially distinct, though ultimately and essentially inseparable'. Matter is not reducible to mind; the world, then, does not consist of minds and their perceptions. Stout is gradually led to the apparently paradoxical conclusion that the sensum is 'material but not physical'. If the sensum were mental, it would be necessary to conclude that we know, and could know, nothing but the mental; if it were physical, then, so diverse and individual are sensa, physical science could never be constructed. The sensum exists in and for the mind, but it is not mental; it points to physical objects, but it is not a physical object. For a sensum is only a conditioned fragment of a physical object, just as a physical object is only a conditioned fragment of the world.

The problem still remains—what is this world like, to which mind, sensum and physical object all belong? Stout describes it in *Mind and Matter*: 'The sensory continua of experiencing individuals are partial extracts from a wider continuum, differing from other parts of the

whole to which they belong, not in their fundamental
nature, but in being actually experienced by individual
selves. The apparent discontinuity and disparity between
the sensa and physical existence which has led to the view
that sensa are not material but "mental", is really due to
a difference in the conditions of our knowledge. Physical
objects are, and sensa are not, phenomena.'[1] Another
problem immediately emerges—how do we know that
there are 'phenomena' (in the Kantian sense) as distinct
from sensa? One can find in Stout's writings a number of
diverse answers, not necessarily inconsistent with one
another, but certainly differing in emphasis. It seemed to
him, at first, sufficient to say that the sensum is apprehended as incomplete, as raising questions which it does
not settle, as needing for its intelligibility the conception
of a physical object of which it is a partial, and conditioned,
revelation. This view is most interestingly worked out in
God and Nature and in his article on 'Distributive Unity
as a Category'. In *Mind and Matter*, however, the emphasis
is pragmatic; 'the only ground for asserting that the
perceptual datum includes more than the mere sensum is
found in the process of correlating perceptual data with
each other so as to guide practical activity in the adjustment of means to ends. If such practical adjustment were
possible in relation to the mere content of sense-
experience taken by itself, subjective sensationalism
would be adequate. But, as we have seen, this is not
so.'[2] The inadequacy of sensa for 'the conduct of life'
(to use Berkeley's phrase) is the best evidence, perhaps
the only evidence, that they are not themselves physical
objects, just as their usefulness as guides is the best
evidence that they point to physical objects.

Thus it is through our own activity that we discover the
real nature of sensa, and the real nature of the world.
Once more, Stout's psychology and his philosophy

[1] (P. 268).
[2] *Op. cit.* p. 269.

supplement one another; the conational theory of mind provides the only firm foundation for an adequate account of the physical world. We need, however, not only the conception of an active mind, but the conception of an active *embodied* mind. As late as 1906, in his 'The Nature of Conation and Mental Activity', he is still talking, in Berkeley's manner, of an activity which is purely spiritual; and Professor Mace, referring to the *Manual*, comments that 'we all read and misunderstood this discussion of the matter as presupposing a Cartesian, perhaps an idealistic philosophy of mind'.[1] In *Mind and Matter*, however, the Cartesian *Cogito* is decisively rejected. |'What self-consciousness reveals is not mere mind or "mental phenomena" but mind and body together in the inseparable unity of the embodied self.'[2]

Not only is the Cartesian wrong about the nature of our existence; he is wrong, too, about the nature of material existence. There are not two worlds: one material, mechanically determined, the other spiritual. There is only the one world, which is through-and-through teleological, through-and-through embodied mind (which is not to say that it consists wholly of embodied *selves*). The monadist is mistaken in so far as he argues that the world is merely mental; he is right in insisting (against the materialist) on 'the omnipresence of mind in nature' and, against the Absolute Idealist, that 'mind in the long run can only be individual mind, and that inversely where there is no mind there is no individuality'.[3]

On any other view, Stout maintains, there could be no such thing as causal connexion. Stout's theory of causality, which is fully worked out in *Mind and Matter*, but is perhaps more clearly presented in his contribution to a symposium on 'Mechanical and Teleological Causality', involves a return to pre-Humean causal theory, although

[1] Obituary Notice, *Brit. J. Psychol.* vol. xxvi, no. 2.
[2] P. 308.
[3] *Op. cit.* pp. 211–12.

in a spirit chastened by Hume's criticisms. 'A cause is such a reason, so that if we had a sufficiently comprehensive and accurate knowledge of what really takes place, we should see how and why the effect follows from the cause with logical necessity',[1] and this kind of deductive connexion between cause and effect is only intelligible if the cause contains an active tendency to give rise to the effect. Hume was right, he thinks, in insisting that only if such an active tendency exists as an ingredient in our experience can causality be anything but constant conjunction; but Hume was wrong in denying that our experience contains any such 'impression' of activity, and wrong in particular in denying that we immediately experience such activity in ourselves.

This activity is not that of a 'free agent' (in Kant's sense of the word). 'The result, whether successful or unsuccessful, never depends wholly on me. My action is, and is experienced as being, only a partial stage in a wider process which expands continuously into the world process.' From this fact we can deduce a conclusion about the nature of the world. 'The world process in general must be so far akin to what I myself experience in being active as to make this continuity possible.'[2] This argument from continuity is taken up on the other side in *Mind and Matter*. There Stout argues that if the human mind were something in all respects distinct from material objects, it could never be in any way influenced by them; only if we suppose that the kind of active tendency we discover in our minds is present in the world as a whole can we understand how the human mind can have a place in the order of nature. Yet some measure of discontinuity we seem to be obliged to admit. For the world, which in so many respects is akin to us, is not constructed wholly of embodied selves. 'In one way embodied selves are of a piece with the rest of the world of finite beings,

[1] 'Mechanical and Teleological Causation', 1935 (p. 46).
[2] *Ibid.* (p. 59).

within which they arise and disappear; in another, there is an abrupt breach of continuity between them and the parts of the same world which are devoid of sentience, feelings and thought.'[1] This discontinuity, Stout maintains, cannot be absolute; but in what sense there is 'a world as a whole' and exactly in what way mind is omnipresent in it were problems left over for *God and Nature*.

There are certain clues to Stout's solution in his theory of the self and in his theory of universals. In both cases, his object was to give an account of a certain kind of unity; in one case, the unity of the human mind, in the other, the unity of a class. The traditional view was that a class could be a unity only if there were some single character which held it together, and in Platonism the multiplicity of particulars is absorbed into that single character; and, again, the traditional theory of self was that if the mind were to be a unity its multiple activities must somehow (when the real nature of mind is understood) be capable of absorption into pure Ego. In a parallel fashion, Absolute Idealism tried to transform the unity of the world into an entity, so that, properly understood, the world was one and was not many.

Now, as against nominalism, Stout insisted that a class had a genuine unity, but it was a unity which involved multiplicity—a *distributive* unity; the characters of things are as particular as the things they characterise, but they are united through being members of a single kind. 'We cannot name them or think of them without referring them to some general class or kind of character';[2] at the same time, they are not themselves universal, but are particular.

It is then possible to regard a particular substance as

---

[1] *Mind and Matter*, p. 313.

[2] 'Things, Predicates and Relations', 1940 (p. 119). This was the last paper Stout ever delivered to a Philosophical Association, although not the last he wrote.

a complex of characters (to reject, that is, a 'substratum'), without being forced to conclude that a particular is wholly constructed out of universals. Stout's theory of the self is an application of this general theory of substances. There is no 'pure ego', no underlying 'real' or 'substantial' self: 'the unity of the self seems to me indistinguishable from the unity of the total complex of its experiences'. At the same time, there is this unity to be accounted for: the adherents of the pure ego are right 'in demanding a condition of unity which does not itself form part of the psychical complex'. Stout's own conclusion is that 'the changing complex of individual experience has the unity and identity uniquely distinctive of what we call a single self or ego only in so far as objects are apprehended as one and the same in different acts or in different stages and phases of the same act'. In the end, indeed, the self can be a unity only because its objects are apprehended as a single object. In the first place, they are apprehended as incomplete and hence as leading beyond themselves, but this apprehension, at the level of 'analytic or reflective consciousness', is explicitly formulated as 'the conception of a Universe'.[1]

Thus the stage is set for Stout's theory of the Universe. It, too, has a unity, but a unity which does not cancel diversity. 'The distinctness and relative independence of partial existences is comprehended within the unity of the whole, but is not and cannot be in any way annulled by it.'[2] It, too, has a ground of unity which lies outside itself. And the ground of unity must be such as to account for the continuity between ourselves and the world in which we find ourselves, between our actions and the reactions they evoke, between our sensa and the objects to which they point. It must, then, be a Mind, but a Mind which immediately apprehends the world not in fragments but as a whole, so that for it there is the one con-

---

[1] *Studies*, pp. 358–61.
[2] 'Distributive Unity as a Category' (p. 12).

tinuum, within which our sensa and physical objects both appear as presentations. In short, it must be God.

Stout's philosophy, then, needs *God and Nature* for its completion. Everything in it leads to the conception of a total Universe, containing whatever is finite, which yet, just because it is finite, demands a ground. The presentation looks towards the object of which it is a fragmentary revelation, the object looks towards the Universe which completes it; every experience is a phase in the history of a self, but a self finds its unity only through the conception of a single object of thought; everything is characterised, but every character is intelligible only in a unity which includes it.

This is a philosophy, then, perfectly definite, systematic, uncompromising. At the same time, we may easily miss the pattern, may easily (however wrongly) think of Stout as an eclectic, or even a piecemeal, philosopher. As Professor Mace puts it: 'He accepted no philosophy but his own, but every other philosophy was grist to his ever-grinding mill. "I have got them all in my system", he once allowed himself to say with the modest and satisfied smile reminiscent of that on the face of the proverbial amiable tiger.'[1] It is this fact which can so easily mislead us; he was not an eclectic, but he found nothing philosophical alien to him.

Pre-eminently, he is a philosopher of the middle way. He would grant you so much, but only so much. Mind is conative—yes, but it is cognitive, too; and cognition and conation are not merely added to one another but mingle in the same process. Characters are particulars, but they belong to kinds; minds are embodied, but mind is not body, nor body mind; things are distinct, but not complete in themselves; we know the world as it is, but it is not only as we know it; to be is not to be known, but whatever is, is known, and whatever is known, is; God is not Nature, but Nature embodies God and God expresses

[1] *Proc. Brit. Acad.* vol. XXXI.

Himself through Nature. The convictions of common sense are preserved, but without disrespect to either science or philosophy. In Stout's philosophy, the ideal of Reconciliation finds its most philosophical expression.

LIST OF STOUT'S WORKS

1884   Critical Notice of H. Maudsley's 'Body and Will'. *Mind* (old series), vol. IX, no. 33.

1887   Critical Notice of W. Knight's 'Hume'. *Mind*, vol. XII, no. 47.

1888   *The Herbartian Psychology. *Mind*, vol. XIII, nos. 51, 52.
Professor Ladd on Body and Mind. *Mind*, vol. XIII, no. 51.
Is Mind Synonymous with Consciousness? *Proc. Ar. Soc.* vol. I (o.s.), no. 1.
(*a*) The Scope and Method of Psychology. *Proc. Ar. Soc.* vol. I, no. 1.

1889   Herbart Compared with the English Psychologists and with Beneke. *Mind*, vol. XIV, no. 53.
Remarks on Mental Association. *Mind*, vol. XIV, no. 54.
The Psychological Work of Herbart's Disciples. *Mind*, vol. XIV, no. 55.

1890   Is the Distinction between Feeling, Cognition and Conation Valid as an Ultimate Distinction of the Mental Functions? (Symposium.) *Proc. Ar. Soc.* vol. I, no. 3.
The Genesis of the Cognition of Physical Reality. *Mind*, vol. XV, no. 57.
Dr Pikler on the Cognition of Physical Reality. *Mind*, vol. XV, no. 60.

1891   Does our Knowledge or Perception of the Ego Admit of being Analysed? (Symposium.) *Proc. Ar. Soc.* vol. I, no. 4.
(*a*) Apperception and the Movement of Attention. *Mind*, vol. XVI, no. 61.
(*a*) Thought and Language. *Mind*, vol. XVI, no. 62.
Critical Notice of A. Lehman's 'Die Hypnose'. *Mind*, vol. XVI, no. 63.
(*a*) Belief. *Mind*, vol. XVI, no. 64.

1892   A General Analysis of Presentations, as a Preparatory to the Theory of their Interaction. *Proc. Ar. Soc.* vol. ii, no. 1.

Is the Distinction between Is and Ought Ultimate or Irreducible? (Symposium.) *Proc. Ar. Soc.* vol. ii, no. 1.

Prefatory Remarks. *Mind* (new series), vol. i, no. 1.

1893   The Philosophy of Mr Shadworth Hodgson. *Proc. Ar. Soc.* vol. 2, no. 2.

Is Human Law the Basis of Morality or Morality of Human Law? (Symposium.) *Proc. Ar. Soc.* vol. ii, no. 2.

Critical Notice of A. Fouillée's 'La Psychologie des Idées-Forces'. *Mind*, vol. ii, no. 8.

1894   The Relation Between Thought and Language. (Symposium.) *Proc. Ar. Soc.* vol. ii, no. 3.

1895   (a) Relative Suggestion. *Proc. Ar. Soc.* vol. iii, no. 1.

Is the Knowledge of Space *a priori*? (Symposium.) *Proc. Ar. Soc.* vol. iii, no. 1.

Critical Notice of O. Külpe's 'Einleitung in die Philosophie'. *Mind*, vol. iv, no. 16.

1896   In what Sense, if any, is it True that Psychical States are Extended? *Proc. Ar. Soc.* vol. iii, no. 2.

*Voluntary Action. *Mind*, vol. v, no. 19.

Analytic Psychology (2 vols.). London: Swan, Sonnenschein (later Allen and Unwin); New York: Macmillan.

1898   Professor Angell's Criticism of 'Analytic Psychology'. *Philos. Rev.* vol. vii, no. 1.

Critical Notice of C. Lloyd Morgan's 'Habit and Instinct'. *Mind*, vol. vii, no. 26.

1899   *A Manual of Psychology*. London: Clive (Cambridge Tutorial Press); New York: Hinds and Noble. (5th ed., rev. by C. A. Mace, with an appendix by R. H. Thouless and a supplementary note by G. F. Stout, 1938.)

Critical Notice of H. Cornelius's 'Psychologie als Erfahrungswissenschaft'. *Mind*, vol. viii, no. 30.

1900   *The Perception of Change and Duration. *Mind*, vol. ix, no. 33.

1901   *The Common-sense Conception of a Material Thing. *Proc. Ar. Soc.* (new series), vol. i.

Articles in both volumes of Baldwin's *Dictionary of Philosophy and Psychology*.

1902   *Alleged Contradictions in the Concept of Relation. *Proc.
        Ar. Soc.* vol. II (reprinted in *Studies* as 'Bradley's Theory
        of Relations').
1903   *Mr Bradley's Theory of Judgment. *Proc. Ar. Soc.*
        vol. III.
        The Groundwork of Psychology. London: Clive; New
        York: Hinds and Noble. (2nd ed., rev. by R. H.
        Thouless, 1927.)
        *Error (in *Personal Idealism*, ed. H. Sturt).
1904   Primary and Secondary Qualities. *Proc. Ar. Soc.* vol. IV.
1905   *Things and Sensations. *Proc. Brit. Acad.* (1905).
1906   *The Nature of Conation and Mental Activity. *Brit. J.
        Psychol.* vol. II, no. I.
        Neo-Kantism as Represented by Dr Dawes Hicks. *Proc.
        Ar. Soc.* vol. VI.
1907   Mr Prichard's Criticism of Psychology. *Mind*, vol. XVI,
        no. 62.
        Critical Notice of F. C. S. Schiller's 'Studies in Humanism'.
        Mind, vol. XVI, no. 64.
1908   *Immediacy, Mediacy and Coherence. *Mind*, vol. XVII,
        no. 65.
        The Nature of Mental Activity. (Symposium.) *Proc. Ar.
        Soc.* vol. VIII.
1909   Are Presentations Mental or Physical? *Proc. Ar. Soc.*
        vol. IX.
1910   Instinct and Intelligence. (Symposium.) *Brit. J. Psychol.*
        vol. III.
1911   Reply to Mr Joseph. *Mind*, vol. XX, no. 77.
        *The Object of Thought and Real Being. *Proc. Ar. Soc.*
        vol. XI (renamed 'Real Being and Being for Thought'
        in *Studies*).
        **Some Fundamental Points in the Theory of Knowledge.*
        Glasgow: MacLehose, St Andrews Quincentenary
        Publications.
        Preface to E. Constance Jones's *New Law of Thought*
        (1911). Putnam.
        Philosophy. In *Votiva Tabella* (pp. 153–66), a Quincen-
        tenary volume of the University of St Andrews.
1913   Can there be Anything Obscure or Implicit in a Mental
        State? *Proc. Ar. Soc.* vol. XIII.

1914   The Status of Sense-data. (Symposium.) *Proc. Ar. Soc.* vol. XIV.

1915   Instinct and Emotion. (Symposium.) *Proc. Ar. Soc.* vol. XV.

      *Mr Russell's Theory of Judgment. *Proc. Ar. Soc.* vol. XV.

      War and Hatred (in *The International Crisis*, ed. E. M. Sidgwick).

1918   Do Finite Individuals Possess a Substantive or an Adjectival Mode of Being? *Proc. Ar. Soc.* vol. XVIII.

1921   *The Nature of Universals and Propositions. *Proc. Brit. Acad.* vol. X.

1922   Prof. Alexander's Theory of Sense-Perception. *Mind*, vol. XXXI, no. 124.

1923   Are the Characters of Particular Things Universal or Particular? (Symposium.) *Proc. Ar. Soc.* supp. vol. III.

1925   *Bradley on Truth and Falsity. *Mind*, vol. XXXIV, no. 133.

1926   *Ward as a Psychologist. *Monist*, vol. XXXVI, no. 1.

      *James Ward on Sense and Thought. (Discussion.) *Mind*, vol. XXXV, no. 140.

1927   The Nature of Introspection. (Symposium.) With a post-script by G. F. Stout. *Proc. Ar. Soc.* supp. vol. VII.

      *In What Way is Memory-Knowledge Immediate? An address to the Scots Philosophical Society (first published in *Studies*).

      [With W. R. Sorley], ed. of James Ward's *Essays in Philosophy.*

1929   [With C. A. Mace], article on 'Psychology' in vol. XVIII of *Encyclopædia Britannica* (14th ed.).

1930   *Studies in Philosophy and Psychology.* London and New York: Macmillan.

1931   *Mind and Matter* (vol. 1, Gifford Lectures). London: Cambridge University Press; New York: Macmillan.

1932   Truth and Reality. *Mind*, vol. XLI, no. 163.

1934   Self-Evidence and Matter of Fact. *Philosophy*, vol. IX.

1935   Mechanical and Teleological Causation. (Symposium.) *Proc. Ar. Soc.* supp. vol. XIV.

1936   Universals Again. *Proc. Ar. Soc.* supp. vol. XV.

      A. F. Shand, A Memoir. *Proc. Brit. Acad.* vol. XXV.

1938   Phenomenalism. *Proc. Ar. Soc.* vol. XXXIX.

1940   Things, Predicates and Relations. *Aust. J. Psychol. Phil.*
         vol. XVIII, no. 2.
         The Philosophy of Samuel Alexander. *Mind*, vol. XLIX,
         nos. 193, 194.
         Samuel Alexander: Personal Reminiscences. *Mind*,
         vol. XLIX, no. 193.
1944   A Criticism of Alexander's Theory of Mind and Know-
         ledge. *Aust. J. Psychol. Phil.* vol. XXII, nos. 1–2.
1947   Distributive Unity as a Category. *Aust. J. Psychol. Phil.*
         vol. XXV, nos. 1–2.

Articles marked (*a*) also appear as chapters in *Analytic Psychology*.
Articles marked with an asterisk werereprinted in *Studies in Philosophy and Psychology*. The dates given in that book are not always identical with those in this bibliography, which refer throughout to the date of publication.

BOOK ONE

INTRODUCTORY

▼

Chapter I

ETHICAL NEUTRALITY AND PRAGMATISM

1. *The Province of the Gifford Lecturer*

Disregarding what may be called side-shows, Gifford
Lectures, whatever titles they have borne, have dealt,
from various points of view, with one main problem:
What is the ultimate nature of the all-inclusive Universe
and what consequently is the status and destiny of human
beings as parts of it? This is to be my central topic also.
The special title [of my first volume],[1] *Mind and Matter*,
only indicates the way in which I approach it. Whether we
consider the relation of mind and body, or the relation of
mind, as knowing, feeling and willing subject, to matter
as its object, the conclusions we reach, whatever they may
be, are bound to influence our whole attitude—theoretical,
practical and emotional—to the universe and to our own
lives. In the present chapter, I shall discuss certain preliminary questions concerning the way in which we ought
to approach this all-important problem of the nature of
the universe and man's place in it.

Even in my initial statement, I have taken for granted
what perhaps I have no right to take for granted. I have
assumed that the universe is a unity in such a sense that
it has a nature as a whole. I have also assumed that it is
possible for us to inquire what its nature is with a reasonable prospect of getting such an answer as will make it
worth while to raise the question. These are no doubt

[1] Bracketed words inserted by Ed.

natural assumptions. The very word 'universe' seems to imply them. None the less they have been and are disputed by acute thinkers whom we cannot disregard. I shall therefore at a later stage[1] consider explicitly how far and in what way the universe can be known as a unity. Meanwhile I shall follow the prevailing trend of common sense and philosophy in presupposing that the Universe of Being is not ultimately a disjointed plurality. I shall assume that it is One, so far and in such a way that we may legitimately inquire into its general constitution as a whole.

2. *The Importance of our Problem for Human Life and Conduct*

There are two introductory questions with which I propose to deal at present. Both are connected with the fundamental importance for human life and conduct of the problem of the nature of the universe and man's place in it. We are sometimes faced with situations which concern us inevitably, so that however we meet them, and even if we ignore them altogether, our action or inaction is charged for us with important consequences. A man in imminent danger of being run over is in such a position; so is the general of an army confronted by a formidable enemy. It sometimes depends on us whether or not we shall place ourselves in circumstances of this sort. For instance, by declining a responsible post we may evade risks and trials which we should have to face if we accepted it. It is otherwise with the urgency of primary bodily needs, such as the need of food to sustain life; we must either bestir ourselves or starve. The need of adopting some practical and emotional attitude in regard to our place and destiny in the universe constitutes an inevitable practical problem of this kind. There is no way of escaping the situation from which it arises; every human being who

[1] [Books ii and iv—Ed.]

has reached a certain stage of mental development must deal with it in some way or other; even to ignore it is by no means to escape it. However a man may meet it, whether by ignoring it or by accepting more or less definite answers in the way of religious belief or unbelief, his procedure affects more or less deeply his general attitude, practical and emotional, to life as a whole. Hence we find generally that when men have reached a certain stage of mental and moral development they have, under the pressure of this practical need, formed what we may call, in a wide sense, religious beliefs, including under this head beliefs which would ordinarily be called irreligious, sceptical or agnostic.

3. *The Formation of Religious Beliefs*

The questions which these beliefs in one way or another answer are fundamentally of the same nature as those which philosophers attempt to answer by systematic reasoning and analysis. But the way in which such results are reached is not initially that of philosophy, and even when philosophers have said their say, their influence on the mass of mankind, though important, is limited and indirect. Religious beliefs are not primarily due to systematic inquiry and reasoning, nor to critical examination of evidence and logical analysis. So far as they are not accepted more or less passively from authority and tradition, they represent the total outcome of the concrete experience and activity of such beings as we are, living in such a world as ours. They express the view which human minds are impelled to take of a situation which they are bound to face, so as to adapt themselves to it in thought and action as best they can. This does not necessarily mean that they are held without valid grounds. It only means that such grounds, so far as they may exist, are not explicitly recognised and analysed, except perhaps in a very partial and inadequate way. It may be, indeed, that they are so deep-seated, of so complex and evasive a character, that they never can be fully displayed so as to be laid bare for scrutiny and criticism. In this respect, they are like many beliefs on which we rely in ordinary life without misgiving.

One of the two questions we have to consider in this introductory chapter is this: how are we, from the point of view of critical reflexion, to treat these precritical unreflective beliefs? Plainly, we cannot accept them without full inquiry. Are we then to set them aside and begin *de novo*? If not, how shall we determine their value in philosophy? This is a topic to which I shall recur,[1] after dealing with the other question, which may be stated as follows.

4. *Pragmatism and 'Ethical Neutrality'*

Seeing that our interest in religious problems is not merely theoretical but, at least for most human beings, predominantly active and emotional, how far, if at all, are we justified in allowing the nature of our practical and emotional needs to determine the nature of our answers to these problems? How far is it legitimate to seek for such answers as will positively satisfy our needs and to reject those which do not? On this issue there is a sharply defined conflict of opinion. We find in the one camp the pragmatists, as represented, e.g., by Mr Schiller, in the other the advocates of 'ethical neutrality', as represented by Mr Bertrand Russell. The pragmatist, as I understand him, urges that we merely blind ourselves to fundamental facts if we attempt to treat practical problems as if they were merely theoretical. It is like the fabled procedure of the ostrich hiding its head in the sand. In a situation calling for practical adjustment, what is required both in belief and in action is a way of satisfying practical needs. Hence in relation to practical interest the true coincides

[1] Pp. 20 ff.

with the useful.[1] At any rate if there is truth which is not useful, it is no concern of ours in the given circumstances. When we say that the truth is what we ought to seek, we imply that it has value for us; and in adapting ourselves to practical exigencies, a truth which does not help us is valueless: therefore it is futile to concern ourselves with it at all. In the only useful sense which we can attach to the word 'true', a belief is true only so far as it is useful and so long as it is useful. This doctrine, as I have stated it, applies only to practical problems. But the pragmatist makes it general, because he holds that all interests are ultimately practical, and for him truth and usefulness, for all practical purposes, practically coincide.

For Mr Russell, on the contrary, and those who think with him, the conceptions of truth and of value are quite separate. In forming beliefs, all that ought to concern us is the question—What is true?—and to this our wants, desires, needs and our view of what ought to be or what ought not to be bear no sort of relevance. So far as any other interest than the purely theoretical interest of discovering what is true leads us to believe what otherwise we should not believe, we are deceiving ourselves; and if we do so consciously we are consciously deceiving ourselves. Any other view must rest on the assumption that the bare fact that we want something to be true or feel that it ought to be true is a valid ground for believing that it really is true. But this, they say, is an utterly baseless presumption in all possible applications. What is, once for all, is quite distinct from and very commonly contrary to both what it ought to be and what we should like it to be. Hence whatever practical and emotional interests may be involved in a question, these ought not in the slightest degree to influence us in deciding what answer we shall give to it, or even whether we shall answer it at all, instead of giving it up as a hopeless riddle. This is

[1] *Useful* in a very wide sense, satisfactory for life and conduct. The word 'practical' has the same wide application in this connexion.

what is called being 'ethically neutral', where the word 'ethical' is, I presume, used to indicate that not only lower interests and values are to be regarded as irrelevant in the search for truth, but also the highest ideals of which human beings are capable.[1]

5. *Emotional and Practical Needs influence the Believer and the Sceptic alike*

Before discussing the issue raised by the opposed theories of 'ethical neutrality' and pragmatism, it will be well to consider a prior question. Whether or not we ought to permit ourselves to be swayed by emotional and practical needs in shaping our view of human life in relation to the universe, it seems clear that in fact we inevitably are so. It is scarcely too much to say that no one quite succeeds in approaching the problem of the existence of God or of a future life as if he were determining an atomic weight or whether the syllogism is a *petitio principii*. This holds good for the sceptic and unbeliever as well as for others—at any rate for those of them who are active partisans of their own views.

That it is true of the adherents of positive dogmas scarcely admits of dispute. It is constantly being urged against them by their opponents; and they themselves explicitly or implicitly confess it. The pitiable state of one 'without God and without hope in the world' is regarded as a legitimate motive for believing in God, even though other views may be theoretically tenable. Similarly with a future life: it would be dreadful, 'if this were all and naught beyond our earth'. Therefore we ought, if we can, to believe that this all is not all and to turn aside from the dismal alternative.

[1] I have throughout put the phrase 'ethical neutrality' in inverted commas. I do so because I deny that those who regard ethical considerations as relevant in philosophy are merely or mainly actuated by the tendency to believe what they would like to be true. To assume this really begs the main question at issue from the outset. I revert to this point on p. 13.

This attitude of mind is found even in those who diverge most widely from traditional standards of orthodoxy. The religious development of Spinoza, no less than that of Bunyan, is dominated by the need to be released from a burden. Bunyan called it the burden of sin; Spinoza called it bondage to passion. But it was in principle the same burden which weighed on both. The position of those who justify this procedure is not of course that we ought to allow ourselves to be swayed by interests of any kind without distinction. We must guard ourselves against being influenced by relatively low, narrow or selfish motives. But if a belief subserves our highest ideals as no other can, if it supports and inspires us in living the best life of which we are capable, this in itself is regarded as a reason for adopting it and clinging to it with a confidence which we may not be able to justify on purely theoretical grounds. Consider, for instance, Dr Ward's picture of what the belief in God may be to men of religious genius. 'There have been men', he says, 'who proclaimed that "they had overcome the world", being in it but no longer of it, had realised "a peace passing all understanding" and found "strength to do all things" in the consciousness of an in-dwelling presence....And their lives confirmed their profession, whatever we may think of the mysterious and seemingly mystical source to which they appealed. They *were* superior to the weakness of the flesh, the fear of men and the temporal anxieties that hold so many in bondage....With a single eye and a single aim their whole being seemed full of light and joy. At one in mind and will with the ground of all reality and the source of all good, as they conceived it, what had they to fear, whoever might be against them? They stood fast, strenuously devoted through life and faithful in death to the widest, deepest and highest that they knew, or indeed—when all is said and done—that it has entered into the heart of man to conceive.'[1]

[1] *Psychological Principles*, p. 469. [Chap. xviii, § 5.]

So far Dr Ward. I need not here discuss how far he is drawing a fancy picture. To me it seems that he is describing an ideal to which some few have approached in an extraordinary degree and many others in a more or less partial and fitful way. But the point I am now concerned with is this. Granting the supreme practical and emotional value of the belief, this value tends to be taken, consciously or unconsciously, by mankind in general as a legitimate motive for accepting it and abiding by it in spite of theoretical doubt and difficulties.

Here we must be careful to avoid confusing two questions which in practice it is difficult to keep apart. It may be held that a belief which works in this way must for that very reason be based on genuine insight into the nature of things, even though the grounds may be such that the believer finds it difficult or impossible to define them so as to make them convincing to others. But quite apart from this, there is in general a strong tendency to treat the value of a belief for human life and conduct as a reason for preferring it to opposing views and for disregarding what may be urged in their favour. This is often carried so far that opposition to a dogma is treated as if it meant antagonism to the good way of life with which it is inseparably connected in the mind of the believer. Thus scepticism or unbelief is taken to indicate some kind of moral perversity or, at least, moral blindness. This is a fruitful source of intolerance and of the heat of theological conflicts.

It must be admitted that believers in God and a future life and in more special creeds are, in general, far from being 'ethically neutral'. But what of their opponents, who are so ready to claim freedom from this sort of bias? I cannot see that their claim is at all justified. They too are nearly always—perhaps always—more or less influenced in forming their views by emotional and practical values. The Epicureans as well as the Stoics recommended their doctrines as leading to the most satisfactory 'way of life'. Lucretius is a typical example. Similarly, in all ages,

we commonly find behind the unbelief of the unbeliever—
at least when he is at all zealous in propagating his views—
strong feelings and convictions concerning social, political
and moral questions and the conditions of human welfare
in general. He may, like the believer, be sometimes
swayed by low, narrow and selfish motives. But often his
impelling interest is worthy of all respect and admiration.
He may think, and historical facts may largely justify him
in thinking, that preoccupation with a supernatural order
leads to error, blindness and a distorted sense of values in
dealing with the actual and verifiable conditions of our
present life. He may be, for instance, indignant and
impatient with those who are content to have the poor
'always with us' because they regard this as a dispensation
of Providence for which they are not responsible. He is,
in general, impatient and indignant at what seems to him
the support lent to an easy-going tolerance of evil and
misery and injustice by the doctrine of a future life, in
which what is wrong in this life will be set right. Such
beliefs appear to him as a sort of drug and soothing syrup
with which humanity has lulled itself to sleep. Like Byron,
he is inclined to couple together 'rum' and 'true religion'.
Hence an attitude of strong aversion to everything of the
nature of religious dogma, which makes it difficult or
impossible to view religious questions in a dry light—
to be 'ethically neutral'.

Another form of bias which works in a similar way
arises from the revolt against tradition and authority, as
opposed to freedom of thought and practical progress.
Rebellion against religious dogmas becomes identified
with freedom to think and live untrammelled by what is
felt as an oppressive bondage to current orthodoxy, not
only in what concerns religion, but generally. For established creeds become inextricably interwoven with, and
both support and are supported by, a complex system of
opinions, sentiments and institutions—of ways of thinking
and acting, moral, social and political, extending to all the

main interests of human life. Hence antagonism to a part of the system almost inevitably tends to become antagonism to it as a whole. It tends to become a more or less indiscriminate antagonism to established tradition and authority as such. Consider for instance the atheism of Shelley or of the early days of the French Revolution. The impelling motives of the unbeliever, like those of the believer, may be and often are of a high and noble nature. But the resulting state of mind is hardly compatible with 'ethical neutrality'. It is hardly compatible with any sustained conscientious effort to examine and sift traditional beliefs in a dry light so as to discriminate what truth they may contain intermingled with error.

6. *'Ethical Neutrality' may defeat itself*

I have so far referred only to the more obvious and palpable forms of bias which may interfere with 'ethical neutrality'. There are others of a kind more subtle and evasive. The very effort to be 'ethically neutral' is apt to defeat itself. Men are being constantly deluded by their natural tendency to assume as true what they think ought to be true or what they want to be true or what it in any way suits them to regard as true. The advocate of 'ethical neutrality' is actuated by a strong desire to avoid this source of error. He has what amounts to a horror of it. This leads him to forget that though apparent accordance with practical and emotional needs may not be of itself evidence of truth, neither is it of itself evidence of falsehood. He rather seems to proceed on the assumption that belief formed under the stress of practical and emotional needs must be untrue or baseless.

A further development of the same bias may impel him, in shaping his own views, to guard beforehand against possible occasions of the fallacy he so much dreads. Take, for instance, Mr Bertrand Russell's denial of the unity of the universe. If the universe of being is merely a collection of items which can only be known piecemeal as they happen to present themselves, there can be no sense in raising questions concerning its nature and constitution as a systematic whole. Mr Russell argues that the so-called universe is such a collection of separate items. He does so on theoretical grounds. But I cannot help believing that if he were disposed impartially to criticise his own reasoning he would find serious flaws in it. I cannot help suspecting that he is influenced by practical and emotional bias. By denying the unity of the universe, he is enabled to get rid at one stroke of all constructive metaphysics, all theology, all positive religious faith. And this suits him both for other reasons and more especially because in this way he escapes embarking at all on what seems to him a troubled sea of passion and prejudice, where 'ethical neutrality' is almost impossible.

I could pursue this topic much further. The ways in which we may fail to be 'ethically' impartial are manifold, diverse and elusive. But I have said enough for my present purpose. I would only repeat, in conclusion, that we equally sin against the principle, as its advocates understand it, whether our impelling motives are ignoble and selfish or noble and unselfish. If butter does not suit the works of a watch, it is no use to urge, like the March Hare, that it is 'the best butter'.

7. *How far is there a Duty to be 'Ethically Neutral'?*

It is now time to turn to the problem with which we started. This is not how far we are able to be 'ethically neutral', but how far we ought to be so. How far is it our duty, however difficult the duty may be, always to do our best to consider all questions, including religious questions, in a dry light? This brings us to the opposition of 'ethical neutrality' and pragmatism. I do not pretend to understand or follow the pragmatic philosophy as a whole. But on one point the pragmatists are clearly right. They are right in insisting that we ought not to proceed as if theoretical interest were the sole or predominant interest where in fact it is not. The aim is to satisfy our needs, and there is no initial reason why curiosity or love of knowledge should take precedence in order of value. Thus, if and when we can really distinguish, on the one hand, a practically useless belief which is most strongly supported by an impartial scrutiny of the accessible evidence, and on the other an incompatible belief which is adapted to fulfil practical and emotional needs of paramount importance, we ought clearly as far as we are able to prefer the second.

But on examination the concession to pragmatism turns out to be apparent rather than real. It presupposes a severance and a possible antagonism of theoretical and practical interest, which if it ever occurs at all, is at least very exceptional and can never be safely assumed to exist. In general, we can count on dealing effectively with a practical situation only in so far as we know what its nature really is; and the best way to ascertain this is to examine the facts as impartially as we can, unswayed by any tendency to believe what we want to be true or what we think ought to be true. Consider the position of a general working amid the fog of war to avoid defeat and secure victory. Whatever else he may do, it is for him a primary and indispensable duty to ascertain, as far as he can, all relevant facts—the intentions of the enemy, the nature, number and disposition of the hostile forces, and so forth. In so doing he must as far as possible only weigh and consider the available evidence and suppress preconceptions arising either from his desires or his fears. Only so can he hope to gain what Marshal Foch called 'assurance' in adjusting his measures to the exigencies of the situation. He seeks truth no doubt only because and so far as it may be useful to him. But he courts failure if he confuses usefulness with truth. The truth is useful inasmuch as it can be used; but this presupposes that truth as such is distinct from usefulness.

It may be said that it is sometimes advantageous for a man to be deceived. This seems to me a very doubtful proposition, if we take a sufficiently comprehensive view of human interests. But even if we grant that it is sometimes good to believe what is false rather than what is true, yet this is a comparatively rare occurrence. In general it is not an enviable state to live in a fool's paradise. Further (and this is the most important point), we cannot tell *when* it is best to be deceived, if it ever is so, unless and so far as we already know what the actual facts are. If, for instance, the universe is so constituted that to know the truth about it would only make men miserable without any compensating advantage, it would be better for them to be deluded. But it would be only through previous impartial inquiry that anyone could ascertain that the universe is so constituted. Thus, even on this extreme hypothesis, it would be the duty at least of some men—those who are to hide the truth from the others—to endeavour to view things in a dry light. This must, on any supposition, be an essential part of the business of the philosopher.

8. *The Common Opposition of what is and what ought to be*

So far I accept the principle of 'ethical neutrality'. But I do so with a reservation which will in the end turn out to be of essential importance. The word 'ethical' in this formula may and does lead to confusion on a vital issue. Granting that in general if we are impartial we shall not believe that anything *is* merely because it *ought to be*, it does not therefore follow that ethical considerations ought to be sweepingly dismissed as merely a source of prejudice. For it may be argued on what pretend to be rational grounds that the common opposition of what is and what ought to be is not always valid; and, in particular, that it is not applicable where the question concerns the nature of the universe as a whole. It may be held that here, if nowhere else, we have good reason for assuming that what ought to be coincides with what essentially is. Whether such reasoning is sound or unsound, it has to be considered on its own merits. Anyone who condemns it offhand, as a violation of ethical neutrality, merely begs the question and may himself perhaps be suspected of bias. With this reservation, I agree that even for the sake of satisfying our practical and emotional needs it is essential, so far as we can, to start from a neutral view of the available evidence. I am trying in the present chapter to be faithful to this principle and I shall do my best to be faithful to it throughout.

9. *The Conflict of Theoretical and Practical Interest*

But after this point has been settled another and a more intricate problem remains behind. How are we to use the result of our impartial inquiry in dealing with practical exigencies? There would be no difficulty if we could reach one definite and unambiguous conclusion of so compelling a certainty as to leave no room for alternative possibilities. But this may not be so. In particular, it may not be so in questions concerning the ultimate nature of the universe and man's place and destiny in it. Here unbiassed scrutiny of the available data together with impartial reasoning may still seem to leave open alternative views. Now if our interest were merely theoretical we might, at least provisionally, rest content with this result, either looking for more light on the subject in the future, or, if there seems no hope of this, giving up the problem as beyond our power to solve. But in adapting ourselves to a situation so as to satisfy, as best we may, our practical and emotional needs, the position is essentially different. In order to have a chance of proceeding efficiently, we must proceed as if one alternative were true to the exclusion of others.

This working assumption may be that which the data at our disposal indicate on the whole as the most reasonable. But in the ordinary business of life it happens not infrequently that our practical needs demand as a working assumption an alternative which is not on the available evidence the most likely. To use our previous example, a general groping his way amid the fog of war may find that there is only one view of the situation which offers him a chance of avoiding ruin and attaining success. He is then bound to proceed as if this view were true, though on the evidence before him it is relatively improbable. If human nature were other than it is, this state of things would present no difficulty to the advocate of so-called 'ethical neutrality'. He might say—'Let us by all means make what practical assumptions we need or seem to need. But let us at the same time bear constantly in mind that our assumptions are doubtful and also the degree in which they are doubtful. Let us remain ready to welcome fresh light and to change our views in whatever way reason and evidence may require.' No doubt this is an ideal which we ought to pursue so far as we can without too great a sacrifice of other interests. But, in fact, human nature and the conditions of human life make it rarely, if ever, possible thus to unite practical efficiency with complete impartiality. When men have once committed themselves to a practical postulate, they can hardly help clinging to it with a confidence and persistence unwarranted on theoretical grounds. The claims of alternative views tend to be dismissed and disregarded. The general who has once committed himself to a plan of operations courts almost certain failure unless he follows his working assumptions in a spirit of assured confidence and communicates a like spirit to others. The same holds good, when the practical issue involves the fundamental and abiding interests—social, political and religious—of great masses of mankind. Current beliefs become interwoven with the whole scheme of life of individuals and of the community of which they are members. Each is impelled to maintain assurance and suppress doubt in others; and the established creed is enforced by the weight of authority and tradition.

10. *The Moral Problem arising from the Evil Effects of this Conflict*

This conflict of theoretical and practical interest is, in itself, a great evil. It tends to fix and confirm men in error and expose them to the risk of painful and disastrous disillusionment. It is also a main source of intolerance, persecution and embittered antagonism. If it seems to a man that for himself and others there is no security against the risk of everlasting torment except in holding, with unwavering confidence, a certain creed, he can scarcely be expected to be tolerant towards unbelievers. He can hardly avoid feeling and acting as if the direct aim of the unbeliever were to bring upon mankind the dreaded doom. If he believes in the efficacy of persecution by burning and slaying, he will burn and slay; or if he fails to do so, through tenderness of heart, he will, under the given conditions, be falling short of his duty. This is an extreme instance. But, in general, so far as a belief comes to be identified with a practical or emotional interest, opposition to the belief tends to be identified with opposition to the interest and to be treated as due to ill-will.

Bias of this kind is no doubt an inevitable evil, inasmuch as we cannot reasonably hope ever to eradicate it entirely. It does not, however, follow that we must or ought to accept it passively, any more than the pain or disease which are also apparently ineradicable. So far as the conditions of life and conduct permit, we ought constantly to strive after an impartial view. We cannot do so under the immediate stress of practical and emotional needs. But we are not always thus intensely preoccupied. There are periods of comparative calm and detachment, which we may devote to reflexion and self-criticism. Further, there may be a certain division of labour. There are some men, among whom Gifford Lecturers ought to be included, whose special business it is to go back upon first principles and submit them to a scrutiny as unbiassed as the frailty of human nature allows.

Still, it must be admitted that the degree in which it is possible thus to keep an open mind depends on the nature of the practical postulates which have already become interwoven with life and conduct. The typical Spanish Inquisitor, for instance, was bound always and under all circumstances to turn a deaf ear and a hostile mind to whatever might tend to weaken his faith. It follows that we ought, in the first instance, to be on our guard against committing ourselves to working assumptions which may lead to intolerance. Other things being equal, that practical postulate is practically the best which most conduces to open-mindedness and friendly co-operation with our fellow-men. If it is not therefore the more likely to be true, it at least affords us the best chance of discovering our errors. Thus if there is a view of the universe and of our place in it which in other ways ministers to our practical needs as well or better than any other, and at the same time disposes us to recognise readily and ungrudgingly the candour and good will of those who disagree with us, to consider attentively and sympathetically all that is said or might be said by them in support of their own position and against ours, and in general to treat them not as enemies but as fellow-workers in the search for what is true and good, it is plain that such a view has an immense practical advantage to recommend it. None the less, it may be false, and if we think it false or most probably false, we must not sacrifice truth in order to be amiable. On the other hand, as I said before, such a view gives us the best chance of correcting our errors.

Further, there is one fundamental assumption in which many of us professedly share, on which the mere fact that a belief favours open-mindedness makes it the more likely to be true. If the universe as a whole is good, if for instance it expresses the supremely good will of a Perfect Being, there can be no ground to fear, but every reason to welcome, whatever reasons or evidence may possibly help further to enlighten us about it. There must, on this assumption, be something wrong in any creed which leads us, for instance, to regard as an enemy of God anyone who denies His existence. If God really exists it must be a matter of comparative indifference whether this or that man believes in His existence or not. What is supremely important both for believer and unbeliever is that they should strive to do His will; and this means that so far as in them lies, they should strive to think truly and act rightly.

11. *The Bearing of the above Discussion on this Book*

The outcome of this discussion in its bearing on my position in this book is as follows. I have primarily to seek after an impartial view of the questions raised. But I have also to recognise that beyond the theoretical problem there is always the practical. The pressure of practical and emotional needs does not permit us to proceed as if only theoretical curiosity were to be satisfied. Where reasons and evidence may not be considered sufficient to remove theoretical doubt, they may yet be sufficient to justify a practical postulate. Where a practical decision is required, it is enough that on the whole such reasons and evidence as are accessible to us point in a certain direction. In following such indications we may run more or less risk of error, but the risk has to be taken.

12. *Can the Truth of Religious Beliefs be tested by Experience?*

In considering working assumptions, I have so far failed to take account of their verification through trial and error. What is initially a practical postulate may in and through

its application lead to experiences which falsify or confirm
it. Indeed, it is a most important advantage of a postulate
that it is capable of being tested in this way. Where the
interest is merely theoretical, this is, I should say, the main
consideration which justifies us in preferring one working
hypothesis to another. But even in pure science, and
a fortiori in matters which involve directly the emotional
and practical needs of mankind, impartial inquiry may not
yield results so decisive as to enable us to dispense finally
with assumptions which are theoretically more or less
doubtful. This clearly holds good for social, political and
ethical questions. When we turn to religious beliefs and
unbeliefs we find ourselves met by a special difficulty; it
may be seriously questioned whether in this region practical
testing of the truth of practical postulates is possible at all.
Their utility may, it would seem, be ascertained by trial,
but not their truth. A man may, let us assume, find by
experience that faith in God enables him to live a good life
and others who know him may recognise that this is so.
But how can he in this way reach experiences either directly
revealing the fact of God's existence or revealing facts other
wise inaccessible, from which this can be inferred? If we
take account only of the ordinary data of sense-perception
or introspection, this seems scarcely possible.

None the less, men in whom the religious consciousness
is especially intense and powerful have always either
expressly claimed or implicitly taken for granted that their
religious experience yields them a direct warrant, not only
of the working value, but of the truth of the faith by which
they live. It is not, they would say, merely the working
value which accounts for the strength of their assurance.
On the contrary, it is only because the assurance arises
from direct insight that its working value can be adequately
accounted for. It is true that this insight, pretended or
real, is of a peculiar kind. It is not founded, for instance,
on sense-perception or logical analysis. Rather it is bound
up with the religious experience itself. Living faith in

God, for example, is felt as direct communion with Him which leaves even less room for doubt of His existence than intimacy with a friend or brother.

13. *The Philosopher's Attitude to 'Religious Experience' and Religious Beliefs*

What ought to be the attitude of a philosopher towards such claims? Proceeding by way of explicit analysis and reasoning, and finding it hard or impossible to include these 'mystical experiences' among the data from which he starts, is he justified in neglecting them altogether, and proceeding as if they could safely be treated as altogether baseless? On the other hand, if he is to take account of them, in what way and to what extent ought he to do so? It is plain, of course, that he cannot accept, as they stand, without searching inquiry, the beliefs in which the religious consciousness actually finds or has found expression. For these differ from individual to individual, from community to community, and from age to age; and what truth there may be in them is mingled and blended with much error. Yet this by itself is no sufficient ground for denying the claim of religious experience as a primary source of knowledge. Even if it is a primary source, there will yet be abundant room for error in the interpretation of its data, just as there is abundant room for error in the interpretation of the data of sense-perception. Further, the errors will be manifold and diverse according to the stage of mental development, the influence of practical interests, and other variable conditions. It is not safe, merely on such grounds, to ignore altogether the claims of the religious consciousness, as represented, let us say, by St Francis, Wordsworth, Spinoza or Gautama, or by a greater than any of those, and to rely entirely on other considerations.

In what way then, and to what extent, ought they to be taken into account? The position of these religious beliefs does not seem to me to differ fundamentally from that of other prescientific beliefs of common sense which human beings have been led to form in their concrete experience of life and the world, without being able to analyse and define their reasons for them.[1] Such are, for instance, the belief in our agency as conscious beings, the belief in a causal order, the belief in external objects. These pre-scientific deliverances of common sense cannot claim to be accepted as they stand by the philosopher. On the contrary, the philosopher or man of science may, from his point of view, freely criticise them and radically recon-struct them. But if he is not to cast doubt on his own methods and results, he must not simply deny them with-out satisfactorily accounting for them, and without sub-stituting for them some view which is capable of taking their place. In particular, if his own inquiry leaves open possible alternatives, there is a presumption in favour of those which are fundamentally consistent with primary beliefs and a presumption against those which are radically irreconcilable with them.

Religious beliefs are, of course, less generally diffused than, for instance, our belief in our own agency as conscious beings. It is possible for men to ignore or neglect their relation to the universe as a whole, as it is not possible for them to ignore or neglect their relations to their immediate

[1] [At this point in the typescript the sentence was inserted in manu-script: 'This whole question will be considered in the following chapter'; and the remainder of this chapter, as printed above, was marked for dele-tion. This seems to have been done in the very preliminary stages of preparing *Mind and Matter*, before Stout decided completely to rewrite the Lectures for publication, and the promised chapter finally appeared as Chapter 1 of *Mind and Matter* ('Common Sense and Philosophy'). This first chapter of *Mind and Matter*, however, deals mainly with the relation of philosophy to prescientific or non-scientific beliefs in general, and makes only a brief reference to religion as one type of such beliefs. For this reason, and because in any case the present chapter would be incomplete without it, I have printed the remainder of the chapter as it stands, in spite of the author's intention that it should be superseded. But it should be read in close connexion with *Mind and Matter*, Chapter 1.—Ed.]

environment. But it does not follow that we may set aside as valueless the claims of those who have most seriously grappled with the religious problem and who seem to themselves to have found in their own experience convincing support for their practical postulates. On this topic it may suffice to refer to what Professor James has said in his *Varieties of Religious Experience*. It is true that such personal experience cannot be expected to have the same weight with others as with the man who himself experiences it, or to have the same weight with outsiders as with those who know him well and are predisposed to trust him. None the less, even outsiders may not be justified in rejecting his evidence as counting for nothing at all.

Besides these special beliefs, there are at least two presuppositions of the religious consciousness in general which may fairly be regarded as primary and universal beliefs. The first is that the universe of which we are part is a unity in such a sense that we are justified in attempting to determine its nature as a whole, and in taking up a certain emotional and practical attitude towards it as a whole. This is also the fundamental assumption of all metaphysical construction. It is common to Bunyan and Spinoza. The second general presumption is that mind is not something merely transient and incidental, but is in some way or other primary and ultimate in the constitution of the universe.

We shall have to deal with both these assumptions by the way of critical reflexion. But, in doing so, we shall do well to remember that the common sense of mankind has also a separate claim to be heard. It has such a claim, because it is by no means always safe to take for granted that the grounds for primary belief, as arising in and through concrete experience in dealing with a practical situation, are, or indeed can be, adequately reproduced and defined in our philosophical analysis.

Chapter II

AGNOSTICISM, LEGITIMATE AND ILLEGITIMATE

1. *If there is no Universe, Metaphysics and Agnosticism are both excluded*

There is one view which, if it could be maintained, would leave no room and no need for an agnostic attitude. If there were no universe at all as an all-inclusive unity, we could neither know nor be ignorant of its nature. There would be only an indefinite multiplicity of items related to each other in space and time; and our knowledge might proceed from item to item in endless progression, as if we were stringing beads. But there would be no universe in any way containing these items within a unity: there would be no whole of being. The very word universe, in its philosophical sense, would have to be banished as covertly suggesting a false or baseless assumption. On this view there would be no positive metaphysical doctrine; and the only task left for metaphysics would be to show that there is no ground for assuming any ultimate and all-embracing unity. Agnosticism too would be excluded. For the agnostic, holding that the ultimate nature of the universe is unknowable, at least presupposes that there is a universe. On the other hand, if there is nothing but an aggregate of particular items with their temporal, spatial and other relations, he can have no ground for asserting that anything is by its own ultimate nature unknowable to finite minds. There is no reason for asserting that anything is unknowable otherwise than the configuration of the other side of the moon is unknowable to dwellers on the earth. Dwellers on the earth cannot know the other side of the moon because they cannot go round and examine it. But in its own nature

the other side of the moon is just as knowable as that
which faces them. From this point of view, it may be that
there is always an unbounded field of ignorance for every
finite mind; but we have no right to say that there is anything which finite minds, as such, are incapable of knowing.

Now I have, so far, not directly examined or criticised
this theory—that there is no universe, but only a collection
of particular items—which may be called pure positivism.
In the next Book I shall come to close quarters with it, and
I shall attempt to show that it is fundamentally untenable.
For the present, I am taking for granted the universe as an
all-inclusive unity. On this assumption, we have to consider how far the nature and constitution of this unity is
knowable or unknowable to such beings as we are.

2. *Spencerian Agnosticism*

There are two forms of agnosticism. There is the modern
form familiar to us, as represented by Herbert Spencer,
and there is that maintained by the great schoolmen such
as Thomas Aquinas and Duns Scotus. The agnostic of the
Spencerian type holds that concerning the ultimate nature
of the universe as a unity we can determine nothing except
that it exists and that it is unknowable. Beyond this we
are necessarily unable to lay down any propositions about
it which are of theoretical or practical value. The result is
that, so far as knowledge and conduct are concerned, we
must proceed as if we were pure positivists, though our
agnosticism is really incompatible with positivism. Only
in one respect is there a difference. The agnostics of this
type recognise everywhere an ultimate mystery which they
cannot even attempt to penetrate; pure positivism, on the
other hand, logically excludes mystery.

Further, some Spencerian agnostics, including Spencer
himself, feel, and hold that it is right and natural to feel,
an appropriate emotion towards this mystery—an emotion
which can properly be called religious. It is sometimes

said by way of a gibe that Herbert Spencer divides all being into two parts, the knowable and the unknowable, and that he assigns all that is knowable to science, and only what is unknowable to religion. If by this it is intended to suggest that in assigning a sphere for religion he is insincere and not to be taken seriously, I cannot agree. We must remember that for Spencer the Unknowable is an all-pervading reality, and in some way the absolute source and presupposition of all finite existence. It is rash to assert that one who believes in such a reality either cannot or ought not to feel towards it a peculiar emotion of awe and reverence. On the contrary, this emotional attitude may be so strong and pervasive as to affect his whole view of the world and of human life.

3. *Criticism of Spencerian Agnosticism*

It is another question whether the Spencerian agnosticism is logically tenable. On what principle can it be justified in stopping short where it does and cutting off all further inquiry as inevitably hopeless from the nature of the case? If we can and do have sufficient grounds for asserting the existence of the universe as an all-inclusive unity, why may not the same grounds justify us in making assertions about its nature? The absolute whole must be such as to contain these partial features and aspects which form the content of our ordinary practical and theoretical experience. It seems purely arbitrary to affirm that the nature of these partial features and aspects can afford no clue to the nature of the unity which transcends and includes them. It is hard to see what right we can have to reject pure positivism and to hold that there is a universe, except on the ground that the field of finite existence in space and time is seen to be by its intrinsic nature incomplete, so that it requires to be conceived as part of a single, ultimate, all-embracing whole. But if finite existence thus points beyond itself to its own completion, why should we lay it down as an *a priori*

principle that it cannot, in any manner or degree, determine the nature and constitution of the whole to which it
belongs? Why should we stop short at the existence of the
universe, and refuse to inquire what sort of universe?
I have argued[1] that as mind is by its nature incapable of
being produced by, or in any way being derived from,
what is not mind, it must be primary and fundamental in
the constitution of the whole. Again, some philosophers,
finding what they take to be contradictions in the nature
of all finite existence, in all that Spencer would call unknowable, argue that if these contradictions are not to be
taken as ultimate, all the objects of thought and knowledge
must be regarded as partial appearances and therefore as,
in varying degrees, unreal appearances of one reality.

Now these arguments may or may not be well founded.
It may even be that all special examples of this type of
reasoning have been unsatisfactory. If this were what the
Spencerian agnostic maintained he might be in the right.
But this is not what he says. What he is committed to is
the proposition that *all* attempts to reason from the nature
of the part to the nature of the whole are, in principle,
wrong. This is mere dogmatism unless it is supported by
a positive and adequate reason. No such reason has ever
been assigned. Spencer, indeed, tells us that the unknowable is unknowable because it is absolute in the sense
of being unrelated, whereas 'to know is to relate'. But it
is plain that if anything is unrelated to what we know, we
can have no ground for asserting that it exists at all. Even
to say that knowable being depends on it is to affirm
a relation. Spencer himself cannot help conceiving this
absolute being as characterised by its relation to what is
knowable. It is for him a persisting power or agency
which manifests or expresses itself in the sphere of existence
accessible to our knowledge. He simply assumes without
discussion that this relation can afford no clue which may
enable us further to determine its nature.

[1] [In *Mind and Matter*.—Ed.]

4. *Scholastic Agnosticism*

Spencerian agnosticism, therefore, is groundless and internally inconsistent. It is otherwise with what I have called Scholastic Agnosticism. This does not deny the possibility of knowing propositions of theoretical and practical value concerning the ultimate nature of the whole within which we live, move and have our being. But it insists that these propositions themselves bring us face to face with the inevitable limits of our knowledge, and raise questions which are, in principle, incapable of being answered by such beings as we are. The reason is that we know the whole only in knowing its partial features. We know it only as that which correlates and combines in a coherent unity such partial features and aspects as we can distinguish within it from our limited position in time and space. It cannot, therefore, be known to us as it would be to a central and universal mind, for which all that is would be completely open and transparent in its unity and in its detail.

The proposition that there is such a mind may be taken to illustrate the range and the restriction of our knowledge in this direction. The proposition is certainly not meaningless, and it is arbitrary to maintain, without special inquiry, that we can have no valid ground for asserting it. We know what we mean by mind, and so far we know what we mean when we say that there is a Universal Mind. We also know what we mean when we say that it is free from the limitations of finite minds. But when we combine these two statements, we are at once confronted with problems which we can never hope to solve. We cannot positively set before ourselves what it is to be a mind and yet free from the limiting conditions of finite thinking and willing. We may say that the Universal Mind is eternal, omniscient, omnipotent. But all that these words convey to us is that it must fulfil certain requirements involved in the very conception of it as universal. We cannot, in thought or

imagination, realise to ourselves in what way these requirements are actually fulfilled.

Here, then, there is a legitimate place for agnosticism.
The schoolmen have ways of stating this position which it
is worth while for us to examine. They sometimes say that
we cannot know God as He is in Himself, but only our
relatedness to Him. They speak of our relatedness to Him,
and not of His relatedness to us; for they mean to deny
that we can know Him as He is related to us, and they
would even hold that He cannot be properly said to be
related to finite beings at all. Such statements seem
needlessly paradoxical.   If A is related to B, B must be
related to A, and we cannot know how A is related to B
without, *pro tanto*, knowing how B is related to A. But we
can get rid of the paradox and yet leave the general position
untouched. We may assert that we know the Universal
Mind only in knowing the relation of finite minds and
other finite beings to it.

Another formula found in the schoolmen is that no
predicate ascribed to finite beings can be ascribed in the
same sense to God. Thus when we say that He knows or
wills or is wise or powerful, the terms *knowledge*, *will*,
power and *wisdom* are equivocal. They cannot mean what
they mean when we say that a man knows or wills or is wise
or powerful. This seems a hard saying and looks as if it
ought to lead to complete agnosticism. For such words as
'knowing' and 'willing' can have no meaning for us
except what is derived from our conception of knowledge
and will in finite minds. If they cannot have this meaning
when applied to the Universal Mind, it would seem that
they can convey no meaning at all. Even the statement that
there is a Universal Mind must be an empty verbal formula
not really expressing a judgment. But this inference is too
hasty. There is a vital distinction between the same
meaning and a derivative meaning. The verb 'to know'
may not have the same sense when we say that the Universal
Mind knows, as it has when we say that a man knows; none

the less the second may be related to the first so as to be derived from it in a definite and intelligible way. As a matter of fact, the ambiguity of which the schoolmen speak is such that we could not recognise its existence at all, if we did not also recognise its source, nature and direction. This enables us, if not completely to get rid of it, at least to allow for it and discount it.

The knowing and willing of the Universal Mind must be altogether free from the limitations and defects of knowing and willing in such beings as we are. In this proposition, taken abstractly, there is no ambiguity. The ambiguity arises only when we attempt positively to realise in thought or imagination what it is to know and will without such limiting conditions. In order to understand the exact position we may with advantage compare and contrast it with that in which we attempt to bring before our mind the state of things which would exist if two contradictory propositions were both true. We may know what 'S is P' means and we may know what 'S is not P' means. Further, we know, in general, what is meant by two propositions' both being true, and *pro tanto* we know what is meant by *these* propositions' both being true. But we cannot bring before our minds anything expressed by their union. We can think of their being combined but we cannot think their actual combination. Similarly with the propositions 'there is knowledge' and 'this knowledge is free from all conditions'. We can think of their being combined, but we cannot think their actual combination. But here the analogy ceases and we find a vital difference. The reason why we cannot think a contradiction is simply that there is nothing to think. The failure, if we may call it a failure, is due to no impotence on our part but to the ultimate nature of being and thought. On the other hand, the reason why we cannot realise in thought what unlimited knowledge is, is not that there is nothing to think, but that there is too much—too much for any finite mind to comprehend. In the attempt to grasp it we substitute for it knowledge as it exists or might exist in a finite being.

Here there is ambiguity which may mislead us if we are not sufficiently on our guard. We may be led to confuse knowing as found in limited beings, such as we are, with the unlimited knowledge of the Universal Mind. But, in principle, it is always possible to avoid this sort of confusion by constantly refusing to ascribe to omniscience whatever defects belong to finite knowledge as such. We cannot, indeed, know what it is to be omniscient as an Omniscient Being himself would know it. None the less we have a valid though always inadequate way of representing what transcends our direct insight. Assuming the unity of the universe, and assuming that the analysis and correlation of its partial features and aspects point to the existence of a Universal Mind as a fundamental condition of this unity, we are bound to ascribe to it whatever belongs to the nature of mind in finite individuals, if and so far as in so doing we avoid ascribing to it the limitations of finite individuals. Thus it is only in so far as our knowledge involves possible ignorance or error that we are debarred from ascribing it in the same sense to the Universal Mind. We are aware not only that our way of representing what transcends our direct insight must be inadequate; we also see the nature and direction of the inadequacy. Thus we can see that, in proportion as finite knowledge is more comprehensive and accurate, the less inadequately it represents omniscience. We can also see that the Universal Mind cannot be incapable of ignorance or error in the sense of being too low in the scale of psychical existence to be capable of knowledge at all. Ignorance and error are excluded only because knowledge is perfect. What owing to our finitude we fail to grasp in thought or imagination is something positive, not a negation or privation. We should be moving still further in the wrong direction if we thought of the Universal Mind as incapable of ignorance or error in the sense in which a stone is so, or a log of wood.

This would mean that it is not a mind at all; and to justify this position, we should have to show that in the world of finite beings mind, as such, arises merely from their finitude, that it does not belong to the ultimate nature of what is limited, but depends only on the limitation. But this is precisely materialism, against which I have already argued.[1]

In dealing with ethical predicates, we must be guided by the same principles; if the most searching inquiry we can make shows that the distinction between moral good and evil is merely incident to the special circumstances and limiting conditions of certain finite beings, such as men, we are not justified in applying ethical conceptions to the Universal Mind at all. We ought to conceive it as ethically indifferent. If, again, we find sufficient reason for asserting that will in finite beings is by its intrinsic nature ultimately directed towards evil, so that it only pursues what is good owing to its defects and limitations, then we are bound to conceive the Universal Mind as perfectly evil, and the world which it wills as a bad world. We should thus reach a metaphysical pessimism resembling that of Schopenhauer. If, on the contrary, we find that will in finite individuals is directed towards evil only because of their finitude, we must regard the Universal Mind as willing what is best, and the whole world which it wills as being good, whatever evil we find it to include. Whichever of these ultimate views we may be led to adopt on general principles, it cannot be upset or at all affected by any empirical balancing of the goods and evils which we actually find in our present circumstances. Such calculation is an entirely insufficient ground either for optimism or pessimism.

It is true that ethical predicates cannot, any more than other predicates, have the same meaning when applied to the Universal Mind as they have when applied to finite minds. But we can discount the difference by keeping in view its nature and direction. If we say that God is just,

[1] [In *Mind and Matter.*—Ed.]

we must not suppose that His justice is the same as ours. But this statement *itself* bears a totally different meaning from what it would have if we made it about a man. If we said of a man that he is not just in the sense in which the word is applicable to finite beings, we should be merely confessing that we are misapplying the word. We could only mean either that he is unjust or that his nature is wholly indifferent to the distinction between justice and injustice, that it is non-moral or ethically indifferent. But to affirm either of these alternatives of God would be an immeasurably greater error than simply to identify His justice with that of a king or a judge. We come nearer to the truth by representing the Universal Mind by what we know of finite minds, and by constantly remembering why and in what way this representation is inadequate.

I have taken as an illustration the conception of a Universal Mind. But the same general principle holds for all attempts to conceive the nature and constitution of the universe as a unity, whether mind is treated as fundamental or only as incident to certain transient finite conditions. We must still start from the nature of finite beings and discount as irrelevant what presupposes or follows from their limitations and defects.

5. The Procedure of Critical Agnosticism compared with that of Science

In some ways, the procedure of critical agnosticism resembles that of science in feeling its way among relatively unknown conditions. The scientific inquirer provisionally accepts and works with hypotheses on the ground that they enable him to account for observed facts and guide him in dealing with them, without assuming that the reality is actually such as he represents it. It is enough for his purpose that his hypothesis should so far agree with the actual conditions as to yield a coherent explanation of the given facts. Similarly, the philosopher, presupposing all data supplied by human knowledge and experience, theoretical and practical, endeavours to represent the unity of the universe as combining these data in a coherent scheme. This is the utmost that can be demanded of him. He need not and cannot penetrate directly into the ultimate nature of the universe as it is in itself, apart from that mode of representing it which alone is possible from the point of view of a finite being. From this point of view, he may reach results which give important help in determining our attitude, practical, emotional and theoretical, towards human life and the world in which we live—our whole view of our duty and destiny. If he can do this, it is unreasonable to complain that he can do no more. A light which is of use to direct our footsteps ought not to be despised merely because it does not illuminate the whole scene. The only difference between the position of the philosopher and that of the man of science, working with tentative hypotheses, depends on the distinction between what is ultimately unknowable to any finite being because of its intrinsic nature, and what is relatively unknowable owing to special circumstances.

6. *The Danger in Agnosticism of evading Difficulties*

If we accept this type of agnosticism, there is a dangerous temptation which we must carefully guard against. We must beware of uncritically evading difficulties by simply asserting that they are solved in a way which is unknowable to us or to any finite mind. This is legitimate for some difficulties, but not for all. It is legitimate where the difficulty is of our own making and arises out of the failure to bear in mind that we are really referring to unlimited being, even when we represent it in terms of limited being. Thus we may find it apparently impossible to conceive that a mind should be eternal or omniscient. If what we are trying to do is to conceive how any finite mind can be omniscient and eternal, and for this reason are inclined to

deny the existence of an omniscient and eternal being,
the difficulty is clearly due to inadvertence and confusion
on our part. It is fully met by pointing out that we are
referring to an unlimited being, and not to a limited one
however superior to ourselves. Here it is legitimate to
apply F. H. Bradley's formula: 'what may be and must be
is, even though we cannot realise in thought or imagination
how it is.' We have no right to assert that an omniscient
and eternal being cannot exist; and if we have grounds
for asserting that it must exist, we have the same grounds
for asserting that it does exist.

On the other hand, we have no right to deal in this way
with problems which concern the nature of finite existence as such. If, for instance, we find what appear to us to
be ultimate contradictions in the conception of change and
succession, it will not do simply to say that in some fashion,
which we cannot comprehend, these contradictions are
resolved in the absolute unity of all reality. Either we hold
change and succession really to exist as such or we do not.
If they really exist as such, they are included as such in
the universal whole. Hence if they are inherently contradictory in their nature, the contradiction remains. The
only way of removing it is by making our conceptual
analysis more adequate. If, on the contrary, change and
succession do not or may not really exist, but only seem to
exist, then there is no reason for surprise that the false
assumption of their reality leads to contradictions.

We may also infer that since there is nothing temporal
all that really is must be eternal. But it is not permissible
to express this by saying that the contradictions supposed
to be inherent in the conception of change are removed
or resolved in timeless being. If they are removed, it is by
showing that events do not really take place at all, or at least
that conceivably they may not take place. But this must
first be shown independently, before we can proceed to the
inference that whatever is real must be eternal. It must be
shown by a direct examination of change and succession as

they appear to us in the world of finite existence. If I can see no possibility that my awakening and getting out of bed this morning were not successive events, or events at all, I must assume that succession, as such, is included in the unity of the universe, and that if succession involves contradiction, the universe contains contradictions and is *pro tanto* itself absurd. Inversely, if the universe cannot be self-contradictory, it follows that succession as such cannot be so either.

Similarly, if someone, starting from the metaphysical position that the world of finite existence must be good, cannot reconcile this view of it with the evil which he finds in it, it is illogical for him to seek a solution of his difficulty by an appeal to the unknowable. Logically only two alternatives are open to him. He is bound either to give up the position that owing to the fundamental nature of the universe the temporal world of finite existence must be good, or he must, in some way, come to see that it may be ultimately good, in spite of the evil which he finds. If it may be so and it must be so, then it is so. But no device can justify him in holding at once that the world is good and that it cannot be good. It is true that in maintaining that, in spite of the evil actually found in it, the world may be good, he has a right to take into account the immeasurable ignorance of man. But the ignorance which he takes account of must be relevant. It must be ignorance within the sphere of finite beings, not ignorance of the ultimate constitution of the universe which transcends and includes this.

BOOK TWO

THE UNITY OF THE UNIVERSE

▼

Chapter III

THE HEGELIAN DOCTRINE

1. *The Russell-Moore Rejection of the Unity of the Universe*

I have so far proceeded on the assumption that the universe is a unity. I have now to show why I hold this position to be justified. There was a time, not so very long ago, when insistence on this point would have been almost superfluous, for almost everybody would have been ready to take it for granted. But in recent years it has been sharply criticised and denied by the new and important school of thought represented by Mr Bertrand Russell and Mr Moore. Mr Russell denies that the universe can be known to us as a unity in any sense which can warrant us in inquiring into its nature and constitution as a whole. 'We are thus left to the piece-meal investigation of the world and are unable to know the characters of the universe that are remote from our experience.'[1] If we may put it so, we are doomed, according to Russell, to live intellectually from hand to mouth. This does not debar him from the use of such terms as 'the Universe', 'the World', or 'the whole of being'. For such expressions, in his mouth, need not be taken to mean more than 'everything' or 'all beings'. The universe so conceived is just a collection of items. Certain of the items are known to us, some by direct acquaintance, others by inference. We can say of these known items that the universe includes them. But we cannot go beyond this. The items which we know can

[1] *The Problems of Philosophy*, pp. 226–7.

supply no clue to the character and constitution of the whole to which they belong. They do not even supply any ground for asserting that the whole, as such, has a character and constitution except that of being all-inclusive. It is in this sense that Russell denies the unity of the universe, and it is only in this sense that I am at present concerned to maintain it. What I am concerned to maintain is that it is in principle possible to have grounds for asserting and denying other propositions concerning the universe, besides the proposition that it includes whatever has being. This is possible because the character of its parts is capable of supplying a clue to the character of the whole.[1]

2. The Hegelian Doctrine of the Unity of the Universe (the Absolute)

Mr Russell, although he means to deny quite generally that there is any good ground for believing in the unity of the universe at all, yet directs his attack mainly against one special form of the doctrine—a special form which I agree with him in rejecting. The point at issue is whether, in upsetting the reasons for this special view, he has also overthrown the general principle. The theory which he assails is one which for a long time had been dominant. I refer to what is known as Hegelianism or Absolute Idealism, in the form in which it is expounded by such writers as Bradley and Bosanquet. Its distinctive feature is that it recognises only one Reality—the whole of being.

---

[1] I am not concerned to decide between various views which may be taken of the character of the whole, such as monism, singularism, dualism. I am not raising the question whether the universe contains ultimately only one sort of being, or two disparate sorts of being—e.g. matter and mind. I am not inquiring whether it contains a real plurality of distinct individuals or only one individual. Thus, arguments which are directed against special theories of the sort of unity which belongs to the universe do not affect my position, unless they can be generalised so as to apply to all theories which presuppose a unity at all in the sense I have defined.

For it, what we ordinarily regard as the partial contents included within this whole, whether particular existences or universal concepts, are, as such, mere appearances falsely taken to be real. Such mistakes are, for certain purposes, harmless, useful and even indispensable. But they are only working hypotheses which cannot possibly be final truth. Now it would seem that if the parts of a whole, as such, are unreal, the whole itself must be unreal. How then can the universe be real, considered as the all-inclusive whole?

This question leads us to the heart of the mystery of Absolute Idealism. The Hegelian who knows what he is about, though he may start with the conception of the universe as an all-inclusive whole, ends by substituting a radically different view. For him, there is in the long run only one Real Being which, properly speaking, has no parts and is therefore not a whole. All our ordinary judgments, in which we assert or presuppose beings other than this sole reality and comprehended within it, are mistaken. But in making mistakes there must be something concerning which the mistakes are made. This something concerning which the mistakes are made is the sole reality —the one ultimate subject of all judgments. If we know it as it is, all the distinct beings which common sense and science erroneously, though conveniently, take for real would be seen to be 'merged and lost' in its unity. Not 'comprehended', but 'merged and lost'. Thus the universe of the Absolute Idealist is not a whole which includes whatever is other than itself, but an Absolute which excludes the possibility of anything other than itself.

The paradox of this position is mitigated and concealed by what has been called the doctrine of degrees of error. To assert the reality of anything other than the Absolute is always a mistake. But the error is more or less in different judgments. Whether I take a stone or an individual mind for real, I must be wrong, because there is nothing real but the Absolute. Both stone and individual mind are mere appearances of it. None the less the individual mind expresses the nature of the sole reality more adequately than the stone. Hence in regarding it as real I am less remote from the truth than in regarding the stone as real. Similarly, though it is ultimately false both that Caesar crossed the Rubicon and that he remained on the other side of it, yet it is nearer the truth that he did cross it. The only propositions which are not more or less false are (1) that there is only one real being, (2) that whatever else we may take to be real is mere appearance, (3) that this or that appearance expresses the reality more adequately than others.

3. *The Doctrine of the Incompleteness of the Parts of the Universe does not imply that the Whole can be known from a Single Part*

This in rough outline is the Hegelian position so far as we are here concerned with it. We have now to turn to the grounds on which it has been maintained, and consider Mr Russell's attempt to show that these grounds are invalid. The question we are interested in is whether Mr Russell's argument can be generalised so as to apply to all those who suppose that they have good reason for affirming the unity of the universe. Now in part the Hegelian reasons for holding the universe to be a unity are such as may be accepted by non-Hegelians, and such as I would accept myself. Only in part are they peculiarly connected with the special doctrines of Absolute Idealism. What Mr Russell calls the main thesis of Hegel is common ground. It is that 'everything short of the Whole is obviously fragmentary and obviously incapable of existing without the complement supplied by the rest of the world'.[1] This general principle must be accepted by all who hold the unity of the universe. The ground for holding that the

---

[1] Russell, *op. cit.* p. 221.

universe is a unity would be destroyed if it were certain, and would be weakened if it were probable, that anything within it could be self-complete and self-contained, if anything in it were capable of constituting a universe by itself —an *imperium in imperio*.

Mr Russell, proceeding in his exposition, says: 'Just as a comparative anatomist, from a single bone, sees what kind of animal the whole must have been, so the metaphysician, according to Hegel, sees, from any one piece of reality, what the whole of reality must be—at least in its large outlines. Every apparently separate piece of reality has, as it were, hooks which grapple it to the next piece; the next piece, in turn, has fresh hooks, and so on, until the whole universe is reconstructed'.[1] It does seem to be part of the doctrine of Hegel himself, at least, that all that we can know concerning the nature of the Absolute can be seen to be true by a process of reasoning which starts from some single datum. But this view, whether it is or is not vital to the Hegelian philosophy, is at any rate not involved in the general principle of the unity

[1] Russell, *op. cit.* This statement goes far beyond what is involved in the unity of the universe and it is, I think, a misleading description even of the Hegelian position, at least as this is represented by Hegel's English followers. All that need be claimed is that we have sufficient grounds for asserting that the universe is a unity, and that the same grounds justify us in laying down certain propositions concerning the nature of the unity. Such propositions need not and do not make the reality to which they refer comprehensible to us. They demand that it shall be such as to fulfil certain requirements; but they give us no direct insight into the way in which these requirements are actually fulfilled. We can only represent this indirectly and inadequately from our finite point of view. The position of such a Hegelian as Bradley does not seem essentially different in this respect. In determining the nature of the Absolute, Bradley constantly applies the formula, 'What may be and must be is'; but he is careful to add that we do not understand *how* it is. The value for us of the theory of the Absolute Being is that it supplies a principle which guides us in distinguishing relative degrees of truth or 'reality' in our ordinary judgments. Plainly Bradley makes no pretence ideally of reconstructing the universe from its parts, as the comparative anatomist ideally reconstructs an animal from a single bone. The reference to a 'single' bone raises another question.

of the universe, as founded in the essential incompleteness of everything short of the whole. Each part through its incompleteness implies the whole of which it is part, and each part in its own way supplies some clue to the nature of the whole. But the clue supplied by any one part is only partial. It need not of itself and by itself constitute a sufficient source of all our possible knowledge of the general constitution of the universe. On the contrary, every partial clue ends, so to speak, in a note of interrogation. It issues in a question, and this question must have an answer within the whole of being. But by itself it does not suffice to determine what the answer is. It prescribes the answer only to this extent, that it must be an answer to the question. It must be such that the hook of interrogation can grapple it. In order to determine as adequately as we can what the answer is, we have to take account of all the relevant data we can command. We cannot determine 'what God and Man is' merely by examining, however exhaustively, the 'flower in the crannied wall'.[1]

Hence in ultimate philosophical inquiries we are bound, as far as in us lies, to take account of the whole range of our knowledge and experience, theoretical and practical. Failure and error will follow if we omit any important feature or aspect of universal being or fail to see its importance; and in order to make good the failure, the whole work will probably have to be done over again in another philosophical system. Even supposing that our survey of all relevant and important data were as comprehensive and complete as it can be made, and that we had gathered from them all that can be gathered from them, we should still be left with a great note of interrogation. For we still have no direct insight into the nature of the ultimate unity which includes and transcends them. We may be able to

[1] We might indeed, *if* we knew it 'all in all'. But the point is that we cannot know it 'all in all' without taking into account other *distinct* data than itself.

say that it must be such as to satisfy the questions which it raises, and such knowledge may be very important to us as determining our entire emotional and practical attitude. But we cannot tell how it does actually satisfy the conditions which it must satisfy somehow. We are in the long run confronted with problems which we cannot hope to solve.

4. The Relation of Self-contradiction to Incompleteness in Hegelian Doctrine

We have yet to consider the most distinctive peculiarity of the Hegelian procedure. This consists not in the assertion that everything short of the whole is essentially incomplete, but in the ground which is assigned for holding it to be so. On the Hegelian view, shared by such writers as Bradley and Bosanquet, the only valid reason for denying anything to be self-complete is that, when considered by itself, it is self-contradictory. What is meant is not that, when it is once admitted that something is incapable of existing by itself, it is a contradiction to regard it as self-complete. On the contrary, we must first exhibit the self-contradiction before we can infer the incompleteness. This seems to me to be an altogether untenable position. Take as illustration an ordinary deductive inference. A is contained in B and B is contained in C. This state of things is essentially incomplete. It implies something beyond itself—the inclusion of A in C. Now, given that the premises imply the conclusion, it is a contradiction to affirm the premises and deny the conclusion. But unless the implication is first independently presupposed, there is no contradiction at all. There is nothing self-contradictory in asserting that A is contained in B and B in C.

We thus see that it is not necessary, in order to show that something is incomplete, first to show that it is self-contradictory. We have now to add that even if we start

with admitted self-contradiction, we cannot from this infer incompleteness. The whole which includes what is
self-contradictory must include the self-contradiction, and
cannot therefore solve it. It is self-contradictory that a man
should make both ends meet by always paying in ready
money and living on the discount. The contradiction
disappears if we take account of a wider range of facts and
find that the man has a large balance at his banker's on
which he freely draws. But it disappears only because the
original proposition is *not* included in the wider whole, but
rather excluded from it as false. If it were included the
contradiction would remain. Hegel and his followers are
fully aware of this. Hence their sole reality does not really
include but rather excludes what they, none the less, call
its partial features and aspects.[1]

The ultimate conclusion of the Hegelian reasoning is,
as Mr Russell says, that 'if we saw the universe whole...
space and time and matter and evil and all striving and
struggling would disappear, and we should see instead an
eternal perfect unchanging spiritual unity'.[2] Evidently,
then, the whole of being cannot include space, time, matter,
evil, striving, struggling, etc.: or indeed anything else
except itself. It is futile to say that other things are included
somehow but not *as such*. What do we mean by saying that
a proposition is true of a thing but not true of it *as such*?
Take an example. A shopkeeper may have a vote in the
House of Commons, but not *quâ* shopkeeper. This means
that his right to vote does not depend on his being a shopkeeper but on some other character—e.g. his being a duly
elected Member of the House. Similarly, if something,
e.g. change, is said to be included in the absolute whole,
but not as such, this can only mean that change, besides
being change, has some other character in virtue of which

---

[1] The so-called partial features and aspects are merely various forms and
degrees of error in our judgments about it, and there is no judgment free
from such error except that which affirms the Absolute Being as such.

[2] Russell, *op. cit.* p. 223.

it is included. But in the Hegelian view every character of finite being is, as such, self-contradictory. There is therefore no character in which the partial features can be included in the whole. The so-called parts are not parts. The so-called whole is not a whole.[1]

Why then contrast whole and part at all? Why not abide consistently by the antithesis of real and unreal? The reason, I take it, is as follows. If the Hegelian could always, to his own satisfaction, show directly that a given concept was self-contradictory, he would have no motive for introducing the antithesis of whole and part. On the ground of self-contradiction he would straightway infer unreality. But he frequently finds this procedure difficult or impossible. He finds that if he is to show self-contradiction he can do so, if at all, only by first showing essential incompleteness. Then in some way or other he attempts to pass from essential incompleteness to self-contradiction. The method used may vary, but it is always invalid. It is indeed a contradiction to assert that what is essentially incomplete is self-complete. But the contradiction follows from the incompleteness and not inversely.

Hegel's *Logic* supplies ample illustration. We may take as an example the first step, in which he attempts to show that the concept of pure being is internally inconsistent. What he has to say is, in fact, extremely simple and obvious. It amounts to this. In merely asserting that something *is* or *has being*, we cannot possibly exhaust its nature. Merely to say that 'something is' necessarily raises the question— 'What is it?' Thus the concept of pure being is essentially incomplete, and, this being admitted, we contradict our-

---

[1] Thus the Hegelian combines two views which are not only different but incompatible. When Dr Bosanquet speaks of the 'one sole reality within which we live, move and have our being', he is uniting inconsistent conceptions. A reality within which we live and move and have our being cannot be the sole reality, for we must be real also. If we are not real, what he ought to have said is 'the one sole reality within which we *falsely seem* to live, move and have our being'.

selves if we say that it is not so. But this is not enough for
Hegel. He has to show not only that it is essentially
incomplete, but that it is self-contradictory. He argues
that since whatever is is something more than *mere* being,
it must be *other than* being. But what is other than being
is not-being. Hence the contradiction: 'being is not-
being' or 'whatever is is not'. The fallacy is not far to seek.
For contradiction we require the union not merely of
distinguishable predicates but of incompatible predicates.
When I assert that something is red I assert more than
when I merely say that it is coloured. But I do not assert
anything incompatible with its being coloured. On the
contrary, there cannot possibly be any incompatibility.
There can be none just because the concept of colour in
general is essentially incomplete, and in asserting that
a coloured thing is red, I supply what is wanting. To be
coloured is to be coloured in this, that, or some other specific
way. There cannot therefore be any self-contradiction in
saying that what is coloured is so in this way or in that way.
To get a self-contradiction we should have to show that what
is coloured is coloured *neither* in this way nor in that nor
in any other. The same holds for the concept of 'being in
general'. As Dr Hutchison Stirling somewhere points out,
it is not enough for Hegel to show that being is always
identical with being of some kind; what he ought to have
shown is that being of some kind is identical with being of
no kind—with no kind of being.

5. *The Hegelian Treatment of Change and Succession*

The Hegelian does not always argue in this way. He does
not always begin with incompleteness and then proceed to
show self-contradiction and unreality. Where he thinks
that he can do so, he attempts to demonstrate self-contradiction directly. It is thus that he deals, for instance, with
time and space and their infinity and infinite divisibility.
These, according to him, are internally incoherent and

therefore cannot be real. Now, we may have views about time which are incoherent, and so far as they are incoherent they must be mistaken. But it is a quite unwarrantable assumption that the error consists in regarding change and succession as real at all. This is a leap out of the frying-pan into the fire, since it commits us to the assertion that there really is no change and no succession. On the other hand, it seems exceedingly rash to assert that no possible view of the nature of change and succession can be free from self-contradiction. Even if it were admitted that no one hitherto has succeeded in giving a coherent account of them, it by no means follows that no one ever will. There must be a key to the riddle, if, as we maintain, change and succession are really partial features of a real universe and not merely regarded as such owing to a blunder.

6. *Self-consistency is not Self-completeness*

Turning now to Mr Russell's criticism of those who maintain the unity of the universe, we find that one important part of what he has to say is relevant only to the Hegelian position and not at all to ours. He points out that 'the whole tendency of modern thought is more and more in the direction of showing that the supposed contradictions in apparent features of the actual world were illusory'.[1] This is, of course, just what I should expect. But I must again insist that what is internally consistent is not therefore self-complete and self-contained. Consider, for instance, the occurrence of an event such as the fall of a stone or a twinge of toothache. There is, as Hume says, no contradiction in the conception of a beginning of existence. Indeed there cannot be, if events do actually occur. But when this is admitted, nothing is yet decided as to the possibility or impossibility of an *absolute* beginning of existence, a beginning which is unconditioned either by previous events, or by something which is not an event at

[1] Russell, *op. cit.* p. 227.

all. Further, when this question is raised, we involve ourselves in a vicious circle, if we attempt to answer it by
saying that the concept of an absolute beginning is or is
not self-contradictory. If we begin by presupposing that
an absolute beginning of existence is possible, it is a contradiction to say that it is not: if we begin by presupposing
it impossible, it is a contradiction to assert that it is possible.
But there is no contradiction without a positive presupposition one way or the other. In order to reach a decision
we must fall back on positive insight. We must see either
that a beginning of existence is something which may be
self-complete and self-contained, or that it is essentially
incomplete and requires to be supplemented by some
condition on which it depends.

7. *The Nature of Self-evidence*

Now when the issue is raised in this form I personally feel
no hesitation. It seems to me self-evident that a beginning
of existence must depend on conditions. In saying this
I know that I am laying myself open to the charge of
dogmatism. The appeal to self-evidence for the truth of
a disputed proposition seems futile. For he who denies it
of course denies that it is self-evident. Indeed, the mere
fact of disagreement seems fatal to self-evidence. For if
a proposition is evident, it ought to be obviously true for
everyone who understands what it means. To persist in
asserting it as self-evident is therefore mere dogmatism.

To this I reply, in the first place, that to be logically
self-evident is not the same thing as to be psychologically
obvious. Moreover, both parties are, in this respect, in
the same position. For both must appeal to self-evidence.
He who denies self-evidence can only do so on the ground
that it is evident that the contradictory of the proposition
may be true or might have been true. He must be reduced
to this unless he can show independent reasons for denying
that the proposition is true at all. This is so in the present

instance. If any one says that 'it is not self-evident that an absolute beginning of existence is impossible', then either his denial is baseless or he must assert that an absolute beginning is evidently possible. He has no reason to assert that it may occur except what is derived from the nature of the case. The appeal to facts is excluded, because the question is not one of fact but of possibility or impossibility. If, then, he is not prepared to assert, as a self-evident proposition, that there may be an absolute beginning, he has no right to deny that an absolute beginning is self-evidently impossible. All that he has a right to maintain is that the self-evidence is doubtful. If he goes beyond this he is as open to the charge of dogmatism as his opponent.

In the second place, an *impasse* of this kind is by no means inevitable. When what appears self-evident to one man does not appear so to another, it by no means follows that further discussion is unfruitful. Discussion would be unfruitful only if each maintained that he was infallibly right. But in holding that an absolute beginning of existence is evidently impossible, I do not claim infallibility. I may be wrong, as the earth-flattener is wrong in holding it as self-evident that if the earth were round, men at the Antipodes would fall off into space. The earth-flattener errs through inadvertence and confusion, leading to unconscious assumptions which beg the question. It is antecedently quite possible that I may be making a similar muddle. But if this is so, it is not enough merely to remind me of my own fallibility. My opponent also is fallible. I have a right to have it shown how my error has arisen— what inadvertence and confusion have led me astray. Hume recognises this when he alleges a fundamental confusion between true self-evidence and an impulse to believe based on customary association. But Hume's explanation seems to break down and only confirms me in my original view that what I took to be self-evident really is self-evident.

Again, my opponent may proceed indirectly. He may try to show that what I take to be evident is not even true, or that if it were self-evident he and others would not fail to recognise it as such. Now, it is plain that no one can point to any verified instance of an absolute beginning of existence; hence the first course is bound to fail. The second too is quite inconclusive. It is so because those who deny the self-evidence of a proposition are fallible in the same way and in the same degree as those who affirm it. They are as liable to be warped by preconceived theories and hardened prejudices; they are as liable to inadvertence and confusion. If I may be misled by confusing with true self-evidence an impulse to believe due to other conditions, it is equally likely that my opponent may be guilty of the inverse fallacy, and be ascribing, let us say, to custom or instinct what is really self-evidence.

Or, again, my opponent may be assuming that if a proposition is self-evident, the denial of it must contain a direct self-contradiction, whereas in fact there will be no such contradiction unless the proposition is already accepted as self-evident.

Further, the advocate of self-evidence may, like his antagonist, have recourse to indirect argument. In particular, he may urge that unless he is right a system of propositions universally admitted as rationally justified lose their logical basis and, so to speak, hang in the air without support. So far as the question of an absolute beginning of existence is concerned, this argument seems to me to be decisive. For the whole fabric of our knowledge of existence or 'matter of fact', beyond the few and scattered data of our own immediate private experience, depends for its logical justification on our right to complete the given in thought, on the assumption that whatever begins to exist presupposes conditions beyond itself. Hume admits and even emphasises this point. He confesses that unless he assumed the 'necessary connexion' of cause and effect, he would have no right to believe in any existence

beyond the immediate contents of his own private experience and memory. He would have no right, for instance,
to believe that in putting his hand into the fire before him,
the hand would be burnt or that he would feel pain.

8. *Can an Infinite Collection or Series be Self-complete?*

If, now, we take for granted that every event or beginning of existence must depend on conditions beyond
itself, we pass to a further question of crucial importance.
Is this demand adequately fulfilled, if we suppose the
series of past events to be infinite? This problem has been
often confounded with another essentially different—the
problem whether the conception of an actually infinite
series is possible at all. It has been maintained that the
conception of an actually infinite series of past events is
internally contradictory and must therefore be unreal;
further, since it would seem that we cannot conceive the
temporal order except as extending infinitely backward,
change and succession must be unreal. Now Mr Russell
tells us in the name of modern mathematics that the
supposed impossibility of infinite collections is a mistake.
'They are not in fact self-contradictory, but only contradictory of certain rather obstinate mental prejudices.
Hence the reasons for regarding space and time as unreal
have become inoperative, and one of the great sources of
metaphysical constructions is dried up.'[1]

This authoritative ruling I am quite ready to accept.
I am ready to grant, therefore, that the conception of an
infinite series of past events is perfectly free from internal
inconsistency. None the less, my own position is untouched. The sources of metaphysical construction remain
for me unaffected. For what I deny is not that an infinite
collection, such as that of past events, is incapable of
existing at all, but only that it is capable of existing by
itself as something self-complete and self-contained. The

[1] Russell, *op. cit.* p. 229.

difficulty is this. If every event *A* is conditioned by a prior event *B* and this by another *C* and so on, then no event can be adequately conditioned even by the totality of previous events, however many these may be. It can make no difference whether they are finite or infinite in number. On either alternative, change and succession finally presuppose an eternal Being without which they are incapable of existing. The world of becoming cannot be regarded as self-complete and self-contained.

9. *The Temporal and the Eternal*[1]

It is another question whether or not we are bound to assume that an infinitely extended temporal process has actually elapsed before the present moment. Granting that this involves no contradiction, and therefore may be so, it does not follow that it must be so. It does not seem strictly necessary to assume an infinite process, if we can refer the first event of a finite process to the Eternal Being as its source. None the less I do not see my way to accept the latter view, even as a possible alternative. I do not see how it is compatible with the conception of the relation of temporal and eternal being to which all my reasoning hitherto points. The temporal and the eternal are mutually complementary and logically interdependent constituents of the whole of being. Each is essentially incomplete, each is incapable of being what it is without the other. But both are equally fundamental and ultimate in the constitution of the universe. It seems irreconcilable with this view to regard either of them as absolutely derived from the other. As a matter of fact, if we attempt to conceive past temporal process as finite, we cannot avoid presupposing a time before the first event—a time during which the Eternal Being has existed before it created the

[1] [The author had marked off with square brackets the whole of this section, after the first three sentences, presumably with the intention of rewriting it.—Ed.]

world. We are thus drawn to regard the eternal as being in its own nature temporal. The reason, I take it, is that the Eternal Being is incapable of existing except in relation to time-process. Hence when we attempt to conceive it as apart from and independent of the time-order of the world of becoming, we must regard it as, in itself, temporally conditioned. In other words, we cease to conceive it as eternal.

Chapter IV

RUSSELL'S SCEPTICAL THEORY OF KNOWLEDGE

1. *Russell's Rejection of the Unity of the Universe and so of Constructive Metaphysics*

In the last chapter I have shown why I agree with Mr Russell in rejecting the Hegelian attempt to demonstrate the unity of the universe and to find a basis for metaphysical construction by showing that everything short of the whole is directly self-contradictory. I am quite prepared to find that the alleged contradictions are illusory and disappear with more exact analysis. But Mr Russell does not stop short at this point. He denies altogether that the universe can be known as a unity in any sense which would justify an attempt to give an account of its nature and constitution as a whole. In other words, he denies the possibility of metaphysical construction altogether. Now others besides Mr Russell have maintained this position. But he deserves and demands special attention because his scepticism is founded on a new theory of knowledge more thoroughly and acutely worked out than that of any other opponent of constructive metaphysics. This theory is taking strong hold of the minds of the younger generation of students of philosophy; and I feel that I cannot and ought not to proceed without taking account of it. Besides this, Mr Russell is so searching and so successful in bringing to light the fundamental questions at issue that in examining his views I shall be the better enabled to show why and how I abide by the principle of the unity of the universe and therefore regard constructive metaphysics as a legitimate adventure.

2. *Russell's Theory of Knowledge.* (*a*) *Knowledge by Acquaintance and Knowledge About*

I shall first expound Russell's theory itself. We have seen that those who regard the universe as a unity do so on the ground that its partial features are incapable of having being by themselves, as self-complete and self-contained. Now according to Mr Russell this view is quite untenable. It derives its plausibility from a fundamental confusion between knowing a thing and knowing truths about that thing. If we begin by assuming that what is asserted in propositions concerning the thing belongs to its own intrinsic being, then it is plain that the thing cannot have being at all apart from these truths about it; and inasmuch as the propositions about it assert its relatedness to other things, it follows that it is incapable of having any being apart from its relations. It is true, for instance, of a man that he knows things and likes or dislikes them. These are ways in which the man is related to what is other than himself. Now if we begin by presupposing that such relatedness forms part of the being of the man himself, we are, of course, already assuming that the man himself is essentially incomplete, and that apart from his relations he can neither be nor be known. Similarly, if I assume that it is part of the being of a present event, e.g. the fall of a stone, to be preceded and followed by other events, it follows that apart from the other events it cannot have being at all. If again I regard it as belonging to the very being of a sensible appearance, e.g. the white appearance of which I am aware when I look at a certain sheet of paper, that it should be the appearance of something, then I cannot consistently suppose it to exist and yet not to be the appearance of anything.

Now all reasoning of this sort rests, according to Mr Russell, on an entirely unsound basis. 'It is of course the case', he says, 'that a truth which connects one thing with another thing could not subsist if the other thing did not subsist. But a truth about a thing is not part of the thing itself.'[1] It cannot be so because 'it is scarcely conceivable that we can make a judgment or entertain a supposition without knowing what it is that we are judging or supposing about'.[2] Knowledge of things must therefore be logically prior to and logically independent of any knowledge about them. Hence it must be logically prior to and logically independent of any knowledge of their relatedness to other things. Thus relatedness cannot possibly be part of the being of a thing. It is always something so to speak superadded from without.

That direct knowledge of things which necessarily precedes all knowledge about them is called by Russell 'acquaintance.' 'We have *acquaintance* with anything of which we are directly aware, without the intermediary of any process of inference or any knowledge of truths.'[3] There are two essentially distinct kinds of being with which we may be thus acquainted, (1) Particulars and (2) Universals (i.e. qualities and relations). As an example of acquaintance with a particular, we may take my awareness of a toothache at the moment when I am actually feeling it—an awareness such as I cannot possibly have of another man's toothache. My immediate acquaintance with the toothache must not be taken to include anything whatever capable of being asserted of it in a judgment. Thus it must not be taken to include the knowledge that the toothache exists, is present, is felt, is mine, or that it is a toothache, or that it is like anything else, or that it has begun or continues. Bare acquaintance with particulars is speechless not merely for want of words, but because it contains nothing corresponding to what words would express— even such words as 'this' or 'that' or 'here' or 'now'. It follows that this sort of knowledge cannot be true or false. For truth and falsity have meaning only where something is asserted, denied or supposed.

[1] *The Problems of Philosophy*, p. 224.
[2] *Ibid.* p. 91.   [3] *Ibid.* p. 73.

Among the particulars with which we can be acquainted, what Mr Russell calls sense-data are very important. By a sense-datum he means what is immediately experienced in perceiving things by the senses—in seeing, touching, hearing, etc. Thus, in looking at the sheet of paper before me, I am acquainted with a certain white appearance diversified by black appearances.[1] After what I have already said, I need not repeat that bare acquaintance with the sense-appearance does not include knowledge that it exists or appears or is black or white, or indeed any knowledge that could be expressed in words. Before such knowledge can begin, there must already be knowledge by acquaintance. Neither must we suppose ourselves to be aware of anything of which it is an appearance, e.g. a sheet of paper or anything else which by an illusion may be mistaken for a sheet of paper. I might be acquainted with a quite similar sense-datum in a dream. Then it would not be the appearance of anything, though I should mistakenly believe it to be the appearance of a sheet of paper. The appearance[2] itself would then really exist and I should really be acquainted with it. The point is obscured by Mr Russell and others when they speak about seeing or hearing or otherwise *perceiving* sense-data. This is contrary to the use of ordinary language. In ordinary language, we do not say that we see what Mr Russell calls sense-data, but rather something of which the sense-datum is an appearance. If we take it to be an appearance of something when it is really the appearance of something else, we are said to see wrongly—to be under an illusion. But there can be no error in bare acquaintance. Again, if in a dream or hallucination the sense-datum is not the appearance of anything at all, then we do not really see anything; it is *as if* we saw something. When the drunkard

[1] [In the typescript, the term 'apparition' was written above 'appearance' where it occurs in this sentence, but 'appearance' was not deleted.—Ed.]

[2] ['Sense-presentation' written in above 'appearance'.—Ed.]

is said to see rats what is meant is that he seems to see rats. He cannot really see them, for they are not there to see. So, when I see a horse in a dream I only dream that I see a horse—but the dream apparition is actually present, just as it might be if I actually saw a horse.

Besides sense-data, there are other particular existences with which we may be acquainted. These include our own present mental states—our desires, feelings, and cognitions at the moment in which they exist. This kind of acquaintance, which may be called self-consciousness, is the source of all our knowledge of mental things. With obvious hesitation Mr Russell also includes, among the things with which we are acquainted, our bare selves as opposed to our particular thoughts and feelings. Finally he recognises what he calls acquaintance by memory. When we remember anything with which we have previously been acquainted we are according to him acquainted with it again, in spite of the fact that it appears as past and not as present. In this, as I shall hereafter try to show, he is too hasty. In the strict sense of acquaintance as defined by Mr Russell for present sense-data and mental states, there is no acquaintance by memory.[1]

Let us now turn to universals. Here the first point to note is that knowledge *about* particulars involves acquaintance not only with the particulars but also with universals. When we assert or suppose anything concerning a particular, we characterise it as having qualities and relations which are not themselves particular. What we assert is that the particulars are instances or examples of universal qualities or relations; and this would be impossible unless we were acquainted with the universals. Consider the proposition: 'this paper is white'. Here I am saying something about a particular which I refer to as 'this paper'. But I can only do so if I am acquainted with the general meaning of the words 'this', 'paper' and 'whiteness'. So too, I cannot understand the proposition 'this

[1] Cf. pp. 69–70.

egg is like that egg' unless I am immediately acquainted with the universal 'likeness'. On the other hand, it is by no means necessary that judgment concerning universals should include any acquaintance with particulars. To understand the proposition $2+2=4$ we must be acquainted with what is meant by 'being two', by 'addition', by 'equality' and by 'being four'; but we need not be acquainted with any particular instance of 'two-ness' or of 'addition' or of 'equality' or of 'fourness'. There is nothing asserted except universal relations between universals. Symbolic logic and pure mathematics consist of such propositions.

Just as with particulars, we must carefully distinguish between acquaintance with universals and knowledge about them. Knowledge about them is knowledge of their relatedness either to particulars or to each other. But this presupposes a prior and independent awareness of each universal in and for itself, apart from anything to which it may be related. Each universal must be separately and self-completely known. Hence it is inferred that relatedness to other things can form no part of its being and that therefore it is in itself a self-contained entity. Its relations are superadded to its own being, which is intrinsically complete without them.

Thus from the simple and apparently self-evident thesis that before we can know about a thing we must first know the thing itself, Mr Russell develops a thoroughgoing pluralism, which is incompatible with any view of the unity of the universe that could justify us in adventuring, however cautiously, on metaphysical construction. If he is right, we cannot say that everything short of the whole is essentially incomplete. On the contrary, we must say that everything is complete in itself.

3. *Russell's Theory of Knowledge.*
(*b*) *Knowledge by Description*

But when Mr Russell confronts his theory with what appear to be obvious facts, he is brought face to face with what looks like an insuperable difficulty. His central and indispensable thesis is that we cannot know about anything unless in knowing about it we are also independently acquainted with it. But we seem to be continually making judgments about things, and especially about particular existences, with which we have certainly no acquaintance as Mr Russell defines the term. Our own selves, our own presently experienced and remembered sense-data—this is the entire list of all the particulars known to each of us by acquaintance. But these form an immeasurably small part of the things which we seem to know about—which we believe to exist and to be characterised in various ways. There are, for instance, minds other than our own, with their perceptions, thoughts, feelings and desires and the sense-data which appear to them and not to us. We certainly believe in the existence of these things and seem to know a great deal about them. Yet we are not acquainted with them. The same holds good for our knowledge of external objects. If we regard our own sense-data as belonging to the material world, then we are acquainted with part of it. But it is, comparatively speaking, a very small part indeed. If, on the other hand, we regard sense-data as quite distinct from physical or material things, then we are not at all acquainted with the material world or any part of it. How then, on Mr Russell's theory, can we know anything about it? In general, the particulars with which we are actually acquainted are only a few scattered dots or specks in the illimitable expanse of knowable existences. By what sort of bridge can we cross, so as to pass from these given items to the others?

Mr Russell is fully alive to the crucial importance of this question and to the necessity of finding a satisfactory answer to it. But for him the problem is obviously exceedingly difficult, if not desperate. It is so for two reasons. He is bound to abide rigorously by his central principle that no one can know about anything unless he is acquainted with it. He is also bound to assume that the actually given items are each of them self-complete and self-contained, so that they cannot point to anything beyond themselves, as required to supplement them within a whole which transcends and includes them.

As he would himself confess, the task before him is no easy one. His first step is to attempt to show how we can truly judge that something with which we are not acquainted exists. This is possible only through inference from the existence of particulars with which we are acquainted. But can there be such an inference if the given particulars are self-complete and therefore point to nothing beyond themselves? Mr Russell meets this difficulty by introducing, as a bridge between the given and what is not given, general principles of connexion, relations of universals as such. The truth of a proposition asserting a relation between universals implies the truth of propositions asserting corresponding relations between actual instances of these universals, as soon as we know that there are such actual instances. Thus the proposition 'two and two are four' expresses merely a connexion of universals and is not concerned with particulars at all. But given an actual couple, Brown and Jones, and another actual couple, Smith and Robinson, then it follows from the universal relation, that Brown, Jones, Smith and Robinson form a group of four. Now there are certain universal propositions according to which the existence of things of a certain sort A is associated, or at least probably associated, with the existence of things of a certain sort B. Such general principles enable us to know that an instance of B probably exists when we are either directly acquainted with an instance of A, or know of its existence through prior inferences, which of course must ultimately lead back to actual acquaintance. We thus obtain the judgment: 'it is probable that something actually exists having a certain character B, and related in a certain way to A.'

We are thus in a position to *describe* what we are not acquainted with. We can describe it as 'that which has a certain general character and is related in a certain way to something else', where the 'something else' is known either by direct acquaintance or by previous inference (ultimately founded on direct acquaintance). Knowledge of this sort is called by Mr Russell 'knowledge by description' or, more exactly, 'knowledge by definite description'. A description is definite when what is described is so related to something else that there can be only one thing that answers to the description. Thus such phrases as 'the man in the iron mask', 'the other side of the moon', 'the author of *Waverley*', 'the present Prime Minister of England', 'the future of Europe' describe definitely. There is only one man in the iron mask, only one other side of the moon. On the other hand such phrases as 'a man' or 'a triangle' describe indefinitely, because they do not mark off this or that man or triangle individually, to the exclusion of all others. Definite description is all that we need here consider. It is most usually expressed by the use of the definite article in any phrase of the form 'the so-and-so'.

Knowledge by description depends on general principles connecting the existence of one thing with that of another. Thus there is a general rule according to which the existence of visual sense-data of a certain kind is very probably associated with the existence of a tree. When, then, we are acquainted with actual data of this kind, we believe that a tree connected with them actually exists. This we express by saying that we *see* a tree. But we are not acquainted with the tree itself; we only gather its existence with a high degree of probability from the sense-data. We know it by description. It is described as the tree connected with the sense-data, or in more familiar language as the tree which we see or which is before our eyes. Our belief in its existence is not more than probably true, because we might be acquainted with quite similar sense-data in dreams and hallucinations, where no tree associated with them actually exists. In general, the existence of sensible appearances is connected with the probable existence of external or physical objects, and in ordinary sense-perception we take it as a matter of course that they exist, without noticing that there is any logical step in the nature of an inference. Yet we are never acquainted with any physical object at all. In some way, we must be in general acquainted with the meaning of the term 'physical object' as a universal. But no physical object is itself directly known to us.[1]

What then, according to Mr Russell, do we know when we know a thing only by description? We are not, of

[1] Obviously this is a difficult position, at any rate for one who holds, as Mr Russell holds, that sense-data are complete in themselves and cannot therefore by their essential incompleteness point to anything beyond themselves. Hence we need not be surprised that since writing *The Problems of Philosophy* Mr Russell has given up the conception of physical objects altogether in the ordinary sense and substituted for it a theory of what is called the external world, and of our knowledge of it, fundamentally akin to that of Berkeley and of J. S. Mill. In *The Problems of Philosophy* he recognises only one great principle of inference which can justify any passing from the existence of things with which we are acquainted to the belief in the existence of things with which we are not acquainted. The principle is called by him the *principle of induction*, which he states as follows; '(a) When a thing of a certain sort *A* has been found to be associated with a thing of a certain sort *B* [Why not also of the same sort?] and has never been found dissociated from a thing of the sort *B*, the greater the number of cases in which *A* and *B* have been associated, the greater is the probability that they will be associated in a fresh case in which one of them is known to be present; (b) Under the same circumstances, a sufficient number of cases of association will make the probability of a fresh association nearly a certainty, and will make it approach certainty without limit.' (*The Problems of Philosophy*, p. 103.) It is on this principle that we believe that the sun will rise to-morrow, although we are not acquainted with to-morrow, or with the sun as it will be to-morrow, or with the event of its rising. We know these things only by description.

course, acquainted with it. But can we be said to know anything *about* it? Now Mr Russell occasionally uses language which implies that this is so: e.g. in one passage he says that 'many things are known about the man in the iron mask'. But such a statement must be due to a lapse of vigilance. For his fundamental thesis is that we cannot know *about* anything unless we are acquainted with it. But we are not acquainted with what we only know by description. Therefore, if he is right, we cannot know any proposition about it. The very phrase 'knowledge by description' is misleading. For in strictness we do not know at all what we are said to 'know by description'; we only know, at the most, the description of it. We believe that something exists and has a certain character, and that there is nothing else having this character. But the meaning of the word 'something' is general. It is applicable in the same sense to many and diverse 'somethings'. Similarly the 'character' ascribed to it is general. So, too, what we mean by 'there being only one thing so characterised' is general: there are many things which can truly be said to be unique in this way—e.g. the present Prime Minister of England, the centre of gravity of the earth, the highest mountain in the world, and indeed everything which is capable of being definitely described.

Thus a proposition expressing a description contains nothing but a complex of interrelated universals. If the proposition is true, then there must be some actually existing particular which the description describes. But we are not acquainted with this particular and consequently we cannot know about it. Consequently we cannot know that anything real is described by the description. Let us suppose the belief to be erroneous—an alternative which is always possible, though it may be highly improbable. Then we are left with a description which describes nothing because there is nothing to describe. All that we can properly be said to know is the description itself—as a complex of universals. Yet what our minds are dealing with may be exactly the same as if the descriptive pro-position were true.

Thus, whether the proposition is true or false, I know only the description and never anything corresponding to it. For instance, I may believe that a certain box contains matches or that I see a rat; and I may speak of 'the matches in this box' or of 'the rat I see'. But the box may be empty and my belief that I see a rat may be due to delirium tremens. Whether the box actually contains matches or not, whether there is or is not a real rat, makes no difference to my mind and its knowledge. On both suppositions, what my mind is dealing with is only a description, and not any actual particular actually corresponding to it. It follows that we cannot know propositions about any particular with which we are not acquainted. It is not true, then, that we know many propositions concerning the man in the iron mask. On the contrary, we know nothing about him. If we say that 'the man in the iron mask' was unfortunate, then inasmuch as we understand the state-ment, we must be acquainted with what we mean by the phrase 'the man in the iron mask'. But this is only a description couched in general terms. We shall always find, if we push analysis far enough, that definite descrip-tion ultimately includes a relation to some particular or particulars with which we are acquainted. This, however, makes no difference. For according to Mr Russell all relations are universal.

Mr Russell admits that we often intend to make a state-ment about an actual thing described and not merely about the description of it. In this, however, we are inevitably doomed to failure. When we say anything about Bismarck, e.g. that he was astute, we should like to make the judgment about the actual person who was called by this name. But we necessarily fail to do so, since the actual Bismarck is unknown. No one can know him except himself at a time when he was alive and self-conscious. We can describe the proposition which we should like to assert; but we cannot assert it. We may describe it as 'the proposition asserting, concerning the actual object called Bismarck, that he was an astute diplomatist'.

Though I am here expounding, rather than directly criticising, I cannot help pointing out on what very thin ice Mr Russell is here treading. If we cannot assert a proposition concerning a thing with which we are not acquainted, the same difficulty ought to make it impossible for us even to intend to assert it. What is really impossible, if Mr Russell is right, is to have a proposition before our minds at all, when we are unacquainted with one of its constituents. But we must have the proposition before our minds if we are *intending* to assert it, just as much as if we were really asserting it. It is useless to say that what we have is only a description of it. For if this were so, all that we could intend to assert would be the description, not the proposition itself.

4. *Summary of the foregoing Account of Russell's Theory of Knowledge*

I may now briefly sum up my account of Russell's theory of knowledge. There is a knowledge of things, whether particulars or universals, called acquaintance, distinct from and independent of any knowledge of their characters or relations. Acquaintance with a thing does not involve acquaintance with anything else or with the thing's relations to anything else. Hence it is inferred that whatever we can be acquainted with is capable of existing or subsisting by itself independently of relation to other things. Besides acquaintance, and sharply distinguished from it, there is also knowledge *about* things—knowledge of them as being 'such and such or so and so related'. We know *about* things only in so far as they are constituents of propositions. But this is impossible, unless we are independently acquainted with them at the moment in which we make a judgment concerning them. Knowledge *about* is absolutely confined to what we are, at the time, acquainted with. But, as a matter of fact, the particulars we are acquainted with are an extremely small selection from those we seem to know. If then we do not really know about the other things, there must be some kind of knowledge of which we have not yet taken account.

This gap is supposed to be filled by what is called 'knowledge by description'. We may know that something probably exists and has a general character, without knowing the thing itself. If it is objected that to know this is to know about the thing itself, which ought to be impossible since we are not acquainted with it, the answer is that knowledge by description is not really knowledge about the thing described, even when the thing actually exists—and it is always possible, however improbable it may be, that there may actually be no such thing. It is only the description we are acquainted with, and it is therefore only the description which can be characterised in judgments. When we assert that 'the author of *Waverley* was Sir Walter Scott', we are not saying anything about the actual person who wrote the novel, we are only affirming a relation between what is meant by 'being the author of *Waverley*' and 'being called by a certain name'. Thus when all unconscious camouflage is cleared away, it turns out that according to Mr Russell we can each of us know nothing about any particulars except our own present sense-data, our own present mental processes and those sense-data and mental processes which we are actually remembering at any given moment.

5. *Criticism of Russell's Theory of Knowledge*

In criticising this account of the nature and conditions of knowledge, our central interest lies in its bearing on the unity of the universe as presupposed in the possibility of metaphysical construction. If it is right, the universe is merely a collection of loose and separate items, each capable of having its own being apart from all others.

What we have to show is that this position is untenable and that a critical examination of it leads rather to the opposite view, that the universe is a unity.

Let us begin with Mr Russell's general reason for holding that every particular with which we can be acquainted is capable of existing by itself. His argument, apart from the assumptions which underlie it, may be stated in a very simple and compact form. In being merely acquainted with an actually existing particular, we are not acquainted with its relatedness to anything else. Therefore it is capable of existing by itself independently of its relations. Is this valid reasoning? It seems quite clear that it is fallacious. In being acquainted with a thing are we acquainted with all of it? This is a mere matter of definition. In ordinary language, when we have direct acquaintance with part of a thing, we do not hesitate to say that through this part we are acquainted with the whole. We say that we are acquainted with a thing when we are not directly acquainted with all of it. It is in this sense that we speak of being acquainted with a person. But if we exclude such indirect acquaintance, there can be no partial acquaintance. It is as if we so limited the meaning of the word *touch* that we should refuse to say that we are touching a table on the ground that our hand is actually in contact only with a portion of its surface. In this sense of *acquaintance*, then, when we are acquainted with what is part of a whole, we shall refuse to say that we are even indirectly acquainted with the whole; and, since we mean to include in the part only just so much as we are acquainted with, it is a mere tautology to say that we are acquainted with all of it, and not with its relation to anything else. Does it follow that it can exist without being related to anything else? Certainly not. All that follows is that its relatedness is not part of it, which is a very different matter. It is as if we were to argue that as my finger is in contact with a surface and not in contact with anything beneath, therefore the surface may exist by itself without having anything beneath it. Whether this is in fact possible or not, the conclusion does not follow from the premises.

It may be said that since, in acquaintance, we know completely what we are acquainted with, we ought to know whether it is or is not capable of existing by itself. The answer is that such knowledge can only be complete in its own peculiar way. In bare acquaintance with a thing we are supposed to know nothing whatever *about* it. But the question whether it is capable of existing by itself or not is, like all other questions, a question *about* something. At the level of mere acquaintance neither this nor any other question can be either asked or answered.

What then are we to make of this so-called knowledge by mere acquaintance, as Mr Russell defines it? Is there such a thing? And if so, is it properly called knowledge? As regards the second question, the answer seems obvious. We cannot be said to know a thing if we know nothing at all about it—if we know neither what it is nor that it exists nor that it is in any way present to the mind. Acquaintance apart from judgment is not knowledge at all. The distinction of true and false has no application to it. None the less, it seems clear that Mr Russell is referring to something real and of fundamental importance. My knowledge of my own present toothache takes the form of judgment about it. In this respect I know it just as my dentist knows it. But there is a vital difference. My actually existing toothache is *given* to me to judge about, as it is not given to my dentist or anyone else. It is existentially present to my mind as it is not to his. It lies open to my inspection and not to his. Now this givenness of existential presence is not itself knowledge; for all knowledge is of the nature of judgment. But it is an indispensable precondition of a certain way of knowing about particulars. It is the indispensable precondition of what Mr Russell calls 'intuitive judgments of perception'.[1] As the word 'perception' suggests that such knowledge is limited to sense-

---

[1] Russell, *op. cit.* Chapter XI.

data, and as it is otherwise ambiguous, I prefer to speak of 'judgments of immediate experience', i.e. judgments referring to what at the moment is immediately experienced, actually given, existentially present.

If we take these phrases as synonymous with 'acquaintance with particulars', Mr Russell seems clearly right when he says that there may be acquaintance, with little 'knowledge about', or even with none. This holds good, for example, for the subconscious contents of sense-experience—those sense-data which we experience without separately discerning them, or in any way judging about them in detail. Take, for instance, the feeling due to contact with our clothes. We do not ordinarily notice this; we do not distinguish or discern it or mentally assert anything about it. Yet when we do happen to attend, we are aware of it not as a quite novel experience, which then begins for the first time, but as having existed before we discerned it. By far the greater part of the detail of our sense-experience at any moment is thus experienced or existentially present, without any judgment that it is present or that it is such and such. Similarly with present subjective states and processes, such as attending, wanting, being angry and all the various ways of being interested. We may be so preoccupied with the objects of these processes—with what is attended to, desired and so on—that we do not at all, or hardly at all, reflect on the processes themselves, so as to know about them. Yet they are of course immediately experienced and may be very intense and complex.

On the other hand, there is no such existential presence of a remembered experience at the time when we are remembering it. My past toothache is no longer felt. In remembering it I need not have a continuation or repetition of it. Even if I did, the continuation or repetition would be distinct from the original experience repeated or continued. What we know in memory is that we have experienced a particular experience of a certain character more or less exactly or vaguely determined, and that it has a certain time-relation, more or less exactly or vaguely determined, to our present experience. Hence Mr Russell seems clearly wrong when he says that we are acquainted with what we remember, in the sense which he gives to 'acquaintance'. From his point of view, he ought rather to have classed remembrance as knowledge by description. The reason why he shrinks from this is not far to seek. Memory-knowledge, though it does not involve direct acquaintance or existential presence, is none the less primary knowledge in the sense that it is presupposed in all other knowledge of past events. Further, it seems to have sometimes, at least, a degree and kind of evidence closely approaching that of the intuitive judgment of immediate experience.

If it be asked wherein existential presence consists, there is a ready and sufficient answer for subjective states and processes. The existential presence to my mind of a pain or pleasure or desire or emotion consists in its being felt by me, so far as it is felt and while it is felt. Nothing more is required than its existence as a present phase of my conscious life. As such, it is an experience which I live through, though I may know little or nothing about it. It is *in* my mind. The same answer cannot be given without reserve for present sense-data. The difficulty here is that it has become the fashion of late to deny that sense-data are in any way mental, or that they can be properly said to exist in the mind. This is a question which I must at present pass by. I must content myself with pointing out that if sense-data are not mental they at least have a relation to the mind analogous to that which psychical states, as such, have, inasmuch as they can come to be known in that peculiar way which I have called knowledge by immediate experience. They are existentially present in some way, and therefore can be known as only what is existentially present can be known.

Let us now consider this sort of knowledge. What are its distinctive features? In the first place it would seem that there is nothing peculiar in the content of judgment. There is nothing which I can assert in reference to what I myself immediately experience which might not be asserted by another man provided that he has had experiences sufficiently akin to it. The other man, according to Russell, would not really know *about* it but only know the description of it. But, waiving this question, the point is that he may describe it just as I describe it. I know that it exists and is directly present to my mind: he also knows that it exists and is directly present to my mind. I characterise it as red, bright, extensive and round; and he may characterise it in the same way. There is no character which I assign to it which he may not also be in a position to assign to it. He may even direct attention to features of my own experience which I should otherwise have omitted to notice, e.g. that the red patch is somewhat less bright in the middle than elsewhere.

But though such judgments do not differ in content from other judgments referring to particulars, they do differ in the kind and degree of evidence which belongs to them. So far as they are really founded in direct acquaintance, so that what they refer to lies open for inspection, they cannot be false. If I assert that the sense-datum which I am immediately aware of is green and another man denies this, he may be right, inasmuch as it is not what *he* is meaning by 'green' or what is generally meant by 'green'. But he must be wrong, if he intends to deny that it is what I am meaning by 'green'. Such certainty is confined within very narrow limits and, taken by itself, may be regarded as unimportant. But it is very important in relation to the whole system of our knowledge. For it supplies the ultimate nucleus of undeniable matter of fact in all observation and experiment. Another fundamental difference between such intuitive knowledge and all other knowledge referring to actually existing particulars is that it is primary. All other knowledge of matter of fact presupposes it and depends on it. It is logically prior to memory, and it is logically prior to all judgments referring to physical objects or to the sense-data or conscious processes of minds other than our own.

So far Mr Russell would agree. But he adds two propositions which require to be carefully examined. (1) That judgment about particulars, as distinguished from knowledge by description, is strictly confined to intuitive knowledge. (2) That this can include no knowledge of the relation of what is immediately experienced to what is not immediately experienced.

As regards the first point, I have insisted that knowledge by acquaintance is not separable from knowledge about. Mere existential presence is not knowledge at all. But when we do know about something which is existentially present the position is different. In the very act of characterising it as such and such, we must know the thing itself which we characterise—the thing itself which is such and such. We must know it as the subject of our judgments concerning it. It would seem then that there is no way of getting rid of this distinction between knowing about a particular thing and knowing the thing itself. Without knowing the thing there is no knowing about it. But we cannot leave the question in this state. There is a further problem which Mr Russell hardly faces at all. What precisely is the distinction between knowing a thing and knowing it as such and such? Only when we have decided this for intuitive knowledge, can we proceed to consider the sort of knowledge which we may have of particulars falling outside our immediate experience, and to inquire whether *this* involves the essential incompleteness of the particular from which we start.

Let us, then, examine the distinction in the case of an existentially present sense-datum, e.g. what we immediately experience in seeing or dreaming that we see a patch of colour. We are aware that it exists, that it is a unique particular, that it is present to be inspected, that it is red, bright, round. Such judgments, according to Russell, presuppose as a distinct logical precondition knowledge of the sense-datum itself to which they refer. In intuitive knowledge, indeed, we are supposed to be concerned only with what may be called intrinsic characters which belong to the content of immediate experience, independently of all relations which it may have to whatever is not immediately experienced. But even these intrinsic characters are quite distinct from that to which they belong. This must be completely known before anything can be known about it. In judgment, we ascribe even its intrinsic characters to it, somewhat as we might hang a hat on a peg. We invest it with them; but all the while it exists naked and is nakedly known inside its clothes. What is it then that thus exists and is known apart from its qualifications? What is the sense-datum apart from its redness, brightness, extension, roundness and all other characters belonging to it—apart even from its existence, for 'that it exists' is a proposition about it, and it is supposed to be something apart from whatever can be known about it?

This is the question which so much puzzled Locke. The only answer he could find was that, so far at least as our knowledge extends, that which has attributes is simply that which has attributes, and there is no more to be said. But this is a very difficult conception, for it supposes a being of which the whole nature consists in relatedness to something else. And even if it were a tenable view in itself, it would be impossible for Mr Russell. For if the whole being of a thing consisted in its having a nature, there could be no knowledge of it distinct from knowledge of its nature. Acquaintance and knowledge about would coincide. Further, it is plain that an actual content of immediate experience, such as a present sense-datum, cannot be identified with the bare abstraction of Locke's formula.

So far as I can see, there is only one possible way out of this *impasse*. The thing itself which we know about is simply identical with its intrinsic characters, taken all together as united in a quite peculiar form of unity, which we can name only by saying that they are all characters of the same subject. This complex unity includes all qualifications which are conceivably capable of being ascribed to it, as a whole includes its parts—as, e.g. the leg of a chair is distinguished from, yet belongs to, the chair. But here there is an obvious difficulty. How, it may be asked, can we refer a part to a whole without first knowing the whole, and how can we know the whole without first knowing all the parts? It would seem that we ought not to be able to know anything about a datum of experience without knowing all about it. Yet this is by no means always necessary, even in intuitive knowledge, though perhaps it is sometimes possible. If, for instance, we set out to examine the total content of our immediate sense-experience at any moment, we find ourselves picking out, in successive analytic judgments, now these, now those partial features and aspects of it; and yet we are aware throughout of these partial features and aspects as belonging to a whole which includes and transcends them. We are aware of this whole as existentially present, though we are very far from knowing all about it in detail.

We are here, even in intuitive judgments of sense, led back to a principle vital to all theories of knowledge which maintain that the universe is knowable as a unity. In order to know a whole as such, it is not necessary to know all its parts severally. I shall point out later that under certain conditions it is not even indispensable to know any one part. But here I would only insist that in order to know a whole as such we need only know a part of it, provided that this part is apprehended as essentially incomplete, as incapable of standing alone and as requiring to be supplemented by something beyond itself.

Now this holds good for the intuitive judgments by which we characterise our own immediate experiences. We start, for instance, with the awareness that there is something existentially present, having a nature which is initially very vaguely determined for us. But such knowledge is essentially incomplete. Of itself, it passes into the question: what, more precisely, is it that is existentially present? How is its determinate nature to be further specified? Analytic attention, following the clue of this implicit question, may develop further knowledge in successive judgments. But each of these is again recognised as merely partial. Thus in knowing about the thing we are constantly aware that there must be more to be known. What we do know, together with whatever else is to be known, constitutes the complex unity which is the subject of our judgments. To know a part of this is not merely to know that part, but partially to know the whole to which it belongs.

Memory, if it is not, as Mr Russell supposes, quite the same sort of thing as knowledge of present experiences, is at least a primary way of knowing. It is, therefore, worth while to note that the same analysis applies here also. In calling to mind past experiences, e.g. what we saw on a visit to London or Paris, we are constantly aware of gaps and deficiencies in our remembrance. On the basis of memory alone we are aware that much existed and was noticed which we now fail to recall. We know that our remembrance is pervaded by indistinctness and vagueness, and here and there we recognise definite gaps. This familiar fact is highly significant for the theory of knowledge. How is it possible to know through memory alone that something is missing, when we do not remember what it is that is missing—when, indeed, if we did remember it, it would not be missing? To use Mr Russell's stock formula, how can we know about it, if we do not know it? We have not spread out before us, on the one hand, the original experience, on the other, our remembrance of it, so as to be able to compare them and note what is absent in the one and present in the other. Our only clue to the original experience is in memory itself.

I have gone through this tedious analysis in order to establish a general principle, and obtain a general answer to the question: In what sense is it necessary to know a thing in order that we may be able to know about it? If the subject in judgment is simply the unity which includes all that may be conceivably known about it, then all that is required in order to know it is that some one or more of its characters should be known as incomplete, and requiring an appropriate supplement which remains to be specified. In dealing with intuitive knowledge of particulars, I have applied this principle under arbitrary restrictions. I have taken account only of the intrinsic characters of a given experience in distinction from all relatedness to other things. Now the distinction between the inner nature of a thing and its relations is legitimate, and for many purposes important and useful. But it is not in place here. If my previous analysis is right, it is not identical with the distinction between the thing and whatever is known about the thing. From this point of view, the thing must, if my previous analysis is correct, be taken to include all that can be known about it, including its relatedness to things outside it. For such relatedness is essentially incomplete and points to the total nature of the thing as what is required to include and complete it. This total nature is the thing itself considered as a subject of judgment. So too, if the internal characters of a directly intuited experience are such that they cannot stand alone apart from relatedness to other beings, then this relatedness must be regarded as contained in the thing itself, considered as a subject of judgment, and the thing itself is known as a whole, not independently, but in and through the very act of knowing about it. Whether this is so or not—whether the several contents of immediate experience are or are not essentially incomplete, whether they do or do not point beyond themselves to a whole which transcends and includes them all—is really the most crucial issue raised by Mr Russell. On the answer to it will depend our view of the unity of the universe. But before grappling with it, we are bound to consider first another problem, the nature of universals and their relation to particulars.

Chapter V

UNIVERSALS, PARTICULARS AND POSSIBILITIES[1]

1. *Universals and Particulars*

When I proposed to identify any particular thing concerning which we judge with the complex unity including all its characters, I passed by a difficulty which, if it were real, would be fatal to any such view. The thing itself is supposed to be particular. But according to Mr Russell, and according to others who differ fundamentally from him in other respects, the characters of the particular are not particular but universal. They are qualities and relations—and these as such are all universals. Are we then to say that the particular is only a complex, an interfusion or interpenetration, of universals? There are philosophers who would not shrink from this. But I am quite unable to follow them. I cannot deny the logical possibility that there may be distinct particulars in every respect of the same kind, except as regards characters which already presuppose their distinct particularity. Two drops of

[1] [This is the first statement of Stout's theory of Universals, which he developed more fully in the well-known British Academy Lecture entitled *The Nature of Universals and Propositions*, published in 1921 (two years after the delivery of the First Course of Gifford Lectures, to which the present chapter belongs), and reprinted in *Studies in Philosophy and Psychology*. A re-statement of the theory, with a reply to criticism, will be found in his contribution to the Symposium 'Are the Characters of Particular Things Universal or Particular?', in the *Proceedings of the Aristotelian Society*, supplementary vol. III (1923), and the theory is further developed in 'Universals Again', in the same *Proceedings*, supplementary vol. xv (1936), in 'Things, Predicates and Relations' (1940) in the *Australasian Journal of Psychology and Philosophy*, vol. xviii, no. 2, and in 'Distributive Unity as a Category', posthumously published in the *Australasian Journal*, vol.xxv, nos. 1 and 2.—Ed.]

water, for instance, may conceivably be exactly alike except that they must have different positions in space, and whatever further differences this may involve. Why must they have different positions in space? Because they are distinct particulars. There is no other reason. This difference then presupposes their particular distinctness and cannot constitute it; but in all other ways there is nothing in their general nature to distinguish them. On this and other grounds, I agree with Mr Russell that the antithesis of universal and particular is ultimate. On the other hand, I flatly deny what he and many others seem to take for granted. I deny that the qualities and relations of particulars are universal. I assert that the qualities and relations are as truly particular as the particular things to which they belong. The loudness of the sound which I immediately experience is its own particular loudness and not loudness in general and not the loudness of any other sound. Similarly the green of this leaf is not the green of a neighbouring leaf, however much alike the two may be. There are two particular greens as there are two particular leaves. The same holds for relatedness. Edinburgh is north of London and so is Aberdeen. But the northness of Edinburgh is one particular instance of northness in general and the northness of Aberdeen is another. We do indeed say that both are in the same relation to London inasmuch as they are both north of it. But by the same relation we mean merely a relation of the same sort; we mean that there are two instances of the same universal which we call 'northness in general'.

It is true that a quality or relation, as distinguished from the particular things to which it belongs, is abstract: abstract, but not universal. Abstractness and universality are by no means the same. On the contrary, every abstract character of a particular subject is itself particular. If we add the length of one ribbon to the length of another ribbon we are not adding the ribbons themselves; we are adding abstract but particular lengths. Each yard is a distinct particular length, and it is these we add when we say that two yards of one ribbon and three yards of another make five yards. Similarly the word 'whiteness', taken by itself, stands for a universal. But the whiteness of this piece of chalk is a particular—a particular instance of whiteness. Adjectives in their distinctive and appropriate use are names of characters of things and not, as the logical text-books teach, names of the things themselves. But adjectives which qualify particulars are not names of universals. They supply an appropriate verbal form for ascribing a particular character to a particular subject, as in 'this horse is white', or 'this white horse'. The same holds good for verbs.

What are universals and how are they related to their particular instances? If I am right so far, there remains, I think, only one tenable view. We have to regard the universal as a very peculiar kind of whole and its particular instances, actual or possible, as its parts. In saying this I am extending the use of the word 'whole' beyond what is felt as natural in ordinary language. I am using it to indicate any connexion of differences within a unity. Now there are manifold ultimate forms of unity. There is the unity of a successive series; there is the unity of a spatial complex; there is the unity of characters belonging to the same thing; and there is also the altogether peculiar form of unity which we may call the distributive unity of a class or kind. The whole constituted by this form of unity is a universal; its parts, as such, may be either concrete things or abstract qualities and relations. When they are concrete, they are called members of a class, and said to be so in virtue of possessing a common character. Members of the class 'all white things', for example, are said to have the common character 'whiteness'. What does this really mean? It will be found that, if we press this question, we are driven back on the other sort of universals, those which have for their traits abstract characters. Each particular white thing has its own particular whiteness. When we say, then, that they have a common character, we must mean not that there is one numerically identical quality in all, but that each possesses a quality of the same sort as a quality belonging to each of the others. In our example, we have to do with that kind of abstract quality which is called 'whiteness in general', or simply 'whiteness'. It is a whole with parts which, being abstract, are called 'instances' of it and not 'members' of it. Every particular white thing literally participates or shares in the universal whiteness. For each has a particular character which is a particular instance of it. Each possesses a part of it and none possesses the whole.

Against this view of universals as wholes with parts Mr Russell would have objections to urge. He would, for instance, point out that there are classes which have no members and that in order to know a universal it is not necessary to know all or any of its instances. I shall have occasion to discuss these points later on when we come to discuss Mr Russell's doctrine of a separate world of universals distinct from the world of particulars. At present it is enough to say that such difficulties disappear if we recognise (1) that there are possible as well as actual instances, and (2) that in order to know a whole, as such, it is not necessary to know any of its parts, except, of course, as being parts of the whole. Such knowledge is essentially incomplete. But all our knowledge is essentially incomplete.

To sum up our results so far. We have seen reason for holding that anything considered as a subject or constituent of propositions is to be regarded as the complex unity including all its characters. This being so, all that is required for knowing the thing as we must know it in order to know about it, is that we should know some character of it as essentially incomplete and requiring to be supplemented by other characters. We know that there are other characters without knowing what they are. This view does not mean that the particular is a complex of universals. For each character of a particular is itself particular: it is abstract but not universal. The union of particular characters in a concrete thing is one ultimate form of unity; the union of a particular character with other characters of the same kind is another form of unity. On the other hand, particulars and universals, though distinct, are essentially connected, at least from the side of the particular. There is no particular quality or relatedness which is not an instance of an abstract universal, and there is no particular thing which is not a member of a class, or rather of an indefinite number of classes. Thus apart from universals there can be no particulars, actual or possible or impossible. There is no separate world of particulars detached from the universals. I am, of course, bound also to assert that there is no separate world of universals detached from particulars, actual, possible or impossible. But, in view of Mr Russell's strong assertion to the contrary, this point will require separate discussion.[1]

2. *The Principle of the Incompleteness of the Data of Experience*

We have now cleared the ground for dealing with our most vital problem. Admittedly all our knowledge about particular existence, all that Hume calls knowledge of matter of fact, begins with and is in some way derived from what are relatively extremely few and scattered data. These primary data include undoubtedly the existentially present contents of our private experiences—our present sense-data and mental states. Provisionally, at least, they may also be taken to include whatever each of us remembers of his past experiences. The question is—How is it logically possible to pass beyond these data of experience so as to know about the vast world of matter of fact, in which they

[1] See § 5, p. 89.

are merely minute specks? To me it seems that no tenable answer is discoverable unless it is presupposed that each datum is known as essentially incomplete, and as continued beyond itself into a whole which transcends and includes it. Further, this whole is apprehended as one and the same for all data. The way in which each is to be continued beyond itself may be, and perhaps always is, in some measure (though never completely) determined for us by its own special nature. A specific sense-datum, for instance, is never as such apprehended as self-complete, but as connected with an unexperienced existence beyond itself, of which it is the appearance. Here we have the rudimentary beginning of the knowledge of external objects—but only the merest rudiment of a beginning, essentially incomplete, and raising further questions. These get partially answered in the process of discovering connexions, according to general rules, between different perceptual data in the context of the one whole which includes them all. However far this process may advance, it remains essentially incomplete and its essential incompleteness is the indispensable principle of its development. It could not even begin unless the primary data of immediate experience were incapable of being, or being known as, self-existent.

3. *Criticism of Russell's View of Descriptive Judgments as asserting Probability and not Necessary Connexion*

This, I take it, is the only tenable view, unless some other can be suggested which will bear examination. The only other alternative which can claim to be seriously considered is that propounded by Russell in his theory of knowledge by description. So far as this theory rests on the impossibility of knowing about a thing without knowing the thing itself, I have already dealt with it. Knowing the thing itself, in the sense required, does not involve its existential presence, but only the knowledge of some character of it as incompletely characterising it. Thus, if we can be sure that something actual, which is not existentially present to consciousness, has a certain character, we both know this actual existence and know about it.

But Mr Russell denies that we ever can know as much as this. He does so on the ground that all descriptive judgments assert only probabilities and not necessary connexion. It is in the highest degree likely that the sun will rise to-morrow and that there is another side to the moon. None the less it is always possible that the sun may not rise to-morrow and that there may not be another side to the moon. Whether this is so or not makes no difference to what we really know. In neither case do we know the thing described and consequently we do not really know about it.

This argument seems to me to involve an elusive but fatal fallacy.[1] It is assumed that we can and do know that our description *probably* describes something actual. But this is impossible unless we know something actual which is known probably to correspond to our description. We must know it in order even to be able to describe it falsely— to make a mistake about it. In believing that the sun will rise to-morrow my belief must refer to some actual situation, whether this is truly described as to-morrow's sunrise, or as the destruction of the solar system, or otherwise. The probability of our description is always relative to the probability of other alternative descriptions of the same fact. The fact itself cannot in the long run be merely probable, because it is presupposed in all probable judgments about it. Further, it cannot be any actual existence taken at random. For our only clue to it lies in its relation to the special data with which we started, and ultimately to the content of immediate experience. So far then as it is determined for us as being related in some particular

---

[1] [For a fuller treatment of the argument of this paragraph see the articles on 'Error' and on 'The Nature of Universals and Propositions' in *Studies in Philosophy and Psychology.*—Ed.]

way to particular data, we cannot be wrong. To this extent we have certain knowledge of necessary connexion. It is only so far as we go beyond this and specify it further, as we constantly do in ordinary judgments, that possible alternatives emerge which have various degrees of comparative probability. It follows from this reasoning that, even as a precondition of probable belief, we must have certain knowledge, however imperfect, of actual existence beyond the limits of immediate experience and memory. Thus the logical edifice erected by Mr Russell, with so much pains and skill, tumbles to pieces like a house of cards.

More detailed examination of probable judgments fully bears out the thesis that they are and must be based on knowledge of necessary connexion.[1] We have no right to assert that anything will even probably take place unless we are prepared to assert that it probably must take place. Probability in matters of fact presupposes necessity.[2] For example, a servant girl on putting a lighted match to a fire in the morning expects it to burn up. If she counts on this with absolute certainty, she is logically bound to hold not only that it will do so, but that it *must* do so. If, under the given circumstances, the fire *may* not burn, there can be no warrant for asserting, without reserve, that it will burn. But if it is untrue that it may not burn, it cannot but be true that it will burn.

Now suppose that what is asserted is that the fire will *probably* burn. Here too, by parity of reasoning, there can be no warrant for affirming that the event will probably

---

[1] [The typescript suggests that the author intended, for lecturing purposes at least, to substitute a shorter version for the passage that follows (down to the end of Section 4). He refers to the treatment of the same subject 'in a previous lecture'; but this treatment is missing. The reader may be referred to the Section on 'Causality and Probability' in *Mind and Matter* (pp. 117–20), which is probably based on the missing passage. I have printed the full version in the text and the shorter version in a footnote following it.—Ed.]

[2] [Cf. *Mind and Matter*, pp. 117–20.—Ed.]

occur which is not a warrant for affirming that it probably *must* occur. In so far as it is possible or in any degree likely that it may not take place, this simply diminishes the likelihood that it *must* take place and increases the probability that it *cannot* take place. The two exclusive alternatives are either that it must or that it cannot, and so far as there is no necessary connexion there is no probability, and no degree of probability. It becomes impossible to anticipate experience at all. But if what occurs, occurs necessarily, there must be conditions which, in some way, make it necessary. Thus, when the servant believes that the fire is likely to burn up, it is on the presumption that there is present some group of conditions such that the event must be of the kind anticipated. If any one of the conditions is wanting, the result will be of a different sort and will not correspond to her anticipation of it. But she does not and cannot know certainly that all requisite conditions are fulfilled. She knows that some part of them is given, but as for the rest, she is ignorant of what they are and certainly has no means of ascertaining by observation whether they are actually to be found or not. She can only have a probable presumption that, whatever they may be, they can be counted on as present. The warrant for this presumption is, in ultimate principle, the same as that afforded by sampling a collection, e.g. a bag of billiard balls or a cart of wheat. The servant girl has found within a certain range of experiences or inductive universe of discourse, that under more or less similar circumstances the fire has burnt up always, or nearly always, or much more often than not. Hence she is entitled to infer that within this range and under like circumstances the unknown conditions of an event of this sort occur with great relative frequency. But the presupposition is that what are sampled are necessary connexions. If, for instance, acts of free choice were absolutely undetermined, they would *pro tanto* not even be probably predictable. The same holds for the sampling of a bag of billiard balls. The underlying assumption is that the result of each act of drawing is necessarily determined by its own direction and by the existing distribution of balls in the bag. If there are ninety-nine white balls and one black, there are ninety-nine possible arrangements of them which would make it necessary that the particular ball selected should be white, as against one possible arrangement which would necessitate its being black.[1]

It will be seen that I have not challenged the general position that all our specific anticipations of particular matters of fact fall short of absolute certainty. This may very well be true. I have not even excluded or intended to exclude the possibility of miracles, as events determined by factors which do not belong to what is known to us as the ordinary course of nature. My point is that all probability and improbability in matter of fact presupposes, and cannot therefore be substituted for, necessity. Further, it seems clear that necessary connexion of particulars must consist in their essential incompleteness apart from each other. An occurrence which is capable of existing by itself apart from anything else cannot imply the existence of anything else.

4. *Russell's Principle of Induction and its Relation to his View of Universals*

Mr Russell would, if I understand him aright, deny this. He would maintain that relations of universals may supply a valid ground for inferring from the existence of one particular at least the probable existence of another, even though the particulars themselves are quite loose and separate. His main example is what he calls the *principle*

[1] [Mr J. L. Mackie has pointed out to me that even if it is assumed (as it is on p. 104) that there are only a hundred 'places' in the bag, each always occupied by one ball, the number of possible arrangements is not 100 but $\lfloor 100$; but it is true that the ratio between the numbers of arrangements with a white and the black ball in the 'place' from which the ball is drawn is 99 : 1.—Ed.]

of induction, which I quoted earlier. He states the first part of it as follows: 'The greater number of cases in which a thing of a certain sort *A* has been, without exception, associated with a thing of the sort *B*, the greater is the probability that they will be associated in a fresh case in which one of them is known to be present.'[1] This, being put forward as an ultimate logical principle and not as derived from experience, ought, of course, to be self-evidently true, if it is true at all. On the contrary, when strictly interpreted in the only sense possible for Mr Russell, it turns out to be self-evidently false. We must set aside all reference to sampling a collection; for we cannot sample the future. As Mr Russell says himself, 'we have experience of past futures, but not of future futures'.[2] We can sample only the conditions of what has not yet happened. But we must not, on Russell's view, assume any connexion in the way of condition and consequence as logically prior to the inductive principle. When a particular *A* occurs together with a particular *B*, the existence of *A* is not to be thought of as having anything whatever to do with the occurrence of *B*. There is not even a question of this being possible. It is taken as final fact that *A* might just as well have occurred without *B* and *B* without *A*. If, then, in a fresh case, *A* is known to be present, whereas it is unknown whether *B* is present or not, our previous experience of the association of another *A* with another *B* can contribute absolutely nothing to determine this question. For we must still assume that the presence of *A* in no way conditions or is connected with conditions which determine the presence of *B*. Evidently, the repetition of instances can in this respect make no difference. If it is hopeless to look for something in two boxes known to be empty, it is equally hopeless to look for it in two million

[1] *The Problems of Philosophy*, p. 103. [The formula given above is a slightly compressed version of the formula as Mr Russell actually gives it.—Ed.]

[2] *Ibid.* p. 100.

equally empty. The general position that the existence of one particular may be inferable from that of another through a universal principle, although the particulars themselves, as such, are loose and separate, evidently rests on a peculiar view of the nature of universals. It presupposes that universals have a separate and independent being of their own apart from particular instances— a view radically incompatible with that which I have maintained.[1]

[1] [The following is the shortened version written to take the place of the above passage beginning at p. 84: 'As I have attempted to show in a previous Lecture [see p. 84, n.1], we have no right to assert that anything will even probably take place, unless we are prepared to assert that it probably must take place. Probability in matters of fact presupposes necessity. Mr Russell, on the contrary, maintains that a general principle may connect particulars which are in themselves loose and separate. His main example is what he calls "the principle of induction", stated as follows: "The greater the number of cases in which a thing of a certain sort A has been without exception associated with a thing of the sort B, the greater is the probability that they will be associated in a fresh case in which one of them is known to be present." This principle, being an ultimate presupposition of inference from experience, cannot, of course, be itself inferred from experience. It should therefore be self-evidently true, considered merely as a relation of universals. The two universals are (1) frequent occurrence of a certain kind of conjunction in past experience, and (2) the probable occurrence of the same kind of conjunction in fresh instances. Now, apart from further assumptions, there is no discernible relation of the two universals such that the one can be seen to imply the other. We must set aside all reference to sampling a collection; for it is admitted that one cannot sample the future. We must also set aside all reference to causal conditions, direct or indirect; for all particulars are supposed to be loose and separate. But if we uncompromisingly exclude such further assumptions, it seems clear that the supposed relation between the universals does not exist. The alleged principle of induction is self-evidently false, not self-evidently true.

'We have yet to examine Mr Russell's general position that the existence of one particular may be inferred from that of another, although the particulars themselves are loose and separate. It presupposes that universals have a separate being of their own, independent of their particular instances.'—Ed.]

5. *Criticism of Russell's View of the Independent Existence of Universals*

As a matter of fact, Mr Russell does hold that universals have a being of their own, independent and self-complete, apart from particulars. As such they form the objects of symbolic logic and pure mathematics. The truths of symbolic logic and pure mathematics consist in relations of universals, and are quite unaffected by the question whether particular instances of these universals actually exist. On the other hand, all knowledge of particular existence which transcends what is immediately experienced presupposes the application of universal principles to given instances, and can never yield more than probable belief—not certain and evident truth. Here we have plainly a very old distinction—the Platonic distinction between ἐπιστήμη and δόξα. It would be interesting to compare the Platonic form of it with Russell's. But this would lead us too far afield. What concerns us here is to determine what it means and how far it is justified. Now I do not see how it can be denied that there is a system of evidently true propositions which are not directly concerned with actual existence. Further, it seems clear that truths cannot be true of nothing. They must express what in some sense has being. We cannot know and yet know nothing. Nor will it do to say that what we are dealing with is a creature of thought. It may indeed be true that all being, including actual existence, is relative to mind, in the sense that it could not be without mind. But what is here suggested is that the process of knowing may make or produce its own object, that the being of a concept may consist of being conceived. This seems a quite untenable position, and has in fact been sufficiently refuted by Plato. To think is to think something; thought, therefore, cannot exist prior to what is thought of; it cannot therefore make or produce what is thought of. The subject-matter of logic and pure mathematics has a nature of its own which our thinking simply discovers and does not, in any sense, create.

There is then a region of being, of vast extent and importance, distinct from that of actually existing particulars. But are these two realms, as Mr Russell holds, each essentially complete in itself apart from the other? This brings us back to the question of the nature of universals. I have given reasons for regarding a universal as merely the distributive unity of its instances. If this be right, it seems to follow that where there are no instances there can be no universal, and that no universal can be known unless its instances are known. Now Mr Russell, with apparently good reason, would deny both these positions. We can know universals and relations of universals where no instances can be given. We know, for example, that 'All products of two integers, which never have been and never will be thought of by any human being, are over 100'.[1] Yet from the nature of the case we, being human beings, cannot give any instance of such pairs of integers or of their products. Apart from such special illustrations it must be admitted that we frequently understand the meaning of general names, without having before our minds any single example of what they mean. I can understand what is meant by 'all men are mortal', or 'more haste less speed' without calling up any man in particular or any death in particular or any particular instance of 'haste' or of 'speed'. All this I readily concede. But it does not really touch my position. To think of a universal is to think of all its instances *as such*, but this does not imply that we know them otherwise than in this essentially incomplete way, as being instances of this universal. Thus in asserting that 'all men are mortal' we assert that that particular man is mortal who was in fact called Socrates and lived and died at Athens at a certain date and under certain circumstances. But our knowledge as expressed in the general proposition is essentially in-

[1] Russell, *op. cit.* p. 169.

complete, inasmuch as it does not include the knowledge that a particular man actually existed with this particular history. The defect is partially supplied by the syllogism with its minor premise 'Socrates is a man'. The reason why such syllogisms contain no *petitio principii* is that the minor premise only serves to complete what is essentially incomplete in the major premise. This account of the matter is confirmed, where we do have given some particular instance—as when, in thinking of 'figures in general', I have in mind a particular triangle. The particular triangle does not help me at all, unless I apprehend it as one instance of figure among others and as *standing for* all the others, which are not themselves separately presented. It must then be possible to think of 'all the others' together without thinking of any one separately.

6. *Possibility*[1]

We have still to face the difficulty that there are universals which have not only no *given* instances but no actual instances at all. There are or may be no frictionless fluids, no levers quite weightless and rigid, no perfectly straight lines. Out of a hundred men no man may be precisely the average height or age or have precisely the average income. Yet these conceptions are of great importance for our knowledge. In general, it is indifferent to the student of logic, mathematics, or mathematical physics whether instances of the universals with which he deals actually exist or not. Even the science of the actual order of the world treats it largely in an indirect way through a conceptual model, which has no actual counterpart. 'How then can it be true that a universal is merely the distributive

[1] [The theory of the status of possibilities developed in the next two sections is to be found also in the articles (reprinted in *Studies in Philosophy and Psychology*) on 'Error' (1903), 'Real Being and Being for Thought' (1911) and in the last pages of 'The Nature of Universals and Propositions' (1921).—Ed.]

unity of its instances?' I answer that just as the universal itself has a being other than actual existence, its particular instances need not actually exist. They too may have a being other than that of any actual thing or event, or any actual quality or character of a thing or event. It is easy to see that this must be so. When we speak, for example, of a perfect fluid, we mean something particular. It is one out of an indefinite plurality of perfect fluids: each of them indeed consists of parts which are themselves perfect fluids. The universal is not any one or more of these, but the class of which they are members. Similarly, each member has its own particular though abstract fluidity, and 'fluidity in general' is the corresponding abstract universal.

The sort of being which belongs to particulars that do not actually exist is possibility, in a wide sense of the word which I shall presently attempt to define. In so far as a universal has not actual instances it must have possible instances; and the problem of the relation of the ideal realm of logic and mathematics to things and events as they really exist and happen ultimately concerns the relation of the possible to the actual. The thesis which I have to make good is that these two regions of being, though distinct, are through and through interdependent, each being essentially incomplete without the other.

To clear the ground, we must first determine more precisely what we mean by possibility, its range and importance, and in what sense it can be regarded as a form of being distinct from and co-ordinate with actual existence. In the first place, it is most important to notice that possibility is always relative to some universal, which may be highly complex or comparatively simple. What is possible but not also actual is possible only from certain points of view, but not from others. Thus, in relation to general geometrical conditions it is possible for a man a hundred feet high to stand upright and walk about; but it is mechanically impossible. Or take the proposition that on an average two-and-a-half men have failed in a certain examination. Though this seems absurd, yet it has meaning and may be perfectly true. It must therefore express a possibility relatively to some general condition, though not to others. The general condition is purely numerical and has nothing to do with the constitution of human beings. A certain number of numbers must be such as to yield a certain sum total; if, for instance, the examination has been held eight times and the total number of the ploughed is twenty, the numbers ploughed on each occasion must together equal twenty. This is a purely arithmetical condition and all other considerations are irrelevant. It may be fulfilled in many alternative ways, and among these is one in which the several numbers are all equal. They are then said to average two-and-a-half. So the cork is buoyant even when circumstances are such that it does not and cannot float. It is so because apart from these circumstances it has a general nature, of which floating on water is a possible special development. Its actual state is only one value of a variable. The same holds for all mere possibility. What is merely possible without being actual is possible only from one point of view and impossible from another. What is possible in all ways is also actual.

7. *Knowledge and the Possible*

We turn now to the range and importance of possibilities in the constitution of the universe. I need not again refer to symbolic logic and pure mathematics. Even the conception of a variable, which is so fundamental in these sciences, is nothing but the conception of alternative possible instances of a universal. But the importance of possible instances is far from being restricted to this purely ideal sphere. The science which sets out to deal with things as they actually exist and events as they actually happen cannot pass beyond relatively rough and provisional generalities, without adopting indirect

methods of approach, in which the possible is substituted for the actual. Thus mechanics formulates laws
which hold strictly not for actual levers, but for ideal
levers supposed to be perfectly rigid and weightless.
Hydrostatics formulates laws not directly for water or
air, but for absolutely frictionless fluids. Newton's first
law of motion asserts directly only what would happen
to a body under the action of no forces in absolute space.
Yet there is no actual body under the action of no forces
and there may be no absolute space. In ways such as these,
what has been called a 'conceptual model' is made to
mediate between the mind and actual things and events.
But it is not interposed as a veil or mask. Its function is
to reveal, not to conceal. By means of the merely possible
we obtain indirectly an insight into the actual, which we
could not have otherwise. Actual levers have more or less
weight and are more or less flexible. But they behave in
such a way that if they *were* weightless and rigid they would
strictly obey the laws of mechanics; and it is from this point
of view that we can best understand the general nature of
a lever. Similarly, in the other illustrations of the perfect
fluid and so on, there is no way of grasping the nature of
the actual except by considering its relation to the merely
possible.

It is mainly exact science which is concerned with such
ideal instances. But in other ways, our most ordinary
familiar knowledge of the actual world of body and mind
and social intercourse includes everywhere what is merely
possible, in inseparable union with what is actual. The
characters we ascribe to things consist not only in their
actual states and modes of behaviour, but in what Locke
called their active and passive powers. Glass is brittle when
it is not actually breaking: it is brittle even though it never
has been and never will be broken—if, for instance, it
ceases to exist as glass before it can break. In the same
way arsenic and prussic acid are poisonous even though
they do not actually poison anyone. An acorn is capable

of growing into an oak, and this remains true even though its actual fate is to be crushed under someone's heel. The sizes and shapes of bodies include or imply all manner of possible relations to other bodies of the same or different shape and size. If we take into account the various possible appearances of things to the senses, it becomes possible, as Mill and Berkeley, and recently Russell, have shown, to describe the material world, from this point of view, as consisting in relatively few actual sensations within an immense system of permanent possibilities of sensation.

On the whole it seems safe to assert that the general nature of material things consists not merely in what they actually are or how they actually behave but in what they may be, might be or might have been, and in the ways in which they might behave or might have behaved. The same holds at least as obviously for mind. We constantly speak of mental faculties, powers, aptitudes, dispositions, propensities. Love and hatred consist not only in what a man actually feels, desires or wills in relation to the object loved or hated, but in what he would feel, desire or will if the appropriate occasion arose: what we call character always transcends the partial expressions of it elicited by actual circumstances. Examples from social relations readily present themselves. It is enough to refer to contracts, to money, to commercial credit. Credit, for instance, consists in a man's power to obtain goods or money, founded on the belief which others have in his power to pay within a certain time.

8. *Practical Activity and the Possible*

I have so far considered the possible only in relation to knowledge. But we should have an extremely imperfect view of its significance if we confined ourselves to this, and failed to take account of the essential part it plays within the sphere of will and of imagination. All practical activity is essentially concerned with possible alternatives. The end aimed at by the agent is that one among these alternatives which he strives to make actual, rejecting others which will remain, so far as he is concerned, mere unrealised possibilities—belonging to the region of what might have been. Where there is, in the proper sense, a voluntary decision, various alternatives are considered and appreciated in relation to each other, so as to lead up to a choice between them. Before the decision is reached the agent has no means of foreseeing what he is going to do. This he can find out only by actually making up his mind. Before he has made up his mind, he must consider the alternatives which are possible apart from his own actual choice. It is for him as a voluntary agent to determine, so far as in him lies, which of these possibilities shall be realised and which shall remain unrealised. In this sense, if in no other, it is always true that he might have decided otherwise than in fact he does decide. Thus in free voluntary activity, the agent is bound to recognise what is possible as having a being distinct from what is actual.

Of course, we have to bear in mind that possibility is always relative. Something may be possible in the sense that only a voluntary decision is needed in order to make it real. Thus I may or may not move my arm according as I choose. The movement is possible relatively to all conditions except my will. This we may call practical possibility. Now it often happens that we attempt what is practically impossible, as when I will to lift a weight which turns out unexpectedly to be too heavy for me. Then I fail instead of succeeding. But no one can really determine to do what he knows he cannot do. I cannot resolve to pluck the moon out of the sky with my hands. As Herbart said, what Napoleon willed as Emperor he only wished or desired at St Helena. What is willed must be possible relatively to those general aspects and features of the given situation which are taken into account by the agent. So far as he really doubts his own power, he does not unreservedly will to do something, but only to make an attempt to do it, so as not to let slip whatever chance there may be of success. Provided that there is a strong enough motive, this may happen even when success appears very improbable. The domain of the possible is the domain of free agency. But it also prescribes insuperable limits to freedom. We are free to choose between possible alternatives. But we are ultimately powerless to determine what is practically possible and what is not.

This seems to follow from the very nature of will as such, and applies also to the universal mind. Even God does not ultimately make or create possibilities. To be omnipotent is to be able to do whatever is practically possible, not anything that is practically impossible. Though I have spoken of this as a limitation of the will, it must be understood that it is so only in a logical sense. It is not a restriction. Will is restricted so far as it is confined to a certain limited range of alternatives. Where all possible alternatives are open to it, it is absolutely free. Hence Leibniz had good reason for conceiving the divine will as choosing the actual world among various possible worlds, and also for denying that God creates the eternal truths.

9. *Imagination and the Possible*

I can only refer very briefly to the free play of fancy and imagination, which yields all that we call fiction, from the idlest day-dreaming to Shakespeare's *Hamlet* and Homer's *Iliad*. The word *imagination* has two distinct senses. In one it means thinking of objects, whether actual or possible, by help of vivid mental imagery. In the other, it means thinking of the possible as distinct from the actual. It is this second use only which concerns us here. In this sense it is plain that imagination is not confined to what we ordinarily call fiction. Perfect fluids and weightless levers are imaginary objects. What is distinctive of such fictions as those of the poet or novelist is that they do not directly aim at the advancement of knowledge or the achievement of practical results. The poet or novelist discovers and contemplates possible being for its own sake, for its own intrinsic interest. On the other hand, it is quite wrong to infer that because the free play of imagination does not directly aim at practical or theoretical results, it is therefore without theoretical or practical significance, bad or good. This is obviously untrue. The reason is that what is possible is always so only as a possible variation of what is actual, considered in certain aspects of its general nature. The actual instances of a universal are only selected values of a variable having other values which are merely possible. But we have no ultimate clue to the possible except in the general nature of the actual, and, on the other hand, as our insight into what is possible widens and deepens, our insight into the nature of the real world widens and deepens with it. In order to be able to imagine the play of *Hamlet*, Shakespeare must have had a profound and extensive understanding of the nature of real men and women. Moreover, in the process of imagining it, his insight would be further increased and deepened. Similar enlightenment comes to the intelligent reader or spectator of the play. On the practical side I need only refer in passing to the influence of the free play of imagination in shaping our ends and ideals. Noble fiction elevates, base fiction degrades. It is largely on such grounds that the study of literature can claim an educational value at least equal to that of science and its practical application.

10. *The 'Reality' of the Possible*

Possibility is, then, of essential importance for knowledge, for practice and for literature and art. But what after all is the status of the possible? Are we prepared to assert that it is real or that it exists? In answering this question, it is essential to distinguish two distinct though connected meanings of *reality*. *Real* is always a relative term. But in one sense it is opposed to the merely possible as its correlate. In another it is opposed to the merely apparent. In the first meaning it is as plainly nonsense to say that the possible, as such, is real as it is to say that the smaller as such is the greater or that right as such is left. It is quite otherwise if we consider reality as opposed to mere appearance. From this point of view, to say that the possible, as such, is unreal, means that the whole distinction between the possible and the real does not belong to the being and nature of the things we know or think of, but is merely something made or generated in and by the process of knowing or thinking. So regarded, it would have being merely for thought, and except as a product of thought it would not enter into the constitution of the universe at all.

I have already pointed out the absurdity of the view that the mind can make its own objects by thinking about them. But the conception of possibility requires special consideration. There are two ways in which the distinction of the real and the possible may be regarded as mere appearance. In one of them, which is represented by Dr Bosanquet, we have a special phase of the general doctrine that all our ordinary knowledge is through and through infected with error. The other, starting from the basis of common sense, simply asserts that possibility is merely subjective, because there would be no possible alternatives apart from our ignorance. On this view, when we say 'Jones is either a knave or a fool', what we mean is that we do not know which he is. If we did know, there would be no question of possible alternatives, and we should simply say 'he is a knave' or 'he is a fool'. The obvious reply is that in order to be specifically ignorant which of two alternatives is real, we must first know what the alternatives are; and this depends not on our ignorance, but (in the given case) on our knowledge of the sort of way in which Jones has behaved, and our knowledge of human nature in general. Further, if it is true that Jones is either a knave or a fool, it remains true even when we know definitely that he is a knave and not a fool; otherwise we have to admit that a valid conclusion may contradict one of the premises from which it is inferred. 'Jones is either a knave or a fool; he is not a knave; therefore he is a fool'. Here the conclusion 'he is a fool', inasmuch as it is not known at all independently of the disjunctive premise, can neither falsify it nor supersede it.

In other propositions, both disjunctive and hypothetical, the reference to ignorance is plainly irrelevant. In asserting that every triangle is either scalene, isosceles or equilateral, I include those particular triangles which I already know as scalene, as equilateral, as isosceles; and even as regards the others, it is no part of my meaning that I do not know which they are. So the statement, 'this stuff is poisonous', means roughly that if anyone takes a sufficient dose of it he will be poisoned. The speaker's knowledge or ignorance whether the poison has or has not, will or will not actually poison anybody is quite irrelevant. In some hypotheticals, possibilities are expressly opposed to known facts. For instance, 'if I were in your place, I should refuse to pay'. Here the speaker is not ignorant whether he is in the other man's place. He knows definitely that he is not and that in view of his past history he could not be so. The possibility he contemplates is known by him to be relative only to certain general aspects of the actual situation. It is compatible with being in the other man's place that he should retain his own character and opinions. He knows quite well that from other points of view what he supposes is out of the question. As further examples of this type of proposition, we may give the following: 'If I had missed the train, I should have been ruined'; 'If the Gallipoli Expedition had been a success, the war would have been shortened'; 'If ice were heavier than water, what are now the temperate regions of the globe would have been uninhabitable'.

I have already dealt generally with what we may call the Hegelian position. According to it, the distinction between the real and the possible is not purely subjective. It is one of the ways in which the one reality is partially falsified for finite individuals: in this respect it is like time and change and spatial relations. After my previous discussion of this doctrine, I need here only refer to one further point— Dr Bosanquet's account of the import of disjunctive propositions. He denies that a true or perfect disjunctive involves the distinction between the possible and the real at all. Rather, it expresses the mutual interdependence and the mutual exclusiveness of the real parts of a real system. He gives as an example: 'The triangle is either scalene, isosceles, or equilateral'. Now what is this statement to be taken to mean? Does it mean that of all conceivable triangles, some must be scalene and some isosceles and the others equilateral? On this interpretation, the words 'scalene', etc., do not stand for possible alternatives which may or may not be real. They are all equally real. But then there is no disjunctive but only a conjunctive proposition. To get a true disjunctive we must mean that each and every particular triangle is either scalene or isosceles or equilateral; and as any given triangle really has only one of these characters, the others must be merely possible alternatives.

To sum up the result of this discussion: It is absurd to say that the possible as such is real in the sense in which reality is opposed to possibility. But in the other sense in which the real is contrasted, not with the possible, but with the merely apparent, the possible is real. It is not a product of our way of thinking, but really belongs to the nature of what we think of.

This, however, is to be understood with two very important reservations. In the first place, I have to say here what I said before in discussing universals.[1] In denying that the difference between the real and the

[1] Cf. p. 89.

posssible is generated in and by the process of thinking, I by no means commit myself to the position that it has being independently of mind. I reserve the question till we come to face the wider problem, whether apart from mind any mode of being, possible or actual, particular or universal, can be self-complete.[1]

In the second place, the possible as such, though it has a distinct being, has no independent being apart from the real, any more than the greater as such has a being independent of the less. Further, the dependence is mutual. The possible and the real are each essentially incomplete without the other. The possible has being only in so far as it is the indispensable correlate of the real. The connecting link is the universal, as the unity of all its instances. There is no real being, whether concrete or abstract, which is not an instance of a universal; and there is no universal which does not include within its unity possible as well as real instances, unless indeed it is expressly so defined as to exclude them, as when we say not 'all ships' but 'all actually existing ships'. On the other hand, there is nothing possible which is not so as a possible variation of something real. The class of 'perfect fluids' may have only possible members: but it has these only because it is comprehended within the wider class of fluids, which contains actual water and air.

11. *Possibilities as Alternatives*

All possibilities fall into special groups, such that the members of each group are related to each other as alternatives; and the precise nature of the correlation of the real and the possible is seen only by examining what we mean by this word 'alternative'. It is the function of a disjunctive proposition to enumerate all the alternatives belonging to a certain group. 'Jones is either merely foolish or merely dishonest or both'. Here we have

[1] Cf. Chapter xviii.

possible alternatives, but they are not so merely in relation to each other; they are so only in their common relation to something real. The proposition is not true unless Jones is real, unless he has really behaved in such a way that his conduct may be truly regarded as due either to folly or dishonesty or both, and unless he really possesses a characteristic which is identical with at least one of these. This is the realised alternative and the others are unrealised. The possible, just so far as it is possible, is possibly real. It is from this point of view that we can best account for suppositions, for erroneous beliefs and for degrees of probability. Since the possible is what may be real, we can think of it as being real. We can do so without forgetting that it is only one alternative among others, and even when we know that it is not the realised alternative. This is what we call supposition. In general the conjunction 'if' means that what follows it is merely supposed, e.g. 'If Jones is or were a knave', 'if he had acted otherwise', 'if ice were heavier than water', 'if this stone moved through a non-resisting medium'. The consequent as well as the antecedent of a hypothetical proposition is merely supposed. What is asserted is that the realisation of one possibility involves the realisation of another, but it is not asserted that either is realised—e.g. 'if he were a knave he would have been less frank'.

In supposal we do not lose sight of the fact that there are other alternatives which also may be real. When we ignore, or fail to notice, or dismiss from consideration other alternatives, our mental attitude is belief. We proceed in thought and action as if there were only one alternative. In other words, we proceed in thought and action as if what is before our mind were not what may be real, but what is real. Then, if the alternative considered to the exclusion of others is not the realised alternative, we are making a mistake. I venture to think that this account of error and no other fairly meets the difficulties raised in Plato's *Theaetetus*, which are at bottom the same as those which trouble Mr Russell, and which lead to his peculiar theory of belief, given in the *Problems of Philosophy*, but now rejected by himself. Socrates in the *Theaetetus* asks—How can we make a mistake? The mistake must either consist in thinking what really is not: which cannot be, because, on this view, there is nothing to think; or it consists in confusing something which is real with something else which is real, which again cannot be; for we can identify one with the other only if and so far as both are present to the mind; and so far as both are thus present, we must distinguish and we cannot confuse them. The difficulty disappears, if what is before the mind is something which may or may not be real.[1]

12. *Possibility and Probability*

The possible as such is more or less probable or improbable; and probability always seems to be founded on some numerical ratio between alternative instances of the same universal. It is here important to distinguish between the probability of a particular fact and the probability of a general character. If we consider only the class 'all balls in this bag', then the more balls there are, the more alternative places there are which any one ball may occupy, and the more improbable it is that any one particular ball should occupy one particular place. If there are a hundred balls, the odds against this are ninety-nine to one. On the

[1] [This sentence is a very short-hand and consequently obscure statement of a theory which is best expounded in the article entitled 'Real Being and Being for Thought' in *Studies in Philosophy and Psychology*. The point is that what is present to the mind in error is a possible alternative which, as such, may or may not be realised. Though it is not in fact realised, this does not mean that it is something unreal, in the sense of being created by or dependent on mind; it has being independent of its being thought of. The 'reality' or objectivity of a possible alternative is bound up with the reality of the universal of which it is one possible realisation among others.—Ed.]

other hand, if the balls in the bag are some white and some black, then it is still true that the more white balls there are, the less probable it is that a particular white ball will occupy a certain place, but the more probable that this place will be occupied by one or other of the white balls rather than by a black one. This is so because the proportion of alternatives belonging to one class is increased relatively to those which belong to the other class. If there are fifty white balls and fifty black the probability that the ball in a certain place is white is one-half. But assuming that it is white, the odds against its being a particular white ball previously marked out from the rest are forty-nine to one. Probability is not subjective, any more than possibility. It is indeed always relative to some universal or universals, and it depends on what universal we take account of; but our selective attention no more makes the universal and its connected possibilities and probabilities than we make a road by deciding to take it. There is a certain probability that a man, inasmuch as he is a man, will die within six months. Inasmuch as he is a man suffering from bronchitis, there is another and a greater probability of this. What we call the probability of the man's dying is still only relative. It is relative to all that we know or can ascertain concerning the man and his circumstances.

13. *Summary*

It is now time to gather up the result of this long discussion in its bearing on the unity of the universe. We began by attempting to show that our knowledge of the actual world logically presupposes that actual particulars are essentially incomplete—are incapable of existing except as members of one whole to which they all belong. But at this point we were confronted by what claims to be an alternative explanation. Actual particulars, it is said, are, in themselves, loose and separate. So far as we know relations between them which go beyond immediate experience or acquaintance, this knowledge depends on an independent knowledge of relations between universals, of which given particulars are found to be instances. Universal principles are thus regarded as a thread on which we can string the loose items together. Herein the doctrine of Mr Russell seems to bear a curious resemblance to that of Kant, and both seem to me to be infected by the same fallacy. They proceed on the assumption that the particular and the universal are not only mutually distinct, but mutually independent. As against this, I have put forward and tried to establish the view that the universal is nothing but a peculiar form of unity, the distributive unity of its particular instances. This plainly leaves it no independent being, though it does leave it a distinct being of its own.

But here arises an obvious difficulty. We have to meet the fact that in the ideal region of logic and mathematics we seem to turn our back on the actual. We deal with the objects of our thought apart from the question whether they actually exist. But on examination it turns out that here also the universal is nothing more or less than the unity of its instances. Only, we must include instances which are merely possible as well as those which are actual. Thus the question of the relation of universals to actual existence resolves itself, so far as the unity of the universe is concerned, into the question of the relation of the possible to the real, and to the actual as what is ultimately real. Hence our long discussion of possibility, in which we were led to deal with such important problems as the use of 'conceptual models' to give insight into the actual course of events, and with the nature of free choice and of belief, error, and probability. We found as the result of this inquiry that the possible and the real are each essentially incomplete without the other. Thus, universals and their interconnexion include the actual and the possible in the inseparable unity of a single system. This view commits us to the apparent absurdity that the merely possible is real. But the paradox is removed if we take reality in the sense in which it is opposed not to the possible but to the merely apparent. When, for instance, Dr Bosanquet speaks of 'the one all-inclusive Reality in which we live and move and have our being', we must maintain that the possible as such enters into the constitution of this reality, and is in this sense real. If the all-inclusive reality did not include possibilities, we could not 'live and move and have our being' in it. We should be suffocated.

The position we have reached as regards the unity of the universe may be stated as follows. Setting aside metaphysical construction, we find that the whole system of our common sense and scientific knowledge presupposes it, and apart from it loses all logical warrant. When what is thus presupposed in all our ordinary knowledge and action is explicitly recognised, a further problem inevitably arises. Can we, from those partial features and aspects of the whole which are accessible to us, venture to form any judgment concerning the nature of the whole in its unity? The attempt to answer this question may be a great adventure and its chances of success initially dubious. But at any rate it cannot be shelved by the *a priori* dictum that we have no reason for regarding the universe as a unity at all, rather than as a collection of separate items which can only be known piecemeal or hand-to-mouth, as they happen to present themselves.

14. *The Purpose and Method of 'Constructive Metaphysics'*

Finally I would remind the reader of what I urged in my first chapter. The question of the unity of the universe is not merely theoretical. It is of the deepest and widest practical and emotional significance. We cannot, therefore, afford to pass it by without coming to any sort of decision one way or the other. A practical postulate is required; and in forming a practical postulate we have to follow whatever clues offer themselves, even though they may leave room for doubt. Besides this, the primary uncritical belief of mankind, arising in its practical dealings with concrete situations, presupposes that the universe is a unity. In particular, this view underlies the ordinary religious consciousness in its historical development. But, as I argued in the first chapter,[1] there is a presumption in favour of such primary beliefs, so that if critical inquiry fails to overthrow them, and *a fortiori* if it on the whole tends to support them, we are justified in accepting them, as least as practical postulates.

When we have said that the universe is a unity we have yet to determine what account we are to give of its nature and constitution as a whole, based on all the data at our disposal. This is the problem of philosophy as constructive metaphysics; and, on the whole, the history of philosophy shows steady progress in dealing with it. Owing to the very nature of the problem itself, partial failures mean that the task as a whole has to be begun afresh. The parts of the puzzle have in large measure to be taken to pieces and put together again. Hence the succession of philosophical systems, in which each new thinker seems to begin *de novo*, accepting hardly anything from his predecessors. But those who make this a reproach also make it a reproach that each new philosopher seems to repeat in a more or less disguised form what has been said by those who have gone before him, and in particular that he studies and feels bound to study the history of philosophy in a way in which the chemist, for instance, is not bound to study the past history of chemistry. The explanation is simply this: when anyone makes a relatively new departure in philosophy, he has from the nature of the case to answer again from a new point of view the whole range of philosophical questions in their systematic interconnexion. But in doing so, if he is to avoid the mere repetition of past crudities and blunders, he is bound constantly to use the work of his forerunners, learning as much from their partial failure as from their partial success, as much from what he

[1] Cf. pp. 20–21.

disagrees with in them as from what he agrees with. Also, he learns as much from sceptical criticism as from constructive systems. Hume was as important to Kant as Leibniz. The constructive metaphysics of the future will, I think, have much to learn from Russell, who is a Hume brought up to date. In this way, and in no other, progress in philosophy is possible; and the careful and competent student of the history of philosophy recognises that such progress is actually to be found. In its nature it is inevitably different from that of the special sciences; but perhaps not in degree, when the conditions of the problem are fairly taken into account.

BOOK THREE

MATTER AND OUR
KNOWLEDGE OF IT[1]

▼

Chapter VI

NEO-REALISM AND THE
BERKELEY-MILL THEORY

1. *Transitional*

In [*Mind and Matter*],[2] I approached the relation of matter
and mind from the point of view of the psycho-physical
union of mind and body. I reached the result that mind
cannot be derived from matter, but must be ultimate and
fundamental in the constitution of the Universe of Being.[3]
Hence the correlation between them must be universal
and not confined to such finite individuals as men and
animals. If then we take the psycho-physical relation as
an adequate clue to this universal connexion, we seem
driven to a doctrine of universal parallelism or of universal
interaction. Further, we saw that this line of thought
ultimately points to an Eternal and Universal Mind as the
source from which finite individuals derive their being.

But in this mode of procedure, which starts with the
psycho-physical relation as if it were an ultimate fact, we

[1] [With the general topic of this Book, cf. *Mind and Matter*, Book IV.—
Ed.]

[2] [The typescript reads 'the lectures of my previous course'. The
present chapter is the first Lecture of the Second Course of Gifford
Lectures, and the particular lectures of the First Course here referred to
were destroyed by the author after the publication of *Mind and Matter*, on
the ground that they had been made obsolete by the further treatment of
the subject in *Mind and Matter*, Book II, and Book IV, Chapter VII.—Ed.]

[3] [Cf. the passage from *Mind and Matter*, pp. 314–15 (quoted in the
Editorial Preface, p. xxi).—Ed.]

gain no insight into the nature and ground of the psycho-physical relation itself. Consequently we leave the general nature of the connexion between matter and mind an unexplained enigma.

We have now to try whether we shall succeed better in this respect by pursuing another line of investigation. We shall begin, not with the relation of mind and body, but with the relation of matter as object known to individual minds as knowing it. We shall inquire what is logically primary in our knowledge of the material world, and examine the logical nature and conditions of the process by which we reach that view of it which is now taken for granted by common sense and the sciences. In this way we may hope to gain some answer to the questions what matter ultimately is, and how it is ultimately related to mind within the unity of the universe. We shall then be in a position from which we can return with advantage to the problem of the relation of body and mind.

2. *Common-sense Presuppositions about Matter*

I start from common sense and science. I do not mean that I rely on any philosophical opinions which the plain man or man of science may hold or may be supposed to hold. I mean that I begin by taking for granted that view of the external world which is essentially presupposed in the practical conduct of daily life, in anticipating the course of events, and in adapting means to ends. Science, when it does not run into philosophical theory, is, I take it, only a highly systematised and generalised development of common sense. Both common sense and science make mistakes, which are such from their own point of view, and not merely for the philosophical critic. But errors of this kind, being errors which the plain man and the man of science are prepared to recognise as such, presuppose a general system of knowledge which alone makes them possible, and which makes it possible to correct them.

It is this general system which I initially assume to be valid.

What then is thus essentially presupposed in ordinary life and in science concerning the nature of matter and the way in which we know it? The material world includes a vast system of things having extension, figure, relative position and motion in space, which exist, change their nature and relations and causally interact, quite independently of being perceived by individual minds such as ours. On the other hand, we are in the first instance conversant with this world only by way of sense-perception. To use Locke's metaphor, our ideas of it come to us only through the channels of sense. Berkeley was true to common sense when he defined matter as what we see and feel, or otherwise sensibly perceive. Yet the range of sense-perception is amazingly narrow as compared with the vastness of the world to which it gives the introduction. It extends only to those things which happen to enter into certain special and transient relations with the body of the percipient, and even of these only such partial aspects and features are perceived as happen to affect our sense-organs in certain peculiar ways. Primary sense-knowledge only gives minute and relatively detached fragments of the material world.

How then do common sense and science transcend these partial data, and pass to the knowledge of the whole which contains them? There is only one way. The partial data are apprehended as being partial, and are completed in thought and imagination by a context which includes and unites them—a context which is itself unperceived and, in part, imperceptible. A primitive and simple form of the process consists merely in connecting an earlier and a later percept by intermediate links filling up the gap between them, as when we fill up the interval between the disappearance and reappearance of a moving object by thinking of it as continuing to exist and to move while it is unperceived. In its latest and most complex stages the same process yields the conceptual construction of the chemist, the physicist or the astronomer. Throughout the whole development from its rudimentary beginnings to the most advanced scientific theories, however far sense-perception may be transcended, it is transcended only by means of itself. The right to supply a context to the perceptual data is logically conditioned by the demand that the context shall connect the data with each other in a coherent order, and that no datum which refuses to fit into the scheme shall be ignored until its claims are satisfied. A datum may indeed be treated as illusion or hallucination. But even then it has to be shown how and why such illusions arise. They too in their own way have to be included, not ignored. It is further to be noted that the nature of the unperceived constituents of the external world are thought or imagined only on the analogy supplied by perceptual data. These may of course be largely modified, transformed and reconstructed. But all these variations are ultimately variations of certain general characters and relations which are primarily given in sense-perception. Extension, motion and relative position are everywhere presupposed, but apart from sense-experience we have no means of knowing what it is to be extended or to move.

3. *The Philosophical Problem*

I have said that I begin by assuming this view of the external world which is presupposed by practical common sense and by physical science. But if we begin with it, why not end with it? What need is there to say anything more? Well, I shall end with it in the sense that I shall reach no conclusions which are incompatible with it, and none which are not required to supplement it. But as it stands it is incomplete, and leaves unanswered very important questions which for the philosopher imperatively demand an answer.

The central problem is this: What account can we give of the logical connexion between the primary data of sense and the vast body of knowledge which claims to be derived from and dependent on them? That this is a serious question may be seen from the difficulties felt by those philosophers who have really faced it, and the variable and conflicting results which they have reached. Descartes, for instance, finds, on critical examination, that sense-knowledge cannot possibly do what is required of it. Through it we apprehend external objects only as they happen to affect our particular bodies. Such limited knowledge, though practically useful, is very confused and full of error. This limited point of view he contrasts sharply with that which we have now reached. We are now in a position from which we can survey the material world as a whole, and our body as only one part among others. From this standing-ground we can know what the sun and moon really are as contrasted with the way in which they appear to the senses. We have transcended the limits of sense-knowledge and we are able to criticise it from a superior and independent position, correcting and explaining the illusions of sense-perception. How can we logically reach this standing-ground if we are supposed to start only from sense-perception itself? Descartes answers that we cannot. The problem cannot be solved unless we suppose a positive source of knowledge, independent of sense. Hence he assumes a comprehensive system of positive ideas and principles, which are due not to sense-perception, but to our nature as thinking beings. It is through an innate idea of this kind that we know the material world as what, according to him, it really is— a spatial system extended in three dimensions and without any other attribute except extension and its modes, all secondary qualities being excluded from it.

Thus the ordinary presupposition of common sense and science, that our knowledge of the external world has developed from sense-perception, turns out, according to Descartes, to be untenable; and other philosophers, such as Leibniz, Spinoza and Kant would so far agree with him.

I do not think that they are right, but the questions they raise do require an answer and cannot be answered merely by restating the ordinary position of common sense and science. Such problems specially concern the philosopher. But he does not, in the first instance, make them or discover them. Rather they are forced upon him by the wavering inconsistency of common sense and by the partial conflict of common sense with science, and even of science with itself. The plain man undoubtedly agrees with Berkeley that his own sensa[1]—the contents of his own immediate sense-experience—are material facts, not mental, as knowing, feeling and willing are mental. Yet he does not consistently identify his own sensa with the objects which he supposes to exist and persist independently of their being perceived. Wherever occasion arises, he is prepared to regard the sensa as merely more or less transitory appearances of bodies and their qualities, appearances which may vary greatly where there is no variation in the things perceived, and which may even be present in dreams and hallucinations when no corresponding external object exists at all. It is easy to perplex him by pressing this seeming inconsistency upon his notice. If he follows his own natural bias, he will probably remain convinced that both positions are true, though he does not know how to reconcile them. But the philosopher cannot rest content with this. He must, if he can, show that the two views can be made consistent with each other. Failing this, he must adopt one to the exclusion of the other, and whichever he rejects he will find himself at variance with the original assumption which formed the basis from which he started. And by casting doubt on this, he so far casts doubt on his own position.

Further difficulties emerge when we consider points on which science finds itself in conflict with common sense.

[1] [Hitherto the author has used the terms *sense-datum* and *sense-data*, which are used in Russell's *The Problems of Philosophy*, which he has been criticising. From now on he uses the terms *sensum* and *sensa*, which he preferred.—Ed.]

From the pre-scientific point of view things are red and hot and sweet, just as they are extended and figured. The physicist and physiologist, on the contrary, draw a sharp distinction between primary and secondary qualities. What we perceive as colour, for example, does not, according to them, really belong to material things. It belongs only to the sense-experience which somehow arises when our body is affected in a certain way by things outside it. It belongs neither to the body which is thus affected nor to the material conditions which act on it. It thus falls outside the world of matter altogether. The plain man is, without much difficulty, brought to see the reasons for this doctrine, and after a fashion to accept it. None the less, when not expressly reflecting on these scientific reasons, he persists in his pre-scientific view, and so does the man of science himself in ordinary life.

4. *Primary Sense-Knowledge*

We have now to grapple directly with what I have described as our central problem. We assume provisionally that it is only through sense-perception that we know that matter exists and what it is. We assume that our knowledge of the material world, so far as it extends beyond the original data of sense, is attained by correlating these data with each other in a coherent context, and that this process is logically valid. The first question we have to answer is this: how must primary sense-knowledge be constituted so as to make it possible for our present knowledge of an external world to be logically derived from it in this way? At the same time, we have also to keep in view another distinct inquiry: whether what direct introspection reveals to us concerning the nature of sense-perception is consistent with the nature it must have, if it is to play the part assigned to it in the development of knowledge.

Our course would be comparatively straight if we had merely to consider sense-perception as we have it now.

But we cannot do so, because what we now call seeing and feeling really include what are logically complex inferences, in which innumerable perceptual data belonging to past experience are combined and correlated. I say, for instance, that I see snow, and I mean that I see it as snow —as something not only white, but soft and cold and powdery. It is only on critical reflexion that I recognise the softness, coldness and powderiness as original data of touch, and not of sight apart from touch. In general, our present perceptual knowledge differs immensely from what it would be on a first perception. It is not only enriched by preformed associations; it is also otherwise profoundly modified. Even the size, shape and distance of things are not purely independent data of present sight and touch, given here and now apart from inference based on previous experience. We cannot now find any instance of sense-knowledge not complicated and modified as the result of a process which begins with the beginning of our intelligent mental life, so that we are now unable to recall its past history by any effort of memory. This being so, we have to determine as best we may the nature of the original data of sense-perception, apart from acquired complexity. For, evidently, we should be moving in a vicious circle if, in dealing with each perception in turn, we accounted for the knowledge conveyed in it as depending on knowledge already acquired in other perceptions.

What then is the nature of primary sense-knowledge? I am using the word 'primary' in a logical rather than in a psychological sense. What is logically primary is to be distinguished from what is merely earlier in the history of the mind. What is logically primary may indeed coincide with what is psychologically primitive; but it does so only in so far as later stages of knowledge are derived from earlier by logical steps. Memory-judgments are undoubtedly primary. But it is quite possible that a rudimentary experience may exist without memory. If this be so, when memory supervenes, it is not only later in time, but is logically a new departure.

A primary way of knowing which is also relatively primitive does not cease to exist in the later stages which logically presuppose it. It still persists, though it may be overlaid, modified and masked by its subsequent developments. Thus each new perception, as it occurs to us now, includes, besides much that is logically inference, a central nucleus which is not acquired, but is primary. It includes a new datum without which the inference would be baseless. It is just this fresh datum which gives it its character of being a perception.[1]

There are then, it would seem, two equivalent ways of approaching our problem. (1) We may inquire what primary sense-perception must be if it is to supply a logical basis for acquired knowledge. Or (2) we may consider our present complex perception, and by direct introspection attempt to distinguish within it the primary nucleus from the acquired complexity. If we could succeed in either of these approaches we should also have succeeded in the other. For the essential aim of both is to find out what we should perceive if this were conditioned merely by the immediate content of present sense-experience apart from other factors.

The method of direct introspection would, no doubt, be best, if we could trust it to give a safe and final decision. But this it cannot do. When we see a thing, we cannot by direct scrutiny distinguish what is due merely to the present visual sensation and what presupposes other perceptual data—visual, tactual and motor. For this we have to use a more circuitous procedure, involving a comparison of different perceptions taking place under variable conditions. When we come to the most fundamental questions concerning primary sense-knowledge, these methods, as well as direct introspection, prove inadequate.

[1] [For a further account of the distinction between the logically primitive and the psychologically primary, see below, pp. 142 ff.—Ed.]

In the long run, there seems to be only one principle on which we can proceed in dealing with points on which introspection may leave us in doubt. We must start from that present knowledge of the material world which we all take for granted in ordinary thought and conduct, and we must consider what primary sense-knowledge must be in order to make this logically and psychologically possible. That theory is, *ceteris paribus*, to be preferred, which solves this problem most fully. On the other hand, theories which upset instead of explaining the fundamental presuppositions of common sense and empirical science are to be rejected—unless, indeed, they can show that these presuppositions are untenable, and can substitute others which will serve instead of them.

5. *Fundamental Alternatives*[1]

There are two ultimately and vitally different ways of regarding primary sense-knowledge. It may be held that what we primarily perceive is merely our own sensa—the existentially present content of our sense-experience—and that on this foundation our whole knowledge of the constitution and course of nature has been built up. We may call this the Berkeleyan theory, because Berkeley was the first to work it out consistently into its consequences. His lead has been followed more recently by J. S. Mill and Bertrand Russell. The other possible view, if indeed it can be shown to be possible, is that even in primary perception we know something more than our own sensa; and that this 'something more' is apprehended as having the distinctive characters of a material object, such as extension, figure, colour, etc. This type of theory is represented by Reid, though he has by no means worked it out in a satisfactory way. It seems to me to be the only one which will cover the facts. But the grounds for holding

[1] [With Sections 5–8, cf. *Mind and Matter*, pp. 162–5.—Ed.]

it will be most clearly brought out if we begin by examining the alternative hypothesis.

What is essential to this is that our knowledge of matter is primarily a knowledge of our own sensa. But philosophers who agree on this point may diverge in other ways. Berkeley, for instance, holds as evident truth that the immediate contents of sense-experience exist only so far as some individual mind actually perceives them—i.e. knows them by acquaintance as they are actually experienced. Thus he has to meet the objection that on his view things are annihilated when they cease to be perceived, and re-created when they are perceived again. But the position that sensa are the sole objects of primary perception and the position that they only exist in being sensed are not inseparable. Some modern writers have indeed separated them. Agreeing with Berkeley that our sense-presentations are material objects, and that they are all we know of matter apart from inference, they assert that their being perceived or otherwise experienced is quite indifferent to their existence. The mind is, so to speak, a stage on which they have their exits and their entrances. But their appearances and their disappearances are only passing phases in their history. This view is attributed by Hume to the plain man. The ploughboy who believes his plough to exist when he no longer sees it or feels it really believes, according to Hume, that the very sense-impressions persist which he had when he did see and feel it. This doctrine, which Hume attributed to common sense, is neo-realism, and we shall begin by examining it.

6. *Neo-Realism*

The neo-realist holds that the immediate contents of sense-experience are themselves material and not mental. He also holds that they are intrinsically capable of existing, whether or not they enter into the experience of any finite mind. Now I am not prepared to deny either of these positions. On the contrary, I shall in the end accept both of them as part of my own view. But, however true they may be in themselves, I must insist that they do not solve the most pressing problem which arises when we seriously attempt to give a coherent account of our knowledge of the material world. The real difficulty is that in practical life and in science we have perpetually to recognise a system of things which in their existence, changes, persistence and interaction are independent of our immediate sense-experience. This physical system, as we may call it, does not include sense-presentations even as parts or partial phases. On the contrary, they seem always to fall outside it. It is true, indeed, that in accordance with the ordinary use of language, we may properly be said to perceive physical facts. But this is just because what we are thus said to perceive is not the immediate content of sense-experience which is present in perceiving it. I see a body as having a certain size and shape. This means that, owing to the presence of certain visual sensa, it appears to me, rightly or wrongly, that there is a body before me having this size and shape. But if I am dreaming there need be no body there, though the visual presentation must actually exist as actually experienced. Further, even when a body really is seen, neither its real nor its apparent shape and size can be identified with the shape and size of the visual presentations. For visual presentations vary perpetually with variations in the position of the percipient's body and eye; they vary also with the variable states of his organs of vision and of his nervous system, and again with differences in the bodily organisation of different percipients. If they are to be identified with the physical objects which are ordinarily said to be perceived, these physical objects must themselves actually change and vary in the same way. The visible chair must actually grow bigger or smaller, as I approach or recede from it. It is needless to point out that any view of this sort flatly contradicts all that we know of

the physical order, and all that we must presuppose concerning it as the basis of our practical conduct in adapting
ourselves to the course of events and controlling them.

For such reasons as these, which will be more fully
developed in the sequel, we must recognise that sensa,
though they may be material and not mental, fall outside
the physical order. If they exist at all when they are not
experienced, they at any rate do not exist as physical facts.
It is just because this is so that our knowledge of the
material world presents a perplexing problem. No one
would even have felt any difficulty, if our own sensa had
been themselves part and parcel of the physical order,
needing only to be ideally extended and connected with
each other by ideally represented links of essentially the
same nature as themselves, but not directly given in actual
sense-experience. Had this been so, as conceivably it
might have been, there would never have been any problem
for the philosophy of perception to discuss.

7. *Berkeley and Mill*

Our knowledge of the physical order cannot then be
explained by assuming that our own sensa exist before and
after they are sensed by us. We have next to discuss the
position of those who, like Berkeley, Mill and Bertrand
Russell, dispense with this assumption, and yet maintain
that we begin by knowing only our own sensa.

The value of Berkeley and Mill to us is that they really
make a serious attempt to show what sort of material
world we should be capable of knowing, on the assumption
that our original data are our own sensa and nothing else.
It is thus possible for us to compare the world as it would
be on this assumption with that which is presupposed by
common sense and science, and to determine how far they
coincide, or are practically equivalent to each other. What
then is the material world for Berkeley? In the first place,
the content of our immediate sense-experience is and must

be part of it; it is the only part which we know directly, and not by inference; and it is the only part which actually exists just as it is experienced. Further, there can be no differences and no relations between sense-presentations as immediately experienced, and no changes in them, which are not differences and relations and changes in the material world. For instance, the extension and figure, the relative situation and motion of visual presentations as such, are quite separate and distinct from the extension and figure, the relative situation and motion of tactual presentations. They come within the continuous unity of the sense-experience of the individual mind, and within this they are related in the way of succession and co-existence; they also in some degree resemble each other. But otherwise they fall apart. They are loose and separate in the same way as colours and sounds. Hence it follows that in the material world also, so far as we directly perceive it, visible extension, shape, motion and position must be quite distinct from tangible extension, shape, motion and position. This seems clearly incompatible with the pre-suppositions of common sense. For we do not take the same body to have two distinct sizes, one perceptible by sight and the other by touch. Rather, the assumption on which we proceed is that there is one size perceived with varying degrees of accuracy in both ways.

So far we have considered only that part of the material world which consists in sensa actually experienced by the individual. But this is admittedly only a very small part of the whole which in some way we come to know. It leaves unexplained the physical order which exists inde-pendently of our actual sense-experience. What account can Mill and Berkeley give of this, and of the way in which we come to know it? It is open to neither of them to say that it is composed of sensa which are not sensed by us, whether these be taken to be the same or different from those which appear and disappear in our own sense-experience. For Mill, at any rate, sensa do not actually exist at all except in so far as actually experienced by us. Berkeley qualifies this position by suggesting that pre-sentations which do not exist in our minds exist in the mind of God.[1] But for both of them the physical order consists and can only consist in a system, not merely of actual but of possible sense-presentations. It includes all the sense-presentations which we may experience, might have experienced, or might be experiencing under certain conditions. It is, in the language of Mill, a system of permanent possibilities of sensation; and these permanent possibilities are regarded as persisting, changing, and mutually determining each other in their changes, just as if they were actual existences. Thus the existence of a chair in the next room, when no one is perceiving it, merely means that such propositions as the following are true: 'If I were in the next room with my eyes turned in a certain direction, I should be experiencing a certain group of visual sensations.' The antecedent in this hypo-thetical proposition must also be interpreted in accordance with the general theory. 'If I were in the next room' can only mean 'if I were experiencing certain sensations' which, in fact, I do not experience. Suppose now that someone, in my absence, removes the chair or puts a cover on it. This means for me that a change has taken place in a possible cluster of sensa which I call a chair, following on a change in another possible cluster which I call a human body.

---

[1] [This commonly given account of the part played by the Berkeleyan God in maintaining the physical world, for which of course there is plenty of warrant in Berkeley's own writings, is specially relevant in the present con-text. But in expounding Berkeley, Stout always gave far greater importance to the causal agency of God in determining the order of actual *and possible* sensa. Cf. *Mind and Matter*, p. 166: 'Berkeley, though he regards the physical world as nothing but an order of actual and possible sensations, yet makes it an essential part of his system that both the sensations and their order shall be referred to a Cause beyond themselves. . . . [He] insists that the cause of our sensations must be a mind: which, as being the author of nature, he identifies with God.'—Ed.]

8. *Criticism of the Berkeley-Mill Position*

I presume that few philosophers are now prepared to defend this view.[1] But it is important that we should clearly understand why the theory is untenable. The fatal objection to it is that it is bound to assume as fact, what it pretends to doubt or deny—the existence of actual physical objects. Unless actual physical things and events are presupposed, we have no means of determining what the required system of possibilities is, and no valid ground for asserting that there is such a system. We know the physical world only in knowing its specific details and their specific relations to each other. But even if these specific details were in fact merely specific possibilities of sensation, and their connexion merely a connexion of such possibilities, still they could not, in the first instance, be known to us in this way. We could not know them unless we represented them to ourselves as dependent on a correspondingly detailed system of actual existences, and unless we apprehended these as having a definite positive nature and definite and positive relations. We could not proceed otherwise than we do in fact proceed—i.e. by assuming actual things and actual occurrences, known as having extension, figure and motion, coexisting in space, and changing and succeeding each other in time. A mere reference to a general agency, such as that of God, on which the world as a whole is supposed to depend, is useless, when what is required is the specific actual conditions on which specific possibilities of sensation depend. 'There is a chair in the next room.' All that this statement means, on Mill's view, can be adequately expressed in such propositions as the following: 'If I were in the next room, and if my eyes were turned in a certain direction, I should be having certain visual presentations.' But I only have ground for asserting that if I were in the

[But as late as 1938 the enemy was still in the field. See the author's article on 'Phenomenalism' in *Proc. Arist. Soc.* Vol. xxxix.—Ed.]

next room I should be seeing a chair, on the assumption that there really is a chair there. It is worse than futile to reply that the existence of a chair in the next room merely consists in certain permanent possibilities of sensation. For then, our original hypothetical proposition takes the following form: 'If there is a possibility of my having certain visual sensations which would be realised if I were in the next room, then it follows that there is such a possibility which would be so realised.' The antecedent has swallowed the consequent, and there is nothing left but the 'if' clause.

To get rid of this futile tautology, we must assume a chair which is no mere possibility, but actually exists. We cannot substitute for this some condition belonging to the agency of unknowable things-in-themselves, or to a plan in the Divine Mind according to which it causes us to have sense-experiences. For antecedently we know nothing about the agency of unknowable things-in-themselves, or of the Divine Mind. What is required is an actual condition which we can represent to ourselves as having a definite nature and definite relations. The same reasoning holds for the supposition 'if my body were in the next room'. My body itself, on Mill's view, must consist in a system of possible sensations, only a small part of which ever become actual. The difference between my body's being here and its being in the next room is mainly a difference in these possibilities, and not in actual sense-experience. But these possibilities presuppose, like others, a corresponding actual existence on which they depend, an actual existence whose nature we can know. And this is found, and can only be found, in what we take to be our actually existing body, as a physical thing.

There is therefore no way of defining or describing the system of possible sensa which it is proposed to substitute for actual physical things and processes, unless we assume them to depend on actually existing factors, having the distinctive characters of physical objects, such as extension, shape, and motion. Nor can we treat this assumption as merely a descriptive device or conceptual construction. It is not a scaffolding which we can remove when the building is finished or a ladder which we can throw down when we have climbed by means of it. This is the position of Mr Bertrand Russell in his elaborate and novel development of the Berkeley-Mill theory. He presupposes that we know that there is an order of possible sensa, such as it would be if physical objects actually existed, although we do not know that they exist. He thus cuts the ground from under his own feet. For unless we accept as fact the actual existence of a connected system of physical conditions, we have no ground for believing that there is such a system of possibilities as the theory posits and attempts to describe.

9. *The Relation of the System of Possible Sensa to the Physical Order*

The general logical position will be made clearer by considering more closely the nature of the system of possible sensa in its relation to the physical order. It is very far from true that every distinction and relation between possibilities of sensation can be matched by a corresponding distinction and relation within the physical world as it exists for common sense and science. Just as a visual presentation, with its own shape, size, position and motion, differs from a touch-presentation with its shape, size, position and motion, so the corresponding possibilities differ in exactly the same way. One is a possible visual experience, the other a possible tactual experience. Similarly, just as one visual sensation differs from another, and as one tactual sensation differs from another, so *possible* visual sensations are distinct from each other, and *possible* tactual sensations are distinct from each other. But for common sense and science it is the very same extension, figure and motion which, in a different way, and with different degrees of accuracy, are perceived both by sight and by touch, and by various tactual and visual sensa. We may call this the physical size, shape and motion. It is this single, physical fact, as contrasted with the manifold possible sensa, which alone enters into, and alone can enter into, our conception of the relation of external objects to each other, as distinct from their relation to our perception. It is, for instance, the physical size which is measured, directly or indirectly, by units of measurement such as a footrule. As measured or measurable in this way, each body has only one size, however variable the actual and possible sensa may be which we have in perceiving it. So, too, in tracing the causal order of the external world, it is the single physical fact which alone makes any difference. It is only the physical size and shape of the key which determines whether it will or will not turn in the lock and open the door.

Can any tenable explanation be given, in terms of the Berkeley-Mill theory, of this distinction between the one physical fact and its manifold ways of appearing through diverse sense-experiences? This may be attempted in two ways. It may be said that what we call the physical fact is in truth only a group of possible sensa, so related to each other according to uniform rules and so associated in our minds that we treat them as a single unity. The objection to this is that the unity of the complex itself presupposes the very distinction which it is supposed to account for, the distinction between different ways of appearing of an identical physical object. The various sensa form a single complex only because of their common relation to what is taken to be the same physical fact perceived by means of them. They group themselves round this as a common centre of reference. Apart from this common centre they have no more unity than the members of a family apart from their descent from common ancestors. But it may be said that the common ancestors are themselves members of the family. Why, in like manner, may not what we have called the physical fact be itself some possible sense-perception, having certain distinctive characters by which it is contrasted with the others belonging to its variable sensible appearances? This brings us to the second view, that maintained by Berkeley.

According to Berkeley, what we regard as the real physical extension, shape, size, distance and motion of a body is the tangible extension, shape, size and motion, and what is tangible is not anything distinct from immediately experienced tactual sensa, but identical with them. Tangible extension, on Berkeley's view, is physically real because it remains constant, while other sensa habitually associated with it vary, and also because it is of peculiar importance, owing to its direct connexion with our bodily pleasures and pains and with our practical activity. Taking for granted that there is an extension which is constant, he insists that this cannot be visual. He therefore concludes that it must be tactual. His proof that it cannot be visual is convincing. 'Suppose', he says, 'I perceive by sight that faint and obscure idea of something, which I doubt whether it be a man, or a tree, or a tower, but judge it to be at the distance of about a mile: I cannot mean, that what I see is a mile off, or that it is the image or likeness of anything a mile off, since that every step I take towards it, the appearance alters, and from being obscure, small, and faint, grows clear, large, and vigorous. And when I come to the mile's end, that which I saw first is quite lost, neither do I find any thing in the likeness of it.'[1]

We must here remember that for Berkeley what we properly see is only the visual apparition itself as immediately experienced. This is what he calls the idea perceived, and all else which we know by sight must be inferred and not directly seen. This of course follows from the general doctrine that the object of primary perception is the present sensum and nothing else. If, then, what is

[1] *New Theory of Vision*, sect. XLIV *ad fin.*

really at a distance remains constant while the visual presentation varies, what is really at a distance cannot be what we directly see, unless what is really at a distance alters in shape, size and distinctness as we approach and recede from it. But to suppose this is to wreck the whole fabric of our ordinary knowledge. The whole system of measurement by such units as feet and inches would become impossible. In particular, the science of optics would be destroyed, and with it Berkeley's initial argument, always assumed to be valid, that we cannot see distance because 'distance being a line directed endwise to the eye, it projects only one point in the fund of the eye. Which point remains invariably the same, whether the distance be longer or shorter'.[1]

For the Berkeley-Mill theory there can be only one way out of this difficulty. Since what we call real size, shape, distance and motion cannot be identified with visual sensa, actual or possible, they must, Berkeley thinks, be identified with tactual sensa, actual and possible, including under this head sense-experiences connected with muscles, joints and tendons. The real size and shape of a body would thus belong to the possible tactual and motor presentations which we should have if we were exploring its surface; its real distance would be constituted by the tactual and motor presentations experienced in approaching it. The fatal objection to this is that tactual and motor sensa vary much in the same way as those of sight, when the physical fact is relatively constant. Touch-sensa vary in extent and shape with the part of the skin used in touching; they differ, for instance, for the nape of the neck and for the tip of the tongue. Motor sensa vary with the varying muscles, joints and tendons which come into action. Thus if Berkeley were right in identifying the distance of a thing with the train of motor and tactual sensa experienced in moving towards it, there would be not one real distance but many. The distance would be different according as a man

[1] *New Theory of Vision*, sect. 11.

walked, crawled, hopped or rode. It would be different for a child, for a man, and for an ant. But a mile remains a mile however we traverse it. What makes the Berkeleyan view plausible and tempting is that, in touch, the surface of part of our body, as an actually existing physical thing, is in direct contact with the surface touched. This makes possible a primitive measurement by superposition, so that we can speak of a hand's breadth or an arm's length. Given superposition, a hand of wood may serve as a measure as well as one of flesh and blood. The presence or absence of touch-sensa is irrelevant, and their variable extensiveness when they are present makes no difference.

I conclude that theories of this type, which substitute the possible for the actual, entirely fail to account for the nature of physical objects, and for our knowledge of them; also, that unless actual physical objects are presupposed, we can neither define what the system of possible sensa is, nor have any valid ground for asserting that there is such a system.

None the less, I do not want to emphasise my disagreement with one to whom I owe so much as to Berkeley. He seems to me to be perfectly right, and to represent the common sense of mankind, in holding as a matter of course that the contents of our immediate sense-experience belong, not indeed to the physical order as such, but to the material world as a whole. When I come to develop my own view it will be found to be in vital respects akin to Berkeley's, so that I may perhaps venture to call myself a Neo-Berkeleyan.

Chapter VII

HOW ARE PHYSICAL OBJECTS
INITIALLY KNOWN?[1]

1. *Physical Objects are not inferred from Sensa*

The previous discussion of Neo-Realism and of the Berkeley-Mill theory shows that physical objects cannot be identified with our own sensa, actual or possible. But our own sensa are the only existences with which we are directly acquainted in sense-perception. How, then, do we know physical objects at all? Do we know them only by way of inference, starting from our own sensa as premises?

To this view there are the gravest objections. If there ever was an inferential process of the kind required, it belongs to a very primitive stage of mental development, and is buried in the remote and forgotten past. From our present point of view we go through processes of inference in determining whether this or that apparently existing physical object really does exist, or whether it has the character which it seems to have. But physical reality in general seems to be directly known in sense-perception

[1] [The doctrine expounded in this chapter is up to a point that of *Mind and Matter* (cf. especially Book III, Chapter V and pp. 296–301). The emphasis on the 'incompleteness' of what is immediately experienced as an explanation of our knowledge of the physical world is central to both. But in *Mind and Matter* 'incompleteness' is finally supplemented by 'active tendency'. The importance given to 'the activity factor' at the end of *Mind and Matter* suggests that Stout had come to regard the earlier treatment of the present volume as in this respect seriously defective. Thus in speaking of memory-knowledge (an example of the function of 'incompleteness' also used in the present chapter) he writes (p. 300): 'The phrases "developed from" and "continued from" lose all relevant meaning if, by excluding active tendency, we dissolve the process of immediate experience into loose and separate parts.'—Ed.]

without any inference at all. This, however, is not in itself an insuperable difficulty. For in our present complex perception there is certainly much acquired knowledge which is now taken for granted as if it were primary. The really vital objection is, that if we begin with the knowledge of only our own sensa, it seems impossible to discover logical steps by which we can be supposed to pass from these to physical facts.

Are physical objects inferred as causal conditions of the occurrences of sense-presentations? This is possible only if the occurrence of sense-presentations is known primarily, and not through inference, as dependent on conditions. For we cannot suppose the primitive mind reasoning as follows: All events have a cause: the occurrence of a sense-presentation is an event: therefore it has a cause. The reference to a cause must therefore be primary. It must be involved in knowing the sense-presentation at all. What remains to be inferred is that the required cause has the character of a physical object. But this is impossible where there is no prior knowledge of physical objects—no prior knowledge either of their nature or of their existence.

2. *The Essential Incompleteness of what is immediately experienced accounts for our Knowledge of the Physical World*

All other attempts to construct a bridge break down in the same way. They all presuppose the very knowledge which they pretend to account for. From the proposition 'my own sensa exist' there are no valid steps to the conclusion that therefore physical things and events exist. Inference being excluded, we seem to be thrown back on the alternative that physical objects are intuitively known, or, as Russell would say, known 'by acquaintance'. But this also is inadmissible. For the only way in which we can be acquainted with actually existing particulars is by directly experiencing them, and physical objects are not directly experienced. How then can they be known at all? There can be no way out of this dilemma, if knowledge by acquaintance and knowledge by inference are the only possible alternatives. No solution is possible, unless there is a mode of knowing which involves neither inference nor direct acquaintance with what is known. Now I maintain that there is such a way of knowing. It transcends the immediate content of actual experience; hence it is not knowledge by acquaintance. It is not dependent on logically prior judgments, and therefore has no premises; hence it is not in any ordinary sense inferential. What in it takes the place of premises is ultimately the essential incompleteness of what is immediately experienced, which cannot be known at all unless in knowing it we know something else connected with it.

3. *Other Examples of this mode of Knowing.*
(*a*) *Knowledge of Universals*

If this mode of knowing were only introduced *ad hoc*, in order to account for our knowledge of the physical world, our right to assume it might be questionable. But this is not so. There are many other examples of fundamental importance, and by considering some of these I hope to make my meaning clear.

(1) Universals are not ultimately inferred, or otherwise derived from prior knowledge. Yet they cannot be said to be known by acquaintance, unless we use the word acquaintance in a loose and ambiguous way. If they are inferred, they must be inferred from logically prior judgments. But all judgments already involve universals. This holds even for judgments about particulars presented in immediate experience. In knowing these as being such and such, we know them as being of certain sorts or kinds; we know them, therefore, as instances of universals. Universals then must be objects of primary knowledge. But, as I have said, they are not known by acquaintance.

Knowledge by acquaintance is not acquaintance itself, and it is not opposed to 'knowledge about' as another distinct way of knowing. Rather it is a peculiar form of 'knowledge about'. It is that form in which the object, by its actual presence within our experience, determines and controls the judgment in which we characterise it—e.g. that it is painful. Thus a toothache which I am actually feeling determines my knowledge about it, as a toothache which I merely remember, or one which is felt by someone else, would not.

In this sense, there can be no acquaintance with universals, distinct from knowledge of them and conditioning knowledge of them. Only particulars exist in such a way that they can be existentially present in immediate experience. Universals then are not known by acquaintance. They are thought, not experienced. Knowledge of them does indeed ultimately depend on acquaintance, but on acquaintance with particulars. Initially they can be known only in knowing particular instances as such. But no particular could be known unless some were immediately experienced.

4. *Other Examples of this mode of Knowing.* (b) *Knowledge of Sense-Impressions through Mental Imagery*[1]

Consider next our knowledge of sense-impressions through mental imagery. What we immediately experience is just the image itself. Thus, in picturing the face of an absent friend, what I immediately experience is not the original sense-presentation which I had in actually seeing the face, but only the revived picture, which may be relatively dim and fragmentary and differs in other ways from the original impression. Yet in all mental imagery the image is apprehended as being the image of impressional experience, past, present, or possible. Even in the freest flight of

[1] [With this and the next section compare *Mind and Matter*, pp. 215–23, and 297–8.—Ed.]

imagination what we imagine is not our own images, but possible impressions which they represent. How is this relation of images to impressions known in the first instance? Certainly not by inference. For this would presuppose that we have other means of ascertaining the connexion, and the only other way would be by direct comparison. But direct comparison is excluded; for when we experience the image we no longer experience the related impression, and conversely. Plainly we cannot say that we compare the image with our remembrance of the corresponding impression. For the remembrance required would have itself to consist in apprehending the present image as being an image of the past impression. Vague forms of remembrance, where there is no experience distinct enough to be called an image, would not serve the purpose. For they are relatively inadequate and rudimentary; they are inchoate stages of the more fully developed memory which works through more or less definite images, and cannot therefore be independent tests of this. The connexion of image and impression is therefore primarily known, and unless we are to regard such knowledge as purely *a priori*, so that every remembrance of a past impression by means of an image is an innate idea, we must account for it by saying that the image is essentially incomplete and cannot be known at all unless it is known as the image of an impression.

5. *Other Examples of this mode of Knowing.*
   (*c*) *Memory-Knowledge in general*

The same holds for memory in general, whatever form it may take. The object more or less adequately remembered is always a past occurrence as it actually occurred. But the occurrence is not actually taking place at the moment in which it is remembered. It cannot therefore be existentially present as an actual content of experience at that moment. Unless, then, we are prepared, as I suppose we are not, to regard all memory-judgments as purely *a priori*, they must depend on the essential incompleteness of some mode of immediate experience, which is such that it cannot be known except as completed by the judgment that a particular event of a certain sort has occurred in the past.

6. *Other Examples of this mode of Knowing.*
(d) *Knowledge of Time-Relations*

Consider finally the primary knowledge of time-relations. This involves even in its most rudimentary form some distinction between present, past, and future, between the 'now', the 'no more' and the 'not yet'. The 'now' cannot be known apart from the 'no more' and the 'not yet'. It cannot be known except as the transition between them. Similarly, the 'not yet' cannot be known except as what is to follow the 'now', and the 'no more' cannot be known except as what has come before the 'now'. The 'no more' is a 'now no more', the 'not yet' is a 'now not yet'. We cannot select any one of these aspects of time and regard it as immediately known and the others as known mediately. Each aspect mediates knowledge of the others and the whole complex is immediately known. None the less the present does occupy a peculiar position within the complex. It does so inasmuch as knowledge of the present is the source of knowledge of the past and future. Only what is present can be immediately experienced. But its being experienced is not the same as its being known. It is immediately experienced in isolation from the past and future. But it cannot be known in this isolation. It is a condition of its being known that past and future should be known in relation to it, just as it is a condition of their being known that it should be known in relation to them. Thus though knowledge of past, present and future mutually mediate each other, it is only the knowledge of the present which is the source of the knowledge of the past and future.

7. *Inference*

This conception of a source of knowledge in other knowledge requires further elucidation; and in considering it
we shall at the same time lead up to the doctrine of primary
sense-knowledge. Let us begin by inquiring in what
sense the premises in an inference are the source of the
conclusion. When the knowledge of *A* is a source of the
knowledge of *B*, this is so because there is some condition
that makes *A* knowable, but does not independently make
B knowable, and this condition is finally found in immediate experience. Consider a simple case of deductive
inference. *A* is taller than *B* and *B* is taller than *C*; therefore *A* is taller than *C*. The conclusion follows from two
propositions called the premises, taken in their relevant
connexion with each other as constituents of a single
complex proposition. Now, of course, the conclusion,
inasmuch as it is known only as inferred from the premises,
is logically implied by them. But it is equally true, though
not so ridiculously obvious, that knowledge of the premises
is similarly conditioned by knowledge of the conclusion
as such. If we cannot know the conclusion as such without
knowing the premises in the requisite connexion with each
other, it is equally true that we cannot know the premises
unless we also at the same time know the conclusion. In
order to be fully aware of the complex proposition '*A* is
taller than *B* and *B* than *C*', I must be aware that *A* is taller
than *C*. We do not first know the whole complex premise
and then pass by a second step to the conclusion. No such
mental operation is required, and if it were required, it
would be impossible. The whole complex premise is
essentially incomplete in such a way that it cannot be
known at all unless at the same time its conclusion is
known. The implication is mutual. Premise and conclusion form an indivisible unity from which neither can
be removed without removing the other.

If there were no more to be said, we could not regard the

knowledge of the premises as a source of the knowledge of what is inferred from them; and not only the syllogism, but all inference, would be a vicious circle. There must be relatively independent grounds for asserting the premises —independent, in the sense that they are not grounds for asserting the conclusion except in so far as they are grounds for asserting the premises. How are these relatively independent grounds supplied? It will not suffice to say that the premises used in one inference are themselves inferred in another. For, as Aristotle long ago pointed out, this would lead to a vicious regress. Plainly we must start with propositions which are not themselves inferred, if we are to start with propositions at all.

8. *Self-evidence, as a Limiting Case of Inference, cannot supply Independent Premises*

We may attempt to supply this requirement by saying that certain propositions are self-evident. Now there certainly is a sort of evidence which can properly be called self-evidence,[1] and it plays an indispensable function in the logical structure of knowledge. Only it must be added that in appealing to it we are as liable to fallacies of ignorance, inadvertence, and confusion as when we rely on inference. Self-evidence is indeed of fundamentally the same nature as inference. It is a limiting case of it. It is the form which inference takes when, instead of connecting one or more distinct propositions with others, it is included within a single proposition. The single proposition has constituents which are essentially incomplete apart from a certain relation to each other which is what the proposition asserts. 'Things equal to the same thing'; this is essentially incomplete: it cannot *be* unless the things are equal to each other, and it cannot be *known* unless the things are known as equal to each other. Now just because self-evidence is of the nature of inference, it cannot of itself

[1] Cf. pp. 47–50.

be an ultimate source of knowledge in the strict sense in which we are using the word 'source'. Given terms actual or possible, of a certain sort and related in a certain manner, there must also be another relation between them. This is the general descriptive formula for self-evident propositions. It therefore presupposes knowledge of terms and relations and a knowledge of them as such and such—as being of a certain sort or kind.

9. *Knowledge of Universals and of Particulars*

What is the source of this knowledge? It cannot be found in any proposition. For all propositions include universals as essential constituents. In the end, universals can only be known at all in knowing actually existing particulars, and particulars can only be known in knowing universals. There is mutual inter-dependence. But it is only the knowledge of universals which depends on that of particulars as its source. This is so because there is an independent and ultimate condition which makes particulars knowable and does not otherwise make universals knowable. This condition is acquaintance or immediate experience. Unless some particulars are immediately experienced they cannot be known, and unless they are known, no universals and no other particulars can be known. So far empirical philosophy is right. The source of all knowledge is knowledge of certain particulars, independently founded on immediate experience.

10. *To assign the Source of Knowledge is not to assign all its Conditions*

In the last resort, then, immediate experience itself is the source of all knowledge. But when we see in what way the empirical philosophy is right we also see in what way it is profoundly wrong. It goes astray in assuming that in tracing knowledge to its source we have assigned all its essential conditions; and Kant also agrees in this with the empirical philosophers, differing from them only in assigning two sources instead of one—the faculty of understanding as well as immediate experience. It ought now to be clear that any such view is quite wrong. There are logical conditions which are not sources, and apart from these conditions a source could not be a source at all. In inference the conclusion as such is not a source of the premises. Yet it is a condition of knowing the premises that in knowing them one should also know the conclusion; and if this were not so, the premises could not be the source of the conclusion. Similarly the particular contents of immediate experience, if they are to be a source of further knowledge, must be essentially incomplete, so that in knowing them we must know something else.[1]

Suppose that we have thus accounted for initial knowledge of universals, we have yet to inquire how we come by knowledge of particulars which are not immediately experienced. It is natural to say that this takes place by way of inference. But what sort of inference? Is it, as Mill would say, from particulars to particulars? But from mere particulars, as Mill's own exposition abundantly shows, nothing can be inferred. The inference, on his own showing, is always from particular facts of a certain kind to other particulars of a certain kind, e.g. from the death of some men to the death of some other men. But if the inference is not merely *from* particulars, neither is it merely *to* particulars. I have no right to affirm that Mr Lloyd George will very probably die some day unless I am prepared to assert that all men similarly circum-

[1] [At this point in the typescript the next three paragraphs were bracketed off, though not deleted, with a marginal direction to begin after the bracketed passage originally constituting the rest of this section. There is no evidence to show whether this was for lecturing purposes only, or whether the author intended to rewrite the passage or even to consider its final omission. I have printed the first two of the bracketed paragraphs (which now complete this section), but have omitted the third, which is confusing and liable to suggest a view about causal inference which the author certainly did not hold.—Ed.]

stanced are very probably mortal. Where Mill is right is in maintaining that the particular instance we start with must not already be known as an instance of the general rule which is inferred. Otherwise this general rule would be itself a premise, and there would be a vicious circle.

There is yet another way in which all inference implies universals. It implies universal principles of connexion between premises and conclusions. These principles are not themselves premises but rather forms of inference. Thus the dictum *de omni et nullo*, or some such proposition, is the form of the first figure of the syllogism. 'There is a penny in my purse and my purse is in my pocket; therefore there is a penny in my pocket' is an inference. 'A part of a part is part of the whole' is the form of it. Both forms are covered by the more general formula: 'If x has a transitive relation to y, and y is in like manner related to z, x is related in the same way to z.' Even the simplest inductive as well as deductive inference must have a form. There must be some general principle justifying inference whenever we have data similar in relevant respects.

11. *The Datum of Primary Sense-Knowledge—the Distinction between the Psychologically Primitive and the Logically Primary*

Let us now apply this principle to the special case in which we are interested—the primary knowledge of physical objects. Unless physical fact is known in primary sense-perception it seems hopeless to attempt to account for our developed knowledge of the physical world. What is the primary physical datum, and how is its existence and nature apprehended? Here we must not lose sight of the distinction, drawn in the last chapter [1], between what is psychologically primitive and what is logically primary. Only that is logically primary which is logically presupposed in subsequent developments. Whatever primitive belief is

[1] Pp. 117–18.

seen to be false at a more advanced stage cannot be logically presupposed in the acquired knowledge which contradicts it. On the other hand, what is primitive may be also primary if it is merely superseded and not falsified from a higher point of view. It is logically primary if and so far as it logically conditions the very knowledge which supersedes it. This applies to the transition from relatively vague and indefinite to relatively determinate and detailed perception.

We may illustrate by transitions of this kind which occur sometimes in our present experience. I hear, let us say, an unfamiliar sound and cannot at first make out what it is. I am at a loss to determine the nature, direction and distance of its source. I apprehend it only as coming from somewhere or other, or possibly as something wrong with my ears. I then happen to catch a glimpse of a lawn-mower in a neighbouring garden, or to remember that there is one there. Straightway a comparatively definite and restricted percept is substituted for the previously vague and indeterminate one. What I now hear is for me the sound of a lawn-mower. But the originally vague sense-knowledge has not been falsified. It has only been specified and limited. The whole development of sense-knowledge, from its primitive beginning to its more advanced stages, involves at every step progressive specification of this kind.

Another illustration which will take us further on our way is supplied by illusions and hallucinations, and the way in which we recognise them as such. In these something is perceived as if it were physical fact, though it is not so. Consider how we know that what appears in sense-perception to be physically real is not so. What tests can we use? Plainly if we take account only of the immediately experienced sensum as affording the sole clue to the existence and nature of the apparently real object, we have no means of judging whether in fact it is real or not. We cannot stir a step without bringing to bear a specialised system of acquired knowledge. If what looks like an apple is so, then it ought to be the possible object of many other perceptions with variable sensa. It ought, for instance, to be perceptible in a certain special way to touch as well as to sight. It ought also to have certain special relations, including causal relations, to other physical facts within the physical order, and the existence of such relations ought to be more or less ascertainable directly or indirectly by sense-perception. It is only by such requirements as these, founded on preacquired knowledge, that what the drunkard seems to see is for him a pink rat, and it is because these requirements are not fulfilled that he is said to be under an hallucination. His pink rats, for instance, are not to be caught in a trap and they don't bite. But if we set aside defining conditions of this sort, there is nothing left to determine, for the percipient, the existence and nature of the perceived object, so far as this transcends immediate experience, except the actual present content of that experience.

This actually present sensum, as entering into and conditioning perception, may be called the perceptual sensum. A reference to anything beyond this presupposes that the perceptual sensum is essentially incomplete, so that it cannot be known at all without the thought of something beyond itself, necessary to complete it in the special way which its own special nature demands. Thus the physical fact must be primarily and primitively apprehended as connected in nature and existence with the perceptual sensum.

12. *The Connexion between Physical Fact and Perceptual Sensum*

What is this connexion? We can answer this question only by considering certain universal and pervasive features of our present sense-knowledge. It is plain that all the characteristics which we now ascribe to physical things are in their general nature ultimately derived from immediate sense-experience. We should not know what is meant by a thing's being extended, figured, blue or smooth or hot, if we had not visual and tactual presentations of like nature. From the point of view of science, it may be denied that some of these characters really belong to the physical world. But in spite of this even the man of science still continues to perceive the sky as blue in the same way as he perceives its extension. We may then take it that in primary and primitive sense-perception the physical object is apprehended as akin in nature to the perceptual sensum.

In the second place, what appears to sense-perception as physically real is apprehended as conditioning the occurrence of the perceptual sensum in the special mode in which it occurs at the moment of perception. This condition is expressed by saying that in sense-experience we feel ourselves receptive. The present sensum would not be such as it is, if it were not determined to be so by the physical fact perceived. This causal reference must be taken as primary, inasmuch as it cannot be otherwise accounted for, and is presupposed in all subsequent developments.

I have stated these two points separately, as if they were independent. But they cannot really be so. The one fundamental fact is that what is immediately experienced is essentially incomplete, and requires completion in accordance with its special nature. Thus the causal reference must be such as to account for the qualification of the physical existence by the character of the correlated sense-presentation. There seems only one way of satisfying this requirement and also of avoiding conflict with common sense. The physical fact and the sensum must be primarily apprehended as continuous in existence, and therefore as more or less akin in nature. The sensum is akin to the physical fact as being of a piece with it. The sensum is the continuation within our immediate experience of something which is not immediately experienced. The physical object is thought of as the prolongation of the content of immediate experience into a region beyond it.

Only in this way can we harmonise common sense with itself and with philosophical analysis. The plain man readily admits and normally takes for granted the distinction between physical fact and sensible appearance, and he is fully assured that in sense-knowledge he knows not merely the sensible appearance but the physical fact. He would be satisfied to accept Locke's formula—that we are 'conversant with external objects by way of sense' without troubling to inquire more precisely what is meant by 'conversant with'. On the other hand, he is perplexed and incredulous when he is called on to treat the whole perceived datum as constituted merely by the physical fact, to the exclusion of his own immediate sensa. He is perplexed and incredulous when he is called on to regard the object perceived as inferred from his own sensa, or to regard the sense-presentation as mind and the perceived object as matter. He will insist that what he primarily knows is what he immediately experiences, and that apart from this he knows nothing, although he still continues to distinguish between an external object and its sensible appearance.

The view for which I am contending makes this position of the plain man consistent and tenable. In primary perception there is no knowledge separable from the knowledge of our own sensa. It is in vain to turn from these and then look for something else. Introspection, when it makes such experiments, will find a blank. But on the other hand the sensum, being essentially incomplete, can only be known at all on condition that it is thought of as connected with something beyond itself, continuous with it in existence and nature. Thus, for primary perception, physical fact and the content of sense-experience form an unbroken unity. The union is far more intimate than that between acquired and primary perceptual knowledge. Hence we cannot reasonably expect that unaided introspection should be able to discriminate the two aspects of what is perceived.

13. *Focal Perception*

The distinction is forced upon me by the further development of sense-knowledge, whereby more specific and determinate objects become substituted for those of primary and primitive perception. The main motive is the divergence of the order and relations of physical facts from the order and relations of sense-presentations, as they are actually experienced in what Dr Ward calls the presentation-continuum. This divergence is found in all physical objects, with one exception—the body of the percipient, as perceived in a peculiar way in which only he himself and no one else can perceive it. If I pass my hand over the surface of a table, tactual impressions partly shift their position, partly arise and disappear in a definite order. But I am not aware of any change or succession in the table and its parts, which are taken to be persistent and coexistent. On the other hand, if I had had the same sensible experience without being aware of the motion of my hand, I should have perceived the table itself as moving.

There are two points to be noticed. The first is the divergence of the physical order from that of immediate sense-experience. The second is that I can be aware of the divergence only because I am in some way perceptually aware of the distinction between the surface touched and my own hand as a means or instrument of perceiving it. What may be called *focal perception* is here of essential importance. Perception is focal when the same thing is perceived as the same through variable sensa. Sometimes what is thus perceived may even be the same part and the same quality of the thing. Thus, the same physical extension and figure are perceived both by sight and touch, though in immediate experience visual extension and tactual extension are quite distinct. Here too, the physical fact is identifiable only because we can account for the difference in sense-experience by difference in the sense-organs through which we perceive it—the eye and the skin. What is focally perceived may, of course, be not the same but different qualities as united in the same thing. But the physical qualities are connected in the physical thing, as the corresponding sensa are not connected in immediate experience. The whiteness and smoothness of a piece of paper have the same place and the same extension. But this is quite untrue of the tactual presentations through which we perceive the smoothness and the visual presentations through which we perceive the whiteness.

So far as focal perception involves a contrast between the physical order and that of immediate experience, the physical object is more determinate than it would be for merely primary sensitive knowledge. The object perceived is marked off and circumscribed as that part of the un-experienced background in which the continuations of several sensa converge, and may even, in part, coincide. It is so marked off in distinction from other perceived physical objects in which they do not as yet meet. These other objects are what we know as conditions of perception, in contrast with what we perceive by means of them. To ascertain accurately what they are requires such sciences as physical and physiological optics. But wherever there is knowledge of an external order diverging from that of immediate experience, such as is probably present even in very primitive stages of mental development, there must be some awareness of conditions of perception as such. There must at least be some awareness of the distinction of the external object from the sense-organ through which we apprehend it, and of the relation be-tween them. The problem which next confronts us there-fore concerns the logical ground and psychological genesis of this distinction. The question is: How do we perceive external objects as such, where the term *external* is taken as narrower than the term *physical*, and means that the physical object is known as external to the sense-organ used in perceiving it? With this question we shall have to deal in the next chapter.

I have here only to add one point in conclusion. It is of great importance to notice that retentiveness, association, and mental imagery tend rather to conform to the external order than to the order in which sense-impressions are originally experienced. Thus, though we can never simultaneously see and touch the same part of the same thing, yet in our mental image of the thing the partial presentations separately traceable to sight and touch, as revived residua of visual and tactual impressions, are united in a simultaneous complex. The experiences connected with the transition from feeling to seeing or from seeing to feeling do not, for the most part, reappear in the image, or if they do they reappear very imperfectly. The like is true of the acquired focal perception of the external thing as uniting different qualities, as when, to quote Dr Ward, 'the sight of a suit of polished armour instantly reinstates and steadily maintains all that we retain of former sensations of its hardness and coldness and smoothness'. Here, too, the intermediate experiences which separate sight and touch tend to be omitted. Similarly, the sights which come to me successively in walking through the streets of a town tend more or less to be mapped together in one simultaneous view when I recall them in imagination. This tendency of retentiveness and reproduction to conform to the external order, rather than to that of impressional experience, seems to me to constitute what Kant calls the productive imagination or the original synthetic function of imagination.

Chapter VIII

EXTERNAL AND INTERNAL PERCEPTION[1]

1. *The Part played by Internal Perception in our Knowledge of an External Order*

If we are to account adequately for the perception of objects as outside the sense-organ through which they are perceived, we must assume some original awareness of the sense-organ itself—an awareness not due to the perception of one sense-organ by means of another, such as arises when we see or touch our own hand. There must be some more immediate awareness of the sense-organs themselves, or at least of some of them, which does not involve the use of one in perceiving others. We must be perpetually aware, for instance, of the seeing eye as such, without seeing it or touching it or otherwise externally perceiving it. We must in this way apprehend the eye as something we see in its distinction from and relation to the thing seen. This peculiar way of perceiving our own body and its parts is what I call internal as contrasted with external perception, and its object, as such, an internal object.

We shall presently inquire into the nature and genesis of internal perception as thus defined. But it will be most convenient to deal first with another question. Taking for granted that there is internal awareness of the sense-organs, how does this enable us to know an external order distinct

---

[1] [This chapter contains a considerably more elaborate and detailed treatment, psychological rather than philosophical, of the distinction and relation between 'internal perception' and 'external perception' than that of *Mind and Matter* (pp. 226–33), where the theory is developed with closer regard to the special part that it has to play in the main argument of the book.—Ed.]

from the order in which sense-presentations actually occur in immediate experience? We come to know this, originally, by experiment, which is possible inasmuch as our movements take place under subjective initiative and control, so that they can be started, continued or suspended at will. Suppose the percipient to be in a situation in which surrounding objects remain at rest and do not otherwise change, while his body and its members are free to move. How does he learn that this is so? The shifting position of his eyes as organs of vision is internally perceptible as he moves at will his head or his body as a whole, or the eyeballs in their sockets. The closing or unclosing the eyelids is internally apprehended, not indeed as a motion of the eyes themselves, but as a motion directly affecting them, and may therefore be included with the others. Suppose the situation to be my own, as I sit in my study. I have at a certain moment a certain group of visual presentations, including, let us say, a sheet of paper which is lying in front of me. This visual sensum is not one which I can command at will under all circumstances merely by opening my eyes. But now that I have it I can detain it constantly by keeping my eyes fixed in the same constant position, and I can make it begin and cease by alternately opening and closing them. Thus even in the intervals during which they are closed I have ground for supposing that, if they were open instead of closed, I should be having the same visual experience. Its coming and going, therefore, are taken to depend on a condition merely affecting the sense-organ, and not as involving any change or alternation in the external object—the sheet of paper. The coming and going of the visual presentation makes no difference to its existence. Suppose next that, with my eyes open, I shift their position in any one of the manifold ways possible to me. As the eyes move, there is a concomitant series of variations within the field of visual sensa. Some shift their place within the field while others keep disappearing from it in successive order and new ones are successively presented. If the process is carried far enough, all the original presentations disappear and are replaced by new. Such variations, affecting the specific content of sense-experience, begin with the movement of the sense-organ, continue while it continues, are suspended when and so long as it is suspended, and recommence when it recommences, and in general vary coincidently with it in a definite order. Whenever it is reversed they are reversed, and whenever it is repeated they are repeated. In all respects they behave as if in the given situation they depended merely on the internally perceived position and change of position of the sense-organ. Hence the presumption that they are dependent is psychologically inevitable and logically justifiable. For the same reason they neither imply nor are taken to imply any motion or succession in external objects, which are therefore presumed to persist independently, and to remain at rest in the same situation relatively to each other.

Sharply contrasted with sensible changes which are thus dependent merely on the variable position of my sense-organs, are changes otherwise similar which, even if they are initiated by me, continue their course independently and end in results which I cannot reverse merely by reversing the movements on which they followed, as when the door of my room blows open or I upset the ink-bottle. I cannot put the ink back into the bottle merely by reversing the movement by which I overturned it. What was previously presentable at will is no longer so, but something else instead of it—a black sheet of paper instead of a white, and a wet one instead of a dry.

The situation I have described is the standard situation. In it there is a system of relatively permanent possibilities of sensation, such that the possibilities can be realised at will in a fixed order by making appropriate movements. Just in so far as this is so, external objects are perceived as stationary and otherwise unaltered. On the other hand, if and so far as the presentational changes do not constantly occur in this regular order on making the appropriate movements, the external objects are themselves perceived as moving or as having moved, or as otherwise changing or changed. If, for instance, when I move my eyes or hand, a visual or tactual impression persistently retains its place in the visual or tactual field, I perceive the external object not as at rest but in motion. Such perceptual judgments are greatly facilitated by the fact that motion is nearly always confined to some of the surrounding objects, while the rest constitute a stationary framework within which it takes place.

2. *Internal Perception as depending on Sensa under Subjective Control*

Up to this point I have taken for granted internal perception of the sense-organs themselves. I have not inquired on what distinctive feature of our sense-experience this internal perception depends. Presupposing such perceptual awareness of the variable positions of our bodies and their parts, the only question I have raised is how we are able to distinguish the degree in which sensible changes are dependent on our movements and the degree in which they are not so; which again is equivalent to the question how, in the first instance, we are able to contrast variation in the external object with its variable ways of appearing to our senses. It is most important to note that even when motor control, as thus defined, is most complete, it is always, in an essential aspect, limited and provisional. We cannot merely by our motor activity determine what specific presentations shall occur, so as always by making the same movement to command the same specific sense-experience. I cannot always command the sight of an inkpot whenever I open my eyes, and I cannot always, by moving them in a certain fixed way, command the sight of the sea. Given a certain specific presentation, we can detain it or make it move within the presentational field until it vanishes. We can also introduce a sequence of new presentations in a permanently possible order. But we have to learn by trial on each new occasion what the specific presentations are, and what is the permanently possible order of their sequence.

What would happen if our subjective control of the flow of immediate sense-experience, instead of being thus limited and provisional, were constant and complete on all occasions, so that by making the same movement we could always get the same sensations? Consider an instance in which this condition is approximately fulfilled. Motor sensa due to muscles, joints and tendons, so far as they accompany the unimpeded motion and freely variable position of my body and limbs, can always be experienced at will under all circumstances. If I am able to make the same movement I can obtain the same train of motor presentations whether I am in London or in Timbuctoo. Now these motor experiences, inasmuch as we can thus always command them at will, yield, of themselves, no perception of external objects, but only internal perception of our own body and its parts. There is nothing to account for this in the intrinsic nature of the muscle, joint and tendon sensa themselves. Experiences essentially similar in kind do give perceptual awareness of external objects, when our movements are impeded by obstacles. It would seem, then, that it is the constancy and uniformity of subjective control which constitutes the only relevant difference. It follows that if all sense-presentations were in the same uniform way producible at will, whenever we were interested in having them, there would be no external but only internal perception. Specific olfactory, optical, tactual and other sensa would then be always freely at our command in the same manner as the muscle, joint and tendon sensa in our unimpeded movement. A certain position of the eye would always give us the same series of sights. A certain mode of sniffing would always give us the same smell, and a certain motion of the head or body would always give the same succession of sounds. Suppose this to hold for all the sensa through which we now perceive external objects. Then all distinction between what is within and what is beyond our own bodies would be abolished. Our bodies would not indeed be those which we now possess. They would not be bounded by our skin. On the contrary, for each of us his own body would be so enlarged as to include the whole physical world as an internal and not at all as an external object. This being so, we should not of course distinguish the body as being our own, and we should have no means of knowing other finite minds to which other bodies could belong.

3. *Internal Perception as depending on Organic Sensibility*

So far, then, as our sense-experience is in regular ways constantly and fully and directly under subjective control, there is only internal perception of our body. But this principle is not by itself adequate. It does not explain, for example, another mode of internal perception, at least equally fundamental—that which depends on organic sensibility. It is the distinctive function of such sensations as those of hunger and thirst, headache, toothache, the smart of a wound or a blow, cutaneous itching, tickling and tingling, etc., to make us internally aware of certain peculiar states and changes of state in our own bodies. But such experiences are the least of all under direct and regular subjective control. They are not even under limited and provisional control, as relatively permanent possibilities. A headache does not regularly begin and cease to be experienced at will, according as I make certain movements. The smooth and cool feel of a knife blade is, in a given situation, presentable at will and capable of being dismissed at will. But if I cut my finger with the edge I cannot get rid of the smart merely by drawing my

finger away. Similarly, if I pass my hand over the surface
of any external object, touch-sensa proper shift their place
in the tactual field, but the smart of the cut does not. It
persistently retains its own presentational position—its
own *local sign*.

4. *The General Principle on which Internal Perception depends*

There are then these two sharply opposed modes of internal
perception. One depends on sensa which are completely
under direct subjective control. The other depends on
sensa which are not thus controllable at all. We have to
find a general principle which will account for both these
ways of being aware of our own body without perceiving
one part of it by means of another.

The general principle is supplied by that conception of
primary sense-knowledge which I discussed and defended
in the last chapter. In primary sense-knowledge there is
nothing to determine perceived relations of physical objects
to each other except the relations of perceptual sensa to
each other, as they actually occur in the flow of immediate
experience. Hence the perceived order must coincide with
the presentational order. What is distinctive of internal
perception is that it is, in this respect, a survival from
primary sense-knowledge. It is that way of perceiving in
which the perceived physical order continues to coincide
with the presentational order. As knowledge begins to
develop, one subject remains for which this persistently
holds good, the percipient's own body as internally apprehended. But we must not suppose that the percipient
himself originally distinguishes between internal and
external perception through any previous and independent
knowledge of what is and what is not his own body. On
the contrary, his own body is originally distinguished
from other things as being what he internally perceives,
whereas external objects are distinguished as having

relations which diverge from the order of immediate experience.[1]

It is true that we perceive our own bodies externally as well as internally, e.g. when I look at my hand. But we then recognise them as our own only because we identify what is externally perceived with something, or with part of something, which is also internally perceived.

If we suppose anything whatever to fulfil this condition, it would *ipso facto* be, for the percipient, part of his body, even though it were spatially separated from other parts. A giant in a fairy-tale may keep his heart, let us say, in a nest at the top of a tree. It is still for him his own heart, because wherever he may be he can still feel it beating and whenever it is touched he feels the smart.

5. *The Part played by Effort against Resistance in distinguishing the Physical Order from the Order of Sense-Experience*

Why then do organic sensa and those which uniformly accompany our unimpeded movements, taken by themselves, yield only internal perception of our own bodies? It can only be because in their case some condition is lacking which is required to enable the individual to know a physical order diverging from that of his own immediate experience. This condition is found, and is only to be found, in the contrast between what depends and what does not depend on subjective initiative or control. But it is not enough that some kinds of sense-presentation should be completely under control, as motor sensa are in our free movements, and others completely beyond control, as organic sensa are. Under neither of these conditions is there ground or motive for distinguishing a physical order

---

[1] As I pass my hand over the surface of the table there is awareness of change in my body, corresponding to the successive changes in my sense-experience; but there is no awareness of change and succession in the table or its parts. The table is therefore for me an external object.

diverging from that of immediate experience. What is required is that the same continued sense-experience shall vary in a twofold way, partly under direct subjective control, and partly independently of it. Only on that condition is there ground or motive for distinguishing between sense-organ as such and external object as such, in their relation to each other. A typical instance in which this condition is fulfilled is that of effort against resistance. The obstacles which interrupt free movement occur occasionally and irregularly in what is otherwise a uniform progression fully under the command of the will. It is possible to anticipate how the train of motor sensa would have been continued if it had not been interrupted. The interruption, being perceptible as such, of itself supplies a ground for recognising the presence of something other than the mobile member.

But the contrast and connexion between what is and what is not due to our action becomes much more marked and complex in the persistent or repeated attempt to continue the impeded movement as it might have been continued if it had not been impeded. There is then a complex experience of motor tension and tactual pressure, which arises independently of our free control. This is further variable in its nature and intensity in two sharply contrasted ways. On the one hand, the tension and pressure increase or diminish in intensity, and are otherwise modified, according as the attempt to continue moving is more or less strenuous, or varies in direction. On the other hand, the subject is powerless to determine whether or not his attempt, however strenuous, will succeed; he is powerless to determine what degree and distribution of pressure and tension is required for success; and when the impeded motion is continued, he cannot determine whether previous pressure and tension shall suddenly cease or persist with diminished intensity and with other variations. Finally, the further presentational changes which follow the movement and persist independently of it, e.g. the upsetting of an inkstand or the bursting of a toy balloon, are determined for him and not by him.

We have here a thoroughgoing antithesis of the kind required. The same complex sensum varies as a whole and at the same time, partially under regular subjective control, and partially in independence of it. There ought to be and there is a corresponding distinction between perceived physical objects. So far as there is dependence on subjective initiative, what is perceived is bodily effort; so far as the course of experience is independent of subjective control, what is perceived is external resistance, differing in character and degree according to circumstances, in the ways indicated by such words as *hard* and *soft*, *solid* and *fluid*, *brittle* and *flexible*, *elastic* and *rigid*. In general, effort is what we make, resistance is what we meet.

6. *Internal and External Perception in Visual Experience*

In this twofold perception of correlated effort and resistance, the essential part is played by muscle and tendon sensa. We pass now to touch proper and to sight. In touching a thing with our hand or other tactual organ, we perceive at once not only what is touched but also our skin as touching it. Even when in ordinary language we are said to be touching nothing, we are still aware, through cutaneous experience, of the surface of our own body, and of the shape, size and relative situation of its parts. In this respect the eye seems sharply contrasted with the skin. We are indeed aware through tactual and motor sensa of our own eyeballs, as they move in their sockets. But we do not seem to be aware of our eye in seeing, through light and colour sensa, as we are aware of our skin in touching, through cutaneous sensa. We have no internal perception of our own retina, such as would at all help us to recognise a facsimile of it if this were before us on a table to examine. We are not internally aware of its shape. It is not perceived as round or square or convex or concave or flat. There is nothing to determine how big it would appear if we could see it or touch it. We are not aware of it as having any visible or tangible qualities.

Are we to conclude that properly visual experiences yield no perception of the organ of vision as such? This inference would be too hasty. We do in fact have internal awareness of the seeing eye as such. We are aware of it as seeing, though not as seen. We are aware of it as a seeing surface confronting the extended field of things seen, and movable relatively to these.

We perceive a visible scene as spread out before our eyes or our view—spread out, as seen, before our eyes, as seeing. The eye embraces or takes in at one glance a wide prospect. This does not mean that the eyeball, as known to us through tactual or motor sensa, embraces or takes in anything. The reference is to the seeing eye as such. 'Things pass before our eyes' or 'our eyes travel over them'. 'We turn our gaze or our view hither and thither.' All such phrases imply perception of the seeing eye as such. We see some things out of the corner of the eye, others from the centre of distinct vision. A very simple experiment will show that motion of the organ of vision is normally perceived through properly visual experience, and not only through motor and tactual experience. When we close our eyes we are still aware of a grey field usually more or less flooded with colour. Keeping the eyes shut we can turn our eyeballs right or left, up or down. In so doing we are distinctly aware of the motion of the eyeball in its socket. But we fail to perceive any change of position in the seeing eye as such. This seems to remain at rest, however the eyeballs move. It does so because the motion of the eyeball is accompanied by no corresponding variation in visual experience proper.

We have then an internal perception of the seeing eye as such. But of what nature? It is apprehended as something extended with locally distinguishable parts, each seeing a locally distinguishable part of the visible scene. There is a central part which sees most clearly, and marginal parts which see most dimly, and other parts intermediate between centre and margin. The parts are of course distinguished merely as seeing, and not as they would be if they were themselves seen. Further, the seeing eye is known as varying in its position relatively to external objects, either through its motion or through theirs. What was seen by one locally distinct part ceases to be so and progressively comes to be seen by others. So far as such changes are in regular ways dependent on subjective initiative and are accompanied by certain motor sensa, we perceive the seeing eye as itself moving. So far as they occur independently, we apprehend things seen as shifting their place relatively to the eye.

What is there in our visual experience to determine this internal perception of the organ of vision? Amid all the variations of things seen the seeing eye as such remains the same. Its position as a whole relatively to external objects is changeable. But otherwise in all our seeing it is apprehended as the constant and invariable factor. Our awareness of it must therefore depend on an aspect of visual experience which is correspondingly constant and invariable. Now, at any moment we immediately experience an extensive presentational field of light and colour sensa. But from moment to moment the specific light and colour sensa which occupy this field change and vary in manifold ways. Nothing that is thus variable can originally condition internal perception of the organ of vision. The colour-quality and brightness of visual presentation, the variable extent of this or that colour-quality and brightness within the presentational field, the variable shape as determined by the way in which qualitatively or intensively different presentations bound each other, their transitions from place to place within the field and in general their local relation to each other when they are presented, as well as the serial order in which they come to appear within the

field and disappear from it, either at will or without subjective initiative—all these variable factors determine
external perception of the colour, shape, comparative size,
rest and motion of visible objects, but not internal perception of the organ of vision.

7. *Local Signs and the Local Sign Continuum*

What then is left which does not vary in this way? I answer
that the extensive field itself is left, in distinction from the
variable contents which occupy it and shift their place
within it from moment to moment. This visual extension
differs from the vague diffuseness of organic and motor
sensa, inasmuch as it includes within it a fixed system of
distinguishable places, which may be successively occupied
by different light and colour sensa. Specific presentations
may move from place to place within the field, but the
extensive field, with its definitely distinguishable diversity
of places, remains constant. This immediately experienced
field has been called a *local sign continuum* and the immediately experienced diversity of places within it has been
called the diversity of *local signs*. The local sign continuum
of sight remains constant, whether I am looking at the
stars or at the carpet of my room, or have my eyes closed.
There is a similar local sign continuum of touch which
remains constant whether I am lying in bed or immersed
in a bath.

Now the local sign continuum is not at all under subjective control. In accordance with our general principles,
therefore, it ought to determine internal perception of the
body of the percipient. In particular, the local sign
continuum of visual experience ought to yield internal
perception of the visual organ as extended, as having
locally distinguishable parts. It ought to yield just such
an internal perception as we in fact have.

But a further condition is required to account for the
inner perception of the seeing eye in its distinction from

and relation to things seen. For this is not an invariable but a variable experience, and one that in its varieties is partly in regular ways under subjective control and partly independent of it. Such an experience is supplied by the coming and going of specific light and colour sensa, their persistence and the shifting of their local sign. This is always partly dependent on our active initiative and partly independent of it. So far as it depends on our active initiative it determines internal perception of the seeing eye, as in motion or at rest relatively to things seen. So far as it is independent of subjective control, it determines external perception of things seen, as in motion or at rest relatively to the eye which sees them.

What has been said of sight applies in principle also to touch. Here, too, there is a local sign continuum which remains constant as specific tactual presentations enter it, disappear from it and shift their local sign, partly under subjective control and partly independently. The touching hand is internally perceived in its distinction from and relation to the external body touched. The only important point which demands discussion is why the internal perception of the touching hand is so much more precise as regards shape, size and other details than that of the seeing eye. It is not enough to say that visual sensa are projected but not localised, whereas tactual sensa are both localised and projected. We must inquire why this is so and what it means.

8. *The External Perception of one Sense-Organ by means of another, and the Relation of this to Internal Perception*

There is an immensely important and very primitive perceptual process which we have not yet considered— that in which two sense-organs are externally perceived, each by means of the other. This complication is found only in touch, as when the right hand is actively drawn over the left, which may itself be actively moved, or kept unmoved, at the same time or alternately. Call one of the mobile members $M1$, the other $M2$.

$M1$ is perceived as external object by means of $M2$, and $M2$ is perceived as external object by means of $M1$; at the same time there is vague internal awareness of $M1$ and of $M2$ each through its own resident sensa, as far as these are uniformly variable under subjective control. This fourfold distinction of two internal and two external perceptions is what our previous discussion would, by itself, lead us to expect. But whatever may be true of the process in its first beginnings, we cannot now by introspection discriminate the four factors, when for example we draw the tips of the fingers across the palm of the opposite hand. The internal perception of $M1$ through its own resident sensa coalesces inseparably with the external perception of $M2$; similarly the external perception of $M2$ by means of $M1$ coalesces with the internal perception of $M2$ through its own sensa. The result is a single perceptual awareness of $M1$, and also of $M2$, which, though internal, has none of the vagueness characterising the internal perception of the eye as the organ of vision. Nor is this all. Even when the tactual organ $M1$ or $M2$ explores a surface outside the body of the percipient, there is still, together with the definite perception of the external object, an equally definite internal perception of the shape of the tactual organ itself, the relative situation of the parts of its surface, and its position as a whole.[1] In this respect touch is quite unique and, in particular, it is sharply contrasted with the other great spatial sense—sight. The contrast can be adequately accounted for only by the conditions under which two organs of touch, $M1$ and $M2$, are perceived by means of each other—conditions which have no parallel in vision. It is the same $M1$ which is externally perceived

[1] Even when, in ordinary language, we are said to be touching nothing, as when we hold our hands above our head, there is still the like spatially distinct and definite perception of the body and its parts, having its sources in resident cutaneous and motor presentations.

by means of $M2$ and internally perceived by its own sensa. If we can show that in the process of perception itself there are sufficiently cogent and primitive motives for identifying it as the same, the problem is, in principle, solved. For, on this assumption, the knowledge of the identical object obtained in one way will blend in the unity of one complex cognition with knowledge of it acquired in the other way. Each mode of knowing—the external and the internal— will supplement and further define the other, so far as this is relatively indefinite or otherwise imperfect. Again, if this takes place constantly and habitually, when one way of perceiving occurs separately the knowledge acquired through the union with the other will be retained and revived, and will continue to define and supplement it. This would explain why in any position of the hand, whether it is touching the other hand or the table, or is held in the empty air, its own resident sensa are the source of a definite perceptual awareness of its shape, the relative situation of its parts, and its position as a whole.

How then is $M1$, as internally perceived, initially known to be identical with $M1$ as externally perceived? The answer is that it is known as identical because it behaves as if it were so. The motion of $M1$, as internally perceived, begins, continues, is suspended, recommences and varies in rate and direction with the beginning, continuance, suspension and variation of the same motion as externally perceived by means of $M2$. The special application of this general principle is complex and takes place under conditions so variable as to make detailed analysis hopeless. I can do no more than illustrate it in its simpler forms. When the left hand, held at rest, is actively explored by the right, the right is internally perceived as moving under subjective initiative and control; the left externally perceives something as passing across it. The inwardly perceived motion begins, ceases, is suspended, reversed, repeated, and otherwise varied at will. At the same time, the externally perceived motion passes continually through the same phases. Hence what is apprehended in the two ways is not two motions but the same motion of the same thing.

Again, consider what happens when the two hands are pushed against each other. For each of them there is effort against resistance. As we have seen, effort is internally perceived inasmuch as the relevant motor and tactual experience is variable under subjective control; resistance is perceived inasmuch as it varies independently. Now, when the two hands push against each other, what is internally felt as effort by one of them increases or diminishes and otherwise varies with what is externally perceived as resistance by the other. Thus, effort in the right hand is identified with resistance to the left, and inversely.

Points of this sort are ridiculously obvious and familiar. Unfortunately that is just the reason why they so often escape notice. Yet they have to be explicitly noticed because, however familiar, they are intensely important. For instance, if what I have been saying is obvious, then nearly all that has been written about the coalescence and projection of sensations is obvious nonsense.

Chapter IX

CORRELATION OF EXTERNAL DATA.
(*a*) CAUSAL RELATIONS

1. *Correlation begins in the Earliest Stages of Perceptual Process*

For primary sense-knowledge, the original unity of sense-experience would have its counterpart in the unity of a single complex physical object. Each distinguishable sensum would indeed have its own continuation in the unexperienced background. But as all sensa are modifications of one presentation-continuum, the total object of primary perception would be correspondingly continuous. This would continue to be so, if we perceived the material world in general as we internally perceive our own bodies.

With the distinction of external object and sense-organ, the continuity of primary perception is broken into a plurality of relatively detached items. But it is so broken up only to be restored in another way, by piecing the fragments together and connecting them with each other by intermediate links. This synthetic process does not involve, as philosophers have often supposed, any synthetic principles due to the nature of the mind, as contrasted with the nature of the data themselves with which it has to deal. The ultimate principle of synthesis is the unity of the universe as a universal form of knowledge, and it is a form of knowledge just because it is a form of the being which is known. A mind which imposed its own synthetic principles on an alien reality would be simply an imposter. The initial data are essentially incomplete, each in its own way, and so raise potential questions which become actual questions so far as the mind is interested in finding answers to them. They are incomplete in such a way that by their own nature they require to be supplemented and connected with each other in a coherent context. In the endeavour to discover this context, an endeavour prompted at first mainly by practical interest, the synthetic process develops. It leads ultimately to the complex ideal and conceptual construction of the physical sciences. But it begins in the earliest stages of perceptual process itself.

Although, for purposes of exposition, we cannot avoid dealing separately with the fundamental factors of perceptual process, giving precedence to those which seem from the point of view of logical analysis to have an ultimate priority, it is important to recognise that in actual mental history these factors are present together and mutually determine each other almost from the outset, so that it seems impossible to mark off a definite stage in which this is not so. Thus, though the distinction between external objects and conditions of perception is ultimately prior, from a logical point of view, to the correlation of external data with each other, yet the first can proceed only a very little way without the second, which virtually from the outset reacts on it and modifies it.

2. *Correlation involved in the Distinction of the External Object perceived from the Conditions of its Perception*

Development in this direction is already implied in the process by which external object is originally distinguished from sense-organ. In particular, this involves focal perception of external data as the same when the sensa experienced in perceiving them are different. Cutaneous and visual impressions, in shifting their local sign, also regularly vary in other ways determined by other differences in the local sensibility of the sensitive surface. Cutaneous sensa, for example, vary in magnitude and shape with the part of the skin used in touching. 'Compare, for example, a corn plaster applied to the back and then to the thumb, or a dental cavity explored by the tongue and afterwards by the finger-tip.'[1] Such differences of presentational size and shape, when they are expressly attended to as such, make the external object appear as if it were correspondingly different. But ordinarily, finding them to depend merely on variation of local sign, we tend to ignore them; referring them to the sense-organ, we perceive the external object as unchanged, except in the way in which it appears to us. Similarly, the visual presentation of the ace of diamonds, which has a certain distinct shape and colour for the centre of distinct vision, passes through intermediate stages into a colourless blur at the periphery. Yet it is perceived throughout as the same unaltered external object. The variation is referred to the sense-organ and not apprehended as variation in the thing seen, but only in the way of seeing it. On the contrary, special features, previously undiscernible, which become discerned as the presentation becomes more distinct, are themselves perceived as externally objective. They are so perceived because it does not depend on the shifting of local signs whether such details shall be distinguished, nor what they shall be when they are distinguished. There is thus a primitive logical ground for preferring distinct perception to indistinct as more precise and accurate. There is a primitive ground and motive for preferring central to marginal vision, and touch with the hand to touch with other parts of the skin. The principle is the same as that which leads us to prefer a magnifying glass to the naked eye where detailed accuracy is necessary.

There is another class of sensible variations, in some respects akin to those which depend on a shifting of local sign, but in other respects essentially different. These occur only when what we ordinarily call the thing perceived, e.g. the bell which we hear or the face which we see, is at a variable distance from the sense-organ, the interval being occupied by an intervening condition of

---

[1] Ward, *Principles of Psychology*, p. 154. [Ward makes a marginal note here: 'Shape, I should say, is not a ''sensum'' or datum.'—Ed.]

perception—air or light. From the point of view of the percipient as distinguished from our own already acquired knowledge, it is just these variations which supply the most primitive way of knowing that the thing at a distance is separated from him by something which is a condition of perceiving it. This is so because they cannot be referred to change either in the sense-organ or in the thing seen.

Changes of the sort we have to consider are manifold and complex. There is the gradual increase in the magnitude of a visual presentation, and in all discernible parts of it, which occurs as we approach the thing seen. This reaches a maximum when we can command certain touch-sensations merely by a motion of the hand or other tactual organ. When we actually experience the touch-sensations, the original visual presentation disappears wholly or in part and that of the hand is substituted for it or for part of it. Reversal of the movements which bring increase are accompanied by a corresponding decrease, passing through the same phases in reverse order, and reaching its limit in the entire disappearance of the visual sensum. Together with these gradual variations in magnitude, there also occur, as we approach the thing seen, gradual change of shape, gradual increase in intensity, and—what is especially important—in detailed distinctness. Similar, though simpler, changes occur in the intensity and distinctness of sounds as we approach or recede from the sounding body, and in the heat which we feel when we approach or recede from a fire.

Now, in one important respect, variations of this type are closely analogous to those that take place when a visual impression passes from the centre to the margin of the visual field, or inversely. In both cases, a presentation changes in character and distinctness while retaining its individual identity. Hence in both cases there is focal perception of one external object throughout the process. But this agreement is accompanied by a fundamental contrast. The series of changes which we are now considering neither consists in, nor is conditioned by, the shifting of visual or tactual impressions within the local sign-continuum. Hence our power to command them by active movement is, in a peculiar way, conditional and provisional. It varies according to circumstances. Given a specific visual presentation in the centre of distinct vision, its varying phases, as it passes from centre to margin, are in uniform and regular ways presentable at will. But the otherwise analogous changes that are independent of local sign are not in this constant way under our subjective control. We can indeed determine their general direction; we can, for instance, determine whether there shall be increase or decrease in intensity, size and distinctness. But we cannot uniformly determine what active movements on our part will be required before a given visual presentation shall reach its maximum or minimum of intensity, distinctness and magnitude, or before we shall reach the stage at which we are able to substitute tactual for visual sensa.

Now so far as the visual series of changes in the same presentation is thus relatively independent of subjective control, it cannot be referred to change or difference in the sense-organ, but must be apprehended as change or difference in something external to the body of the percipient.

We have still, however, to show how this external something is distinguished, as a condition of seeing, from the thing seen. The reason is that what we call the thing seen is a focal object, taken to be identical as regards shape, size and other spatial characters, both for sight and touch. This focal perception, in its primitive form, depends on such conditions as the following: (1) The fact that when the visual presentation reaches a limiting stage of distinctness, intensity and size, we can command, by appropriate movements, certain tactual presentations; (2) that these tactual sensa show a systematic correspondence with the visual in their spatial order and relations, which is most evident when the eye follows the hand as it explores the surface of a body, and especially our own body; (3) that alterations in the tangible object, such as follow effort against resistance, entail corresponding alterations in the visual appearance which affect all phases of the visual series, so far as these are distinct enough to make the difference discernible.

This identical focal object of touch and sight is what we call the thing seen. Change in the focal object, so far as its tangible and visible aspects correspond, must be a change in both at once. Otherwise it is perceived as remaining constant. The variations in visual experience, as we approach or recede from the point where the corresponding tactual experience begins, cannot therefore be referred to change or difference in the thing seen. But we have already shown that they cannot be referred merely to the motion of the body of the percipient. Hence they must determine awareness, however vague, of something else, as making a difference to the sense-organ, but not to the thing seen— an awareness of light as a medium of vision. Such awareness is in its nature and conditions essentially akin to inner perception of the sense-organ, and may be called medial perception. When it is present, objects are perceived as remotely external.

There is an important difference between light as a means of seeing and the air as a medium of the other distance-senses. Heat and sound are apprehended as belonging not only to the remotely external thing which we call their source, but also to the surrounding air itself. The reason is that the air is also perceptible in other ways. It is perceptible to touch proper and may even offer varying degrees of resistance to movement. Hence it is itself a focal object to which heat and sound may be attributed. But light is not thus focally perceived as a thing, but only as a means of seeing things.

3. *The Apprehension of Causal Relations depends on the Incompleteness of Temporal Events*

Up to this point I have treated external objects only in relation to sense-experience. Their relation to each other has been considered only so far as it is implied in the process by which we come to distinguish thing perceived from sense-organ and other conditions of perceiving it. But with the emergence of this distinction, it becomes possible to discover an externally objective order connecting external data with each other, independently of whatever is known as a condition of perception. Conditions of perception are discounted as irrelevant. I have next to give some general account of our knowledge of this independently external order. For this purpose I shall deal mainly with two topics: (1) causal relations between physical events, and (in the next chapter) (2) quantitative relations as measured by superposition, and the secondary qualities.

Causality is not here introduced for the first time. Indeed, I have not been able to stir a step without it. It is, for example, included in the account I have given of logically primary sense-knowledge, as one aspect of the original connexion of the immediately experienced sensum and its continuation into a sphere of existence beyond itself—the primary physical object. And it is again involved in the distinction between what does and what does not depend on subjective initiative.

A rudimentary beginning of the apprehension of causal relations is thus traceable to primary sense-knowledge, and is further involved in the distinction between external object and sense-organ. Its further development rests on the same principle of the essential incompleteness of temporal occurrences, including all beginning, cessation and change, and all continuance of changeable states and relations. At all stages of mental development the very nature of temporal occurrences as such involves a potential

question concerning their causal conditions and consequences. Whether the question shall be actually asked
depends, of course, on the appropriate direction of interest
and attention on the part of the subject. Where and as
far as the subject is not interested he will not inquire.
But so far as he is urged by relevant practical needs or
theoretical curiosity, he will be on the alert to seek for
causal relations. We are at present concerned with causal
relations between physical occurrences more or less dis-
engaged, in the way already described, from the conditions
of perceiving them.

We have no right to assume that such occurrences are
to be accounted for purely by physical factors. They may
also depend in part on mental agency. From a purely
a priori point of view it is just as possible that they might
be entirely so conditioned. Further, we have no right to
presuppose that the conditions of a temporal occurrence
must consist entirely in other temporal occurrences. It is
possible, and I believe true, that temporal process in
general is conditioned by a being which is not temporal
but eternal, and that it would otherwise be essentially
incomplete. Still, the detailed development of causal
knowledge from its primitive perceptual stages to its
culmination in the sciences consists in finding *temporal*
conditions and consequences for temporal occurrences
and, in particular, *physical* conditions and consequences
for physical occurrences. Our immediate problem is how
this development takes place at the level of perceptual
consciousness—how certain perceptual data come to be
perceived as causally conditioning other perceptual data.
For convenience we may confine ourselves to the causation
of changes or events, as distinct from persisting states or
relations of things. It is with the conditions of changes
that the primitive mind at least is mainly concerned. Apart
from special motives, mere persistence is taken as a matter
of course.

4. *Antecedence in Time as the Ground of the Distinction between Cause and Effect*

Let us begin by asking how, within the causal relation, what belongs to the cause is distinguished from what belongs to the effect. I can only give the natural and obvious answer—by its antecedence in time. Only this requires some explanation. For there are difficulties which have led certain philosophers to assert that cause and effect are simultaneous, or that time-relations are irrelevant. Now, so far as causality involves interaction between distinct things, this view is justified. The relation of interaction as such seems really to be simultaneous. When a moving stone impinging on a pane of glass breaks it, the glass does not begin to be broken until the stone begins to break it, and while the stone is breaking it, it is simultaneously being broken. At the same time the motion of the stone is being more or less retarded. What then do we mean in speaking of the impact of the stone as an antecedent condition? What we mean is simply that the impact occurs as a phase in the course of a previous change. The motion of the stone, and its tendency to move when it reaches the window, is a continuation of an anterior motion, and varies according to its momentum. For this reason the stone is regarded by common sense as an active factor, whereas the glass, as it does not thus initiate the change which takes place in itself or in the stone, is regarded as passive. Where two bodies collide in consequence of the previous motion of both of them, each is regarded as both active and passive in relation to the other. Consider again what takes place when I lift to my mouth the fork which I already hold in my hand. The motion of fork and hand go on contemporaneously. But the motion of the hand is initiated by my will, or by some other prior process which does not independently initiate the motion of the fork.

Besides active there are also passive antecedents. The state of the glass when a stone begins to break it is a passive antecedent. It is antecedent because it is continued from the previous existence of the glass. It is passive because there is no prior change in the glass initiating the interaction. It should be added that in so far as an interaction takes time, it consists in a continual series of interactions in which those which precede condition those which follow.

5. *The Linking of Specific Causes with Specific Effects*

We now come to the crucial question. How does the primitive mind proceed, even at the perceptual level, in linking this or that specific event with this or that specific antecedent as its causal condition? Our fundamental view of causal unity, as one aspect of the unity of the universe, does not of itself suffice to solve this problem. Each specific event is essentially incomplete, and requires completion by its specific conditions. But its essential incompleteness does not of itself determine what specific conditions are required to complete it. It raises a possible question to which it does not itself supply an answer. Nor is the answer directly given even when we perceive both a physical event and a causal condition of it. For we are not directly aware of the causal connexion, as we may be, for example, of temporal sequence or of resemblance. Something in the nature of inference is required—inductive inference.

This holds at least for physical causation. For voluntary activity we have to make an important reservation. We can directly see that conscious striving or appetency has an intrinsic tendency to realise itself, so that if other conditions are present, the event which fulfils it will occur. This is implied in saying that the striving is unsuccessful when it is not fulfilled. The distinction between success and failure is meaningless for other causal conditions, except through anthropomorphic analogy. But we must be careful to notice how far this direct insight extends. All that we can directly know in this way is that conscious striving is by its intrinsic nature capable of being a factor in its own realisation, and will be actually so if other factors are present. But it does not follow, even when an event fulfilling it actually takes place, that it must have contributed to the occurrence of this event. For the event may be due to a complex of conditions of which it forms no part. The fly on the revolving cart-wheel may will the wheel to go round, and it does go round. But the will of the fly does not contribute to cause its revolution. In any case, we are here concerned not with mental but with physical causation.

6. The Conception of 'Force' does not help at the Perceptual Level

There is indeed a factor entering into causal connexion between physical facts, the concept of which seems ultimately to be derived from mental agency. I refer to what is commonly called 'force', regarded as something actually existing, and not merely as a mathematical formula. Force is an actually existing tendency to a process which does not or need not actually occur. When the window is broken by the impact of the stone, it is the tendency of the stone to continue in motion, rather than its actual motion, which overcomes the resistance of the glass. The actually continued motion is only such as remains after the resistance of the glass has been overcome. Similarly, when a spring is held down under a superincumbent weight, we regard this as due to a balance of opposing tendencies or forces. The presence of force in this sense is constantly recognised by common sense and in ordinary sense-perception; and I shall try to show in another place[1] that when its nature and the logical motive for assuming it are properly explained, it may be maintained and successfully defended against the charge of crude anthropomorphism. It does not, however, yield that direct insight into causal connexion between physical facts which we are now seeking. It does not do so, because it has no counterpart in the content of immediate

[1] Cf. Chapter xvi, §§ 5 ff.

sense-experience, and cannot therefore be perceived in the same way as sequence, co-existence, resemblance, motion, etc. It is indeed known in perceptual process, but only by perceptual inference, however primitive and obvious this may be. The presence, direction and degree of physical forces is gathered from other physical indications; if this holds for force, it must *a fortiori* hold for physical causation in general. Causal connexion between the physical occurrence and its physical antecedents can be gathered only from other relations discernible between them. In determining what these relations are and what is their relative value, we must avoid *a priori* dogmatism. No doubt they ought to be such as the nature of causal unity itself demands, but it is altogether unsafe to attempt to define in advance what is thus required, apart from the actual development of knowledge through experience. We may indeed say that the claims must be distinctive, so as to mark off antecedents which are causal from those which are not. We may also say that, other things being equal, the more manifold, varied, complex and precise the relations are, the stronger will be the evidence.

7. *Temporal and Spatial Proximity*

The sort of clues which guide the primitive mind even at the perceptual level are for the most part such in their general nature as continue to operate also in later stages. In the absence of other indications, close temporal sequence may be sufficient, when a certain antecedent is the only one which presents itself so as to arrest interest and attention. If I merely tap the table with my hand and a loud crash immediately follows, I may feel for the moment as if my action gave rise to the noise. I have an illusory perception of causal connexion which I correct without delay. But if there were no grounds for making the correction, the first impression would maintain itself unchallenged. Thus to the child the watch-lid appears to fly open because he blows at it. Such inferences are by no means always misleading. The tap on the table, for instance, does cause a noise immediately following it. Whether misleading or not, such indications, in the absence of other evidence, at least yield what may from a logical point of view be regarded as hypotheses to be further tested in subsequent experience. As I have shown in speaking of primitive credulity, it makes no essential difference that the hypotheses are not consciously entertained as such. The primitive mind is justified in following with primitive credulity whatever clues offer themselves to it, until it has more and better. I have spoken of this one as the most meagre possible. None the less it is virtually the same as that used in Mill's method of difference, so far as this is purely inductive, and does not consist in deduction from a preacquired system of knowledge.

The evidence is greatly strengthened if spatial proximity is added to temporal, as when a change beginning in one body is immediately followed by a change in another, when they come into contact or close proximity, and not before. Or, if they are already in contact, it is sufficient that change initiated in one body should spread in the first instance to that which is next to it. For example, I strike a thing and it moves; or, if I already grasp it, its motion follows the motion of my hand. The moving stone and the breaking of the glass is another illustration. So is the motion of a cork drifting downstream. The evidence is further enhanced when the ensuing changes are perceptible in both bodies. In striking or pushing with the hand, for instance, besides the motion or other change in the thing pushed or struck, there is also for the most part perceptible alteration affecting the hand itself. Its motion may be perceptibly retarded, and its altered state may be perceived through the altered motor and organic sensations. So when two bodies collide, both may be broken. With the advance of knowledge this has led to the general principle that all physical action is interaction.

8. *Persistence in Change*

We can also discern at this stage the beginning of another criterion of causal connexion which becomes increasingly important, until it takes shape in such principles as the persistence of matter and the conservation of energy. I mean the traceable persistence in change of the things which appear to act on one another. Hand and thing pushed perceptibly persist in, through and after the complex process into which they enter. They persist, though altered in position and otherwise modified through interaction. Other examples are supplied by the stone and the glass, the wetting of the ground when rain falls on it, or the blot which follows the dropping of ink.

9. *Concomitant Variation*

Any distinctive correspondence or agreement between the nature of the occurrence and the nature of the antecedent has a value dependent on the closeness and complexity of the agreement or correspondence. Take, for instance, the distinctive correspondence between the shape of the foot which stamps the sand and the footprint which follows, or between a drawing and what on that account we take to be its original, or between the structure of a fossil and that of animal or plant organisms, or between what is willed and what actually takes place. Consider the method of Zadig in Voltaire's fable, which for Huxley is typical of the method of science in general. Under this head we have to bring all concomitant variations. Causal laws or rules in general assert not merely that a certain kind of antecedent is followed by a certain kind of consequence, on the assumption that other conditions known or unknown are present; they also formulate with more or less precision how change or difference in the special nature of the antecedent, or of the other factors combined with it, determine corresponding change or difference in the consequent. We can thus show why, through specific variations of the same general conditions, a balloon rises and a stone falls.

Now concomitant variation of an occurrence, as its antecedent varies, is present, not only at the scientific level, but in the most primitive stages of mental development both in animals and men, and it forms for both from the outset an essential and most important clue to causal connexion. In lifting a stone, the motion of the stone varies concomitantly in direction and rapidity with the motion of the hand, and this is true also of a dog carrying a bone in its mouth. The same holds good, though less exactly, if the stone is thrown or pushed. In general, the practical motor activity of men and animals in relation to their environment varies in its result concomitantly with the degree and direction and the successive and simultaneous co-ordination of muscular effort, and also with the variable nature of the situation and of the materials to be dealt with. It thus involves an immensely complex system of finely variable adjustments, which have to be learnt by experience as far as they are not initially provided for by instinctive endowment.

10. *Constant and Frequent Repetition*

So far I have said nothing of the clue which is commonly regarded as being by itself of primary and essential importance—constant and frequent repetition. Given that one sort of occurrence A is within the limits of observation constantly or frequently followed by another B, how far is this evidence that A is part of the cause of B? Note that this question must be kept quite distinct from another with which it is too often confused—what warrant have we for believing that when A occurs B will probably follow? We may know that A is a causal condition of B; yet unless we have ground for believing that all other necessary and sufficient conditions are probably present, we have no logical warrant for believing that A will be followed by B. If any of these is absent, B cannot take place. As a matter of fact we can never know that A, however complex it may be, is the entire cause, and we can never ascertain exhaustively what this is. We can only presume on the probable presence of unspecified conditions as an unexplored background. Now, constant or even relatively frequent repetition is of the greatest value in supplying grounds for this probable presumption. It is so inasmuch as it enables us to sample the distribution of causal conditions within a certain range of observation. We have reason for anticipating, within this range, that when A occurs all the conditions on which B depend are, more or less probably, present also. Now such anticipations, be it noted, are not necessarily based on any assumption that A is even part of the cause of B. A may be merely a sign of the presence of the unknown cause. Thus men expected, and had good reason for expecting, the sun to rise after a certain interval of darkness, although they did not know or suppose that the night was a causal antecedent of the sunrise, and although they did not know even partially what the causal antecedents were. It was enough that they could presume on their presence as somehow included in the ordinary course and constitution of things, falling within the range of their experience. Anything strikingly strange and unprecedented in the behaviour or appearance of the sun in the daytime would justifiably have cast more or less doubt on its rising again as before. The ebb and flow of the tides, the phases of the moon and the succession of the seasons illustrate the same point.

It would seem, then, that the repeated conjunction of two occurrences, however frequent, has of itself little or no value as evidence of causal connexion between them. All depends on what it is that is repeated, and the way in which it is repeated. If I happen to press a button and a ringing sound immediately ensues, this of itself, in the absence of reasons to the contrary, indicates my action as a causal condition of the ringing. Yet the ringing may be entirely due to other causes which occur coincidentally with my pressure of the button. But this becomes exceedingly improbable if the sound recurs on my renewing the pressure at irregular intervals, and if it continues while I press, and ceases when I cease to press. Thus the value of repetition depends on the presence of other relatively independent clues. We may regard repetition itself as a minimum case of concomitant variation. It is the case in which concomitant variation consists merely in a regular coincidence of the times in which the two events happen.

11. *Summary*

To sum up. The demand for causal connexion is ultimately founded on the essential incompleteness of temporal occurrences, each requiring to be completed by its own special conditions and consequences within the unity of the universe. But inasmuch as causal connexion between two distinct physical occurrences has no counterpart within the immediate content of the sense-experience through which we perceive them, it cannot be apprehended with the same kind of directness as coexistence or sequence or extension or motion. It has to be inferred from other special and distinctive relations between them.

I have not attempted an exhaustive list. But I have enumerated, as obviously of primary importance, temporal and spatial proximity, persistence in change, and above all differential correspondence and concomitant variation. Constant repetition is also very important indeed. But its value as direct evidence of causal connexion mainly depends on what it is that is repeated, and on the way in which it is repeated. Though knowledge of causal relation is due to inference, it does not involve conceptual thought or even free ideas. It begins in primitive perceptual process and it pervades the conscious life of animals as well as man. As sense-perception advances in complexity with growing experience, knowledge of what Locke calls active and passive powers of things plays an ever-increasing part in it.

We have now to go back to the position from which we set out in this inquiry. We began by showing that knowledge of external causation involves from the outset some distinction between (1) change and difference due to variable conditions of perception and (2) change and difference in the external things themselves which are touched or seen or otherwise perceived. At the same time we said that this distinction itself becomes further defined and developed by growing knowledge of the relations of physical facts to each other, and more especially of their causal connexions. It is sufficiently obvious, at the stage of ideal and conceptual construction, that coherence of what claims to be physical fact with its context of physical conditions and consequences is a test of its physical reality. At present we are specially concerned with the use of this test in the growth of sense-perception itself. Here too, much of the highest importance is too obvious to dwell on.

Chapter X

CORRELATION OF EXTERNAL DATA.
(*b*) NON-CAUSAL PROPERTIES OF PHYSICAL OBJECTS

1. *Increasing Knowledge of the Objective World depends on Causation*

As knowledge of the externally objective order, and especially of the causal order, advances in range and complexity, it supplies a relatively new and increasingly important test of what is or is not externally real, so that all our knowledge of the external world beyond the range of present perception and memory of past perception stands or falls with the causal order connecting external occurrences. No one has realised this more clearly than Hume, and I cannot do better than quote an illustration from him. 'I am here seated in my chamber with my face to the fire; and all the objects, that strike my senses, are contained in a few yards around me....I hear on a sudden a noise as of a door turning upon its hinges; and a little after see a porter, who advances towards me. This gives occasion to many new reflexions and reasonings. First, I never have observed, that this noise could proceed from any thing but the motion of a door; and therefore conclude, that the present phaenomenon is a contradiction to all past experience, unless the door, which I remember on t'other side the chamber, be still in being. Again, I have always found, that a human body was possessed of a quality, which I call gravity, and which hinders it from mounting in the air, as this porter must have done to arrive at my chamber, unless the stairs I remember be not annihilated by my absence. But this is not all. I receive a letter, which upon opening it I perceive by the hand-writing and subscription to have come from a friend, who says he is two hundred leagues distant. Tis evident I can never account for this without...spreading out in my mind the whole sea and continent between us, and supposing the effects and continued existence of posts and ferries.'[1]

Hume's illustration is taken from ordinary life. It is still more evident that the work of physical science, with its atoms and molecules and other existences and processes, which have not been and cannot be perceived by any human being, is a causal construction serving to correlate the external data of sense-perception with each other. The only ground for asserting the existence of such scientific objects is that they are required for the coherence and completeness of the causal order.

But it is not only at the level of ideal construction that causal connexion supplies a criterion of what is externally real. It fulfils the same function even in primitive stages of perceptual process. Clearly, what is taken as externally objective size, shape, distance and motion is size, shape, distance and motion, so far as they count as factors in the external order of causation. And what is most important to begin with is our own practical activity in overcoming resistance by effort. Change and difference to which we have to adjust our action are externally real. Change and difference in the way in which things appear to the senses, which do not affect the result of our practical activity, are referred to the conditions of perception.

2. *Measurement by Superposition*

I turn now to the development of knowledge of quantitative relations, and particularly the part played in it by measurement by superposition. The function of measurement by superposition is to fix positively by reference to constant standards what the physical magnitudes of things

[1] *A Treatise of Human Nature*, Book I, Part IV, sect. 2 (Selby-Bigge's ed. p. 196).

are, and thus also to determine their shape, in so far as this depends on the relations and dimensions of their parts. Even apart from such measurement we are not altogether without means of determining what we call real size and shape. All apparent differences in size, shape, or indeed any other characters of perceived external objects are taken as externally objective differences, if and so far as the conditions of perception are uniform, or if and so far as we have learned to allow for variations in these conditions. But it is plain that this test by itself is limited in its application, and more or less precarious unless it is confirmed by the causal test and by measurement. Uniformity being presupposed, there are special conditions of perception which are selected as yielding results more true to physical fact than others. Thus shape and related size and position are seen most accurately when we look straight at an object within a relatively short distance. Why are such conditions preferred? Partly because they give relatively distinct and detailed perception. But it is also essential that the shapes, relative sizes and positions appearing under these conditions shall be found to be such as count in the process of physical causation, and also such as agree with the results of measurements by superposition.

3. *How Superposition is itself perceived*

Measurement of this kind is fundamentally important even in primitive perceptual process. First of all we have to consider how superposition itself is, in the first instance, perceived. The vital point is that it cannot be known, to begin with, in any single perception, but requires a series in which the conditions are varied. This is most obvious for sight. It is not enough that one thing A should intercept the view of another B. Otherwise the hand I hold before my eyes would be superimposed on the mountain in the distance. What is required is that from all points of view, varying with variable conditions of perception, A alone shall be visible instead of B. But this, to begin with, can be found out only by trial, even with the degree of accuracy sufficient for practical needs. It is true indeed that, as perceptual knowledge develops, a single glance becomes sufficient. But this is because we have learned by experiences which begin with the beginnings of mental life that what intercepts the view of a thing under certain conditions will also intercept it under others.

The same is also plainly true for tactual perception, when the objects superimposed are themselves external to the body. But we are apt to take for granted that there is something in the intrinsic nature of tactual sense which reveals that the skin is in direct contact with the thing perceived. This view breaks down when we consider indirect perception by an instrument, such as occurs when we feel our food with our knife and fork or touch things with a gloved hand. But all cutaneous perception is really indirect, as the outer layer of the skin is insensitive, so that there is no immediate contact with the sense-organ. It is of course the most familiar of facts, taken for granted even in early stages of perceptual process, that when certain tactual sensations are experienced, a certain part of the skin is superimposed on part or all of the surface of the perceived external object. It is, however, a fact which is primarily learned by experiences in which we find that, however free movements may be varied, perception by means of one part of the skin prevents otherwise possible perception by any other part, or by sight. In this way the presence of tactual sensa comes to mean the spatial coincidence, and therefore the equal extent, of the tactile surface with the surface of the thing perceived. Thus tactual perception comes to include measurement by superposition.

Such measurement, be it noted, is independent of the variable extent of cutaneous sensa themselves. A hand made of wood serves as well as one of flesh and blood, provided that superposition is assumed. The measurement depends on a relation of external things to each other, not to our sensibility. Hence it enables us ordinarily to neglect and discount local differences in the extensiveness of tactual sensa. By superimposing one part of our skin on another, or one object on both parts, we are enabled to interpret sensa, varying in bigness for immediate experience, as indicating the same determinate physical magnitude. We thus obtain what Professor James calls[1] a system of cutaneous equivalences, and come more or less to ignore immediately sensible differences, except when our attention is expressly directed to them. When 'a certain length of thigh surface is in contact with the entire palm and fingers' we take the surface covered by the hand to be equal to the surface of the hand that covers it, although the resident sensa of the thigh surface are much less extensive than those of the hand.

4. *Rejection of the Berkeleyan View of the Relation between Visible and Tangible Extension*

From what has been said it is finally clear that the Berkeleyan view of the relation of visible and tangible extension is untenable. Berkeley and his followers on the one hand identify tangible extension with the immediately experienced extension of tactual sensa, and visible extension with the immediately experienced extension of visual sensa. On the other hand, they identify tangible extension with the externally objective extension as measured in feet and inches, and regard the visible extension as merely a sign of this. This is all wrong. The external magnitude does not belong distinctively either to sight or touch, and is independent of their variations. It is rather determined by the relation of physical things to each other, subsisting independently of their relation to our sensibility, and therefore presupposing the independent existence of the things.

[1] *The Principles of Psychology*, Vol. ii, pp. 177–8.

5. *Our Knowledge of Matter is Relative, Partial and Schematic*

If we now review the whole preceding discussion of the nature and development of our knowledge of the material world, one result emerges clearly. Our knowledge of matter, so far as it transcends the content of immediate sense-experiences, is through and through more or less relative, partial and schematic, rather than positive, concrete and determinate. Its ultimate logical basis and presupposition is primary sense-knowledge, in which the physical object is known merely as the continuation of the actual sense-experience beyond itself into a region of existence which is not immediately experienced—the world. Further development consists in making this initially vague background articulate by marking off within it relatively distinct parts, and in learning their relation to each other. Every step in the process is such that it can only yield relative, partial and schematic knowledge. The distinction between sense-organ and what is perceived by means of it depends on the distinction between two partial aspects of concrete presentational experience, in one of which it is regularly under subjective control and in the other not. Similarly, all focal perception of an identical physical fact through variable sensa—e.g. the perception of the same extension both by sight and touch—involves the like distinction of partial aspects within the concrete unity of sense-experience.

It is through the correlation of external data with each other, and not directly through their relation to sense-experience, that our knowledge of the external world becomes, at least in certain directions, precise and determinate. But this way of determining physical existences through their relation to each other, e.g. in the causal order or in measurement by superposition, can from the nature of the case only yield relative values and not direct apprehension of the nature of the terms related. Thus in measurement by superposition what we learn is only comparative and not absolute magnitude. For such measurement it would make no difference if all physical magnitudes were increased or diminished together, provided that they retained the same proportion to each other. On the other hand, we can know by acquaintance and memory the absolute extent of our visual and tactual presentations, though we cannot know their comparative magnitude with anything approaching the exactness of physical measurement. If knowledge of the external world is thus relative, partial and schematic even at the perceptual level, it is still more obviously so for ideal and conceptual construction, and especially for the exact sciences with their doctrines of the relativity of space and time and motion, culminating in such results as those reached by Einstein. Einstein tells us, for instance, that for the purposes of physical science the concept of simultaneity must be redefined in such a way that A may be simultaneous with B and B with C though A is not simultaneous with C. The ultimate conditions of physical measurement are such that they can only determine simultaneity as thus conceived, and not in the sense in which for immediate experience the loudness of a sound is simultaneous with its pitch, or the black of the paper before me is simultaneous with the ink.

6. Our Knowledge of Secondary Qualities is even more imperfect than of Primary

So far I have referred only to the primary qualities of matter. But our knowledge of the secondary is far more imperfect and indeterminate. This has led to the traditional view of science that only what are called primary qualities, such as size, shape, position and motion are physically real, and that the other qualities called secondary, such as colour, sweetness, hotness, coldness, odour and sound, only belong to our sense-presentations and have no counterpart at all in external objects. Now it is plain that we perceive things and cannot help perceiving them to be red or green, hot or cold, just as we perceive them to be extended and figured.

Further, this is true of the man of science himself when he is not theorising, just as it is true of others. What grounds has he for regarding the apparent evidence of sense-perception and the natural view of common sense as illusory? One reason commonly urged is certainly quite inadequate. It is that the secondary qualities are perceived through variable sense-experiences. If this argument were cogent, it would be equally fatal to the primary qualities, since for these also the perceptual sensa are very variable. What is proved in both cases is not that there is no physical fact perceived, but only that it cannot be identified with any content of immediate experience. There may be a secondary quality connected with the perceptual sensa, as physical extension is connected with the extension of visual and tactual presentations. The really important difference is that we have not the same means of fixing determinate values for the secondary as for the primary qualities. Measurement by superposition is obviously inapplicable. The causal test seems also to fail, in view of the development of the physical sciences.

It is true that for the pre-scientific mind some secondary qualities, at least, appear to count as factors in physical causation. Butter will melt on a hot plate but not on a cold plate. Colour as well as shape is reflected in a mirror. But, even at the primitive stage, what is taken as the causal function of secondary qualities is much more restricted in range, and less systematic in character than that of the primary. In particular, it does not affect the practical adjustment where resistance is overcome by effort. It makes no difference to the motion of a billiard ball whether it is white or red. Modern science has found it possible to dispense, for its own purposes, with even this limited causal function of the secondary qualities. By a bold use of hypotheses it has been able to formulate a relatively comprehensive and unified conception of the executive order of nature in which various modes of the primary qualities take the place of the secondary. Molecular motion, for instance, is substituted for heat as sensibly perceived.

7. *Criticism of the Denial that Secondary Qualities are Physically Real*

Hence there has arisen the denial that anything of the nature of secondary qualities is physically real at all. They are accounted for as due merely to conditions of perception, and especially to the structure of the sense-organs. But the inference is clearly precipitate, even if we fully concede the premises. All that we have a right to assert is that only the primary qualities lend themselves to the purposes of science, inasmuch as it is only in terms of these that we can formulate a positive view of the general causal order of nature in a more or less definite, precise and detailed way. We have no right to assume that we can trace in this definite manner the operation of all conditions which enter into physical processes. The mode of motion which constitutes heat for the physicist, may be correlated with variations in an intensive quality, akin rather to what we feel as heat, than to any primary quality. It is even possible that there really is only the intensive quality, which behaves in such a way that it can be represented for scientific purposes as a mode of motion. It certainly seems rash to affirm that all modes of energy must consist merely in energy of motion or energy of position. Further, even if we deny causal efficacy to secondary qualities, it does not follow that they do not exist, or that the primary can exist without them.

On the other hand, there is very strong reason for denying that primary qualities isolated from secondary can exist independently, as the sole characters of physical things. This point has been strongly urged by Berkeley. 'I desire any one to reflect and try, whether he can, by any abstraction of thought, conceive the extension and motion of a body without all other sensible qualities. For my own part, I see evidently that it is not in my power to frame an idea of a body extended and moved, but I must withal give it some colour, or other sensible quality......'[1] It follows

[1] *Principles of Human Knowledge*, sect. x.

that either both primary and secondary qualities are physically real, or that both merely have their being in the sense-experience of the percipient. Berkeley, taking for granted as universally admitted that the secondary exist in the mind alone, infers that the same must be true of the primary. For us only the alternative is open. As primary qualities are physically real, secondary qualities must be physically real also.

The point is that the primary qualities, when analysed, turn out to be merely relations, so that the terms related require to be otherwise specified. Quantity, whether extensive or intensive, is a more or less of something or other, so that there must be an answer to the question what this is. The like is true of relative position and in general of spatial order. There must be terms to be ordered, and their nature cannot be constituted by their relation to each other. Motion, again, is only change of relative position, and therefore raises the same question.

We are then bound to regard secondary qualities as physically real. On the other hand, it must be admitted that for us they are on a very different footing from primary. Our knowledge of the primary characters is relative, partial, and schematic; but our knowledge of the secondary is much more so. The reason is that after discounting the variable conditions of sense-perception, including the structure and state of the sense-organs, we have not the same means of fixing determinate values for them through such physical relations as causality and superposition. The only principle on which we can proceed is that, given uniform conditions of perception, what differences appear to exist in sense-perception are physically real. Thus colour-differences discernible for a normal eye at a certain distance from the things seen, and in ordinary daylight, really exist independently of our sensibility. They exist in this way even though they may not be discernible in a twilight, or at a greater distance, or by one who is colour-blind. On the other hand, differences not perceptible by the naked eye none the less exist if they are discernible with the aid of a microscope. What is discerned in this way is only relative distinctness, not the specific intrinsic nature of the qualities themselves. This remains more or less undetermined. We could know it definitely only if we could have the same direct acquaintance with the physical facts as we can have with our own sensa.

Chapter XI

THE STATUS OF SENSA

1. *Sensa belong fundamentally to Matter, not to Mind*

The world of physical reality is primarily known as the continuation of the content of immediate sense-experience into a sphere of existence which transcends and includes it. The two are so continuous in existence that the nature of our own sensa supplies a clue, and ultimately the only clue, to the nature of physical existence as extended, figured, coloured and so on. Physical facts being thus of a piece with our own presentation-continuum, we must begin by recognising this unity in existence, and consequent community of nature, in our way of naming them. There must be a common name for both, as contrasted with individual minds as knowing, feeling and willing subjects. This requirement is best satisfied by applying the words 'matter' and 'material' to both. In the fundamental antithesis between mind and matter our sense-presentations belong to the side of matter, not of mind.

A mind is individual in the sense that it cannot contain other minds as parts of it, without thereby breaking up into relatively distinct minds. Matter, on the contrary, is a diffused total, including parts such that each is matter in the same sense as the whole to which they belong. There is the same fundamental distinction between the knowing and willing subject in his individual unity, on the one hand, and his presentation-continuum on the other. I might by a nervous lesion be deprived of half my field of visual sensa, leaving the rest. But an act of volition could not thus be divided so as to take away a portion of it, and leave the remainder. Our own sense-presentations, then, are material and not mental. They are that portion of matter which we immediately experience—which therefore we can know about by acquaintance or memory.

2. *Though Material, Sensa fall outside of Physical Existence*

On the other hand, though our own sensa are material, they seem always to fall outside the domain of physical existence. It is through them and only through them that we are conversant with physical fact, but they are never themselves identical with the physical facts which we know by means of them, whether these concern our own bodies or things external to our bodies. Thus physical science, proceeding in its own way and strictly confined to its own data, and aiming only at knowledge of the externally objective order, can find no place for them any more than for knowing, feeling and willing minds. Sentient organisms are indeed external objects, and as such are investigated by the anatomist and physiologist. But the anatomist and physiologist cannot, merely by anatomical and physiological methods, either of observation or experiment, discover within the organism the sense-presentations which somehow arise in connexion with it. These crop up, so to speak, as epiphenomena, as foreign and disturbing factors obtruded from an alien source into the coherent development of physical knowledge. It is true that without sense-presentations physical science itself would be quite impossible. But, apart from this slight drawback, it would, from the physical point of view, be simpler and more convenient if they did not exist at all.

3. *Sensa are a Part of the Material World as a Whole*

Keeping in view at once this thoroughgoing distinction between sense-experience and physical objects, and also their continuity of existence and community of nature,

I submit that there is only one account of the material world in general which satisfactorily covers the relevant facts. The relation of sense-presentations to the material world is ultimately that of part to whole. The private sensa of the individual percipient constitute that part of the whole which is existentially present in his experience. If we suppose a mind for which the whole material world is existentially present and therefore intuitively knowable, as our sensa are to us, for this mind there would be no distinction between physical fact and sense-presentation. There would only be one immensely complex sensum, having a unity and continuity analogous to the unity and continuity of the content of our own sense-experience. But for us only a tiny fragment of the whole is existentially present; and it is only in this that we have any clue to the existence and nature of the rest. The possibility of knowing more than the immediate content of sense-experience is founded on its essential incompleteness. Owing to this, the original datum of primary sense-knowledge includes not merely the experienced sensum, but the fact that there is something beyond this, continuous with it in existence and nature. This fact may be called the primary physical datum.

The further development of knowledge of the material world depends on the essential incompleteness of the physical data themselves, which is such that they require to be correlated with others in a context which includes and connects them—a systematic order of temporal, spatial and causal relations. This development begins with the beginning of intelligent mental life, and is continued with the ideal and conceptual construction of the sciences. It is abstractly conceivable that sensa might themselves have been directly included in the same order as that which comprehends and unites physical data. Had this been so, the distinction between the content of sense-experience and physical fact would not have existed at all. Instead of it we should only have had a distinction between physical facts immediately experienced and others required to combine

with them in a coherent context. But, as we saw in criticising neo-realism, this view is quite untenable. If it had
been true, everybody would have known it to be true, and
no difficulty or doubt would ever have arisen concerning
the nature of matter and the way we know it. As a matter of
fact we find that the externally objective order does not
connect sensa with each other, but only the external data
which we know by their means. Sense-presentations are
the ultimate source of all knowledge of physical objects;
but they are never physical objects themselves. None the
less the distinction does not concern the ultimate nature of
what is known; it is rather between two ways of knowing
which mutually exclude each other.

4. The Distinction between Knowledge of Sensa and Knowledge through Sensa compared with that between Matter as Phenomenon and Matter as it is in itself

It is plain that this contrast between the two ways of knowing corresponds more or less to the time-honoured antithesis of matter as phenomenon and matter as it is in itself.
I cannot better explain my own view than by showing how
far I accept this antithesis, and in what I differ from the
well-known doctrine of Kant. For Kant, as for me, to know
matter as phenomenon is to know it as characterised by
characters drawn from the content of our immediate sense-
experience—to know it only in relation to our sensibility.
But he also holds that such sensible characters cannot, in
any manner or degree, really belong to the things as they
are in themselves. There is no way of discovering what their
intrinsic nature is. Instead of the things as they are in their
own intrinsic nature, there is substituted a phenomenal
object, interposed, like an opaque screen, between us and
them.

The distinction which I am making is, in this respect,
radically different. It is essential to my position that we can
and do know matter as it is in itself, however limited and

imperfect such knowledge may be. In the first place, our own sensa belong to the domain of matter in its distinction from mind. Now, it is plain that we cannot define phenomenal knowledge as relative to our sensibility, and at the same time assert that our own sensa are known only as phenomena. The intuitive knowledge of existentially present contents of sense-experience is therefore a knowledge of matter as it is in itself—fully determinate, concrete and positive, not relational, abstract and schematic. In the second place, even external objects are known as they are in themselves, in so far as they are apprehended as sharing a common nature with the sensa through which we perceive them. We could not have known what it is to be extended, to be figured, to have relative shape and position, if these characters had not belonged to our own sense-presentations. It is true that externally objective size, for example, is not determined only by the extension of the present sensum. It is also determined by the demand that physical facts shall be connected with each other in a systematic order, temporal, spatial and causal. But this order itself presupposes at least the primary qualities. We must, then, in the absence of cogent reasons to the contrary, assume that in ascribing these primary qualities to physical objects we know them as they are in themselves. But this knowledge is so conditioned that it must be partially inadequate and schematic, as compared with that which we should possess if what we apprehend as physical fact were existentially present within our sense-experience. It extends only so far as there is community of nature between that part of the material world which we immediately experience, and those parts of it which are known as physical phenomena.

But what means have we of determining the degree of this community? There seems to be only one ultimate criterion. We have the right to assert community of nature so far as this is required in order to trace the external order, the system of externally objective relations, spatial, temporal and causal, on which the practical conduct of our lives and the development of the sciences depend.

The general conclusion is that though we have more or less knowledge of physical objects as they are in themselves, yet the knowledge is partial and inadequate even for the primary qualities, and still more so for the secondary. There may be, and must be, aspects and features of matter as it is in itself, which escape us from the phenomenal point of view.

If we take the time-honoured distinction between matter as it is in itself and matter as phenomenal to mean only that phenomenal knowledge by its intrinsic nature and conditions is necessarily partial and inadequate and, in a sense, abstract, we may still retain it. The old formula is so convenient that it is better not to drop it altogether. Only it must be remembered that the distinction is not between two things known, but between two ways of knowing the same thing. Further, the phenomenal way is not so called because it includes no knowledge of matter as it is in itself, but only because this knowledge is essentially imperfect, schematic and abstract.

BOOK FOUR

THE UNIVERSAL CORRELATION OF MIND AND MATTER

▾

Chapter XII

THE RELATION OF THE MIND TO ITS OWN SENSA

1. *The Neo-Realist Challenge to Berkeley*

The whole of the foregoing discussion of the nature of the material world and the way in which we know it has been mainly undertaken, not for its own sake, but in order to prepare the way for dealing with the fundamental question of the connexion of matter and mind. We have reached the result that for each individual mind the primary and direct connexion is with that part of the material world which is constituted by the content of his own immediate sense-experience. We may therefore hope to find here the key to the general problem.

It is in the first place of vital importance to decide between two sharply opposed views of the relation of sensa to the subjective mental life of the individual whose sensa they are. There is on the one hand the traditional view represented by Berkeley, and on the other that of neo-realism, as represented by Professor Alexander, and, in an earlier phase of his thinking, by Mr G. E. Moore. Berkeley with unhesitating confidence and without fear of contradiction asserts that sensa or, as he calls them, ideas, can exist only in some mind. Both to him and to his opponents this seemed evident. This position has been recently challenged by the neo-realists. According to them, Berkeley and his followers and opponents fell into a fallacy due to failure to distinguish clearly between objects known and the act of knowing them. The cognitive act does indeed presuppose a cognitive subject; but it makes no difference to the being and nature of what is known. What is known is entirely independent of anyone's knowing it. Applying this principle to sense-presentations, they maintain that the sensa may exist though no one perceives or otherwise knows them.

2. *Sensa and Subjective States are experienced in the same way*

I shall later show reason for rejecting this neo-realist analysis of knowledge, and for regarding the supposed cognitive act as a mere figment.[1] But it is not necessary to discuss this question at present. For the status of sense-presentations does not depend merely on their being perceived or otherwise known. Besides this, and as a condition of this, they are immediately experienced. They are immediately felt, as subjective states are. I am aware that Professor Alexander has attempted to draw a hard and fast line of distinction between acquaintance with sensa and acquaintance with what belongs to our subjective life. In his language, we are said to contemplate sensa, but not to enjoy them, and to enjoy subjective states and processes, but not to contemplate them. Now, I would not assert that there is no basis for this distinction. But I submit that Alexander has mistaken its nature. What we have to discriminate are not two fundamentally different ways of being experienced, but two fundamentally different kinds of existence. Subjective states and processes are states and processes of that individual unity which he calls the self or 'I'. Hence they can only exist in being experienced by the individual to whom they belong. Sense-presentations, on the contrary, are objects of knowledge and interest to the self, but they are not adjectives of it as an individual unity. When I experience pleasure I am pleased; when I have a sensation of

[1] Cf. pp. 272–8.

white, I am not myself white, or whitened. There is then a vital difference between what we experience in experiencing sensa, and what we experience in experiencing our own states and activities. None the less they are both immediately experienced in the same way, and Alexander's distinction between enjoyment and contemplation is from this point of view untenable. Further, though what is sensibly experienced does not belong to the constitution of my individual self, yet my experiencing of it does.

3. *Can Sensa exist unexperienced? The* prima facie *Difference between Visual and other Sensa*

What ground is there for holding, on the one hand, that the quality and intensity of a feeling of pleasure is incapable of existing without being experienced and, on the other, that the quality and intensity of an immediately experienced sound or smell may so exist? Apart from some special reason which we have not yet found, the distinction seems quite arbitrary. It is futile to urge that the pleasure is a subjective state and that the sound is not. This does indeed make an important difference. My subjective states can exist only in being experienced by me and yours only in being experienced by you. My sensa, on the other hand, inasmuch as they are separable from my being as an individual, may conceivably exist before and after I experience them, provided that they are experienced by some other mind. It is even possible that the same sensa may be or might be simultaneously experienced by different individuals. But this does not help us to understand how sensa could exist without being experienced at all.

There is, however, one way in which this reasoning might be upset. It would lose force if, by direct appeal to introspection, we could clearly discern that whereas subjective states can exist only in being experienced, neither this nor any other relation to mind is essential to the existence of sense-presentations. This is the position of

Mr G. E. Moore. To Berkeley it seemed evident beyond dispute that sense-presentations, though they are not themselves mental but material, can exist only in a mind. To Moore it seems clear that all relation to mind is accidental to their being. Why this discrepancy? In part, I suppose it may be accounted for by a difference in the question which Berkeley and Moore put to themselves. Moore is taking account only of his own mind; Berkeley is considering mind in general. But this explanation does not go far enough. We must look into the question more closely, and repeat the introspective inquiry for ourselves. When we attempt this, a curious and significant fact comes to light. The *prima facie* result of a direct appeal to introspection appears to differ for different kinds of sensa. If, for instance, we consider visual presentations, we may be inclined to agree with Moore that they might exist without being experienced by anyone. If, on the other hand, we consider organic sensa, such as the nausea we feel when a feather tickles our throat, or cramps or headaches, it seems absurd to suppose that the quality and intensity of what we immediately experience could exist either in our own bodies or elsewhere without being experienced at all. For other presentations the *prima facie* deliverance of introspection is less decided. We may hesitate in varying degrees whether in this respect to class immediately experienced warmth and coolness, smells, tastes and sounds with visual sensa or with organic sensa such as cramp and nausea.

Now, we can hardly admit so vital and ultimate a distinction between special sorts of sensa, all of which meet in the unity of one complex sense-experience, and arise, as Dr Ward has shown, through the gradual differentiation of a relatively homogeneous presentation-continuum. There must be a fallacy of introspection on one side or on the other. The test as between Berkeley and Moore is to be found in the question which of them can best explain how the other goes wrong. Now it seems to me that a plain and adequate explanation is open to the Berkeleyan, and that none is open to Moore. When we examine the above distinction between different sorts of sensa, we find that in its varying degrees it corresponds in the main with the distinction between relatively higher and lower senses. At the bottom of the scale there is organic sentience;[1] sight is at the top; and between these come other modes of sense-experience in a more or less roughly graduated order. One kind of sense-presentation is higher than another when it yields more complex, systematic and finely discriminative knowledge of the physical world, and when it is less obtrusive on its own account through its own intensity and painfulness or pleasantness. Hence the higher a sense is in the scale, the more difficult it is by simple introspection to separate, even roughly, the sensa as immediately experienced from the physical objects perceived. This applies above all to sight: it is virtually impossible, without the aid of involved and circuitous methods, to disengage visual presentations as such from things seen and qualities and relations of things seen. Hence the direct appeal to introspection almost inevitably raises a confused issue. The question whether visual sensa can exist without being experienced is almost inevitably confused with the question whether the physical phenomena perceived by means of them can exist without being experienced.

The natural answer of the plain man is that physical phenomena do so exist. That this is the natural answer follows from the very constitution of the physical phenomenon as such. From the phenomenal point of view, interest and attention are concentrated on tracing the externally objective order, causal, spatial and temporal, and for this purpose the reference to an experience other than our own would be a useless encumbrance. Again, the characters of the physical phenomena as such, being derived only from certain partial aspects of sense-experience, are themselves

---

[1] [Ward has a marginal note: 'No, better to say "general sentience"'; organic sensations are of many sorts (cf. Horwicz, e.g.) and unicellular organisms like the amoeba appear to have no organs.'—Ed.]

relatively abstract and schematic, incapable therefore of actually existing by themselves, and *a fortiori* of being immediately experienced by themselves. It follows that a simple appeal to introspection is of little value where there is a strong tendency, as there is in the case of sight, to confuse sense-presentations with the physical objects perceived by means of them. We ought rather to trust its deliverance for the lower senses, where the issue is comparatively distinct. Yet even for the higher senses, including sight, its verdict is by no means consistent. It appeared at least as evident to Berkeley that visual sensa cannot exist without being experienced, as it does to Moore that they can.

4. *The Relation of Sensa to Subjective States and Processes*

It would seem, then, that in this respect sensa do not differ from subjective states and processes. The really fundamental distinction is that sense-presentations are conceivably separable from the subject as an individual unity, whereas subjective states are inseparable. This position is strongly confirmed when we consider certain distinctive ways in which the contents of sense-experience are connected with the mental life of the individual. Take first their peculiarly intimate relation to pleasure and pain. Other objects condition pleasure and pain only because they are known. But the mere existence of sensa as immediately experienced is pleasant or painful. A toothache itself, or a bad smell, and not merely the knowledge about them, affect us disagreeably. Nor is this all. It is a prevailing psychological doctrine that pleasure and pain are always purely subjective, and as such quite distinct from the objects with which we are pleased or pained, towards which we feel agreeably or disagreeably affected. But it is very difficult to maintain this view without very important restrictions, when we confront it with what seems to be the clear testimony of introspection. Some sensuous pleasures and pains seem themselves to be sensuously presented as well as, or instead of, being subjective states. The pain of a toothache seems to belong to the sensation itself, and to be localised like it in the tooth. In the language of Wundt, the painfulness belongs to the sensum as its feeling-tone. The fusion is so intimate that it is arbitrary to break up the whole into two parts so fundamentally distinct that the one may, and the other may not, exist without being experienced. There is thus a real point wrapped up in Berkeley's argument that as a great heat is a great pain, and as pain can exist only in a mind, so heat can exist only in a mind.

Emotions again are generally regarded as subjective states, which exist only in being experienced. Yet it is at the same time recognised that organic and motor sensa enter as contributory factors into the constitution of such emotions as fear and anger and grief, and help to determine their specific character.

Consider finally the status of what are called mental images, and their connexion with the original sense-impressions. Such images are themselves sensory presentations, though derivative and dependent. On the other hand no one, I presume, would assert, unless in the interests of a preconceived theory, that images can exist without being experienced by some mind. But we cannot consistently hold this to be true of images and deny it to be true of the impressions of which they are revivals.

If we fairly take into account all the reasons which I have adduced, we seem bound to conclude that sense-presentations, though they are material and not mental,[1] yet exist only in being experienced by some mind. At least, the *onus probandi* lies heavily on those who deny this.

5. *The Evidence that Sensa exist only as experienced is also Evidence that the Material World exists only as experienced*

We have now to combine this position with the other, that the material world in general is ultimately known as con-

[1] Cf. Chapter XI.

tinuous in nature and existence with our own sensa. An immensely important consequence seems to follow inevitably when the two views are taken together. Inasmuch as our own sensa are of a piece with the whole material world as it is in itself, being partial excerpts from it, and so to speak samples of it, whatever presumption there may be that they exist only in being experienced by a mind is a presumption that the material world as a whole exists only in being experienced by a mind.

There are two main difficulties likely to be felt in accepting this view. The first arises in the failure to distinguish matter as physical phenomenon from matter as it is in itself. In tracing the physical order, reference to mind as correlated with matter yields no help. It would be a useless encumbrance. Further, phenomena as such are essentially incomplete and schematic, in such a way that they are incapable of being immediately experienced by themselves. From the phenomenal point of view therefore, matter is, by a natural and inevitable abstraction, regarded as if it existed independently of mind. But this ought not to prejudice the question what matter is in itself. The second difficulty is the startling nature of the conclusion. Is the argument sufficient to justify us in taking so vast a step? I answer that there are other cogent grounds for holding the universal correlation of mind and matter. The present is only one line of inquiry out of several converging towards the same conclusion. One other such line of inquiry I have already followed out in my criticism of materialism[1]. I am now adding to this whatever presumption may be derived from the mind-dependence of sense-presentations. Other reasons, and those the most important, I have yet to consider.

[1] [In *Mind and Matter*—Ed.]

Chapter XIII[1]

MIND-STUFF THEORIES
AND MONADISM

1. *The Dependence of Mind on Mind*

Negatively, the result of the [discussion and rejection of Materialism in *Mind and Matter* was][2] that mind cannot owe its existence to merely material conditions. But matter, for the purpose of the argument, includes whatever is not mental—whatever does not partake of the nature of knowing, feeling or willing, or of experiencing in the widest possible sense of the term. Hence our negative conclusion has a most important positive counterpart. Wherever a mind such as yours or mine comes into being, it must have its source in mind which already exists. But we cannot stop here. Not only the beginning but the continued existence of our conscious life must be similarly conditioned. It must be conditioned by mind other than our own. All the evidence on which materialism relies to show the dependence of mind on matter for its beginning, continuance and discontinuance becomes from our present point of view evidence for the dependence of mind on mind. This is a very far-reaching proposition. But as it stands, it is extremely vague; and in the attempt to make it more definite we are confronted by a series of difficult problems.

---

[1] [For the position of this and the following chapter see Editorial Preface, p. xxii.—Ed.]

[2] [The typescript reads 'preceding discussion is'. This 'preceding discussion' of Materialism was rewritten and elaborated in *Mind and Matter* and the original treatment in the Lectures was later destroyed by the author. The transition from the argument against Materialism to some of the main problems discussed in the remainder of the present volume is indicated in the passage, quoted in the Editorial Preface p. xxi, from pp. 314–15 of *Mind and Matter* (last Section: 'Ultimate Problems')—Ed.]

First and foremost, how are we to conceive the mind which we assume to exist as a condition of the existence of our own? Are we to posit a single universal mind, without beginning or end, on which all finite minds depend? Or are we to suppose, either beside this or instead of it, a multitude of psychical individuals having each a unity and identity more or less like our own? Or are we to regard individuals as arising from the union and interaction of simpler modes of mental existence which have no individual unity and identity?

2. 'Mind-Stuff' Theories

It is this last alternative which most naturally suggests itself to those who approach such speculations from the point of view of physical science. They tend to cling as closely as possible to the analogy of material processes and, more especially, the processes through which our bodies arise and are maintained in existence, and cease to be. Just as in the brain we appear to find only an immensely complex and elaborately organised system of matter and energy arising from relatively simple combinations, so the minds of men and animals are represented as arising from the complex union of simpler modes of mental existence everywhere correlated with matter and passing through corresponding changes. We thus reach those vague doctrines of universal parallelism or universal interaction which have been called 'Mind-stuff theories'. Their distinctive character is that they derive individual minds from a diffused mental material which has not even in the most rudimentary form anything analogous to the unity of consciousness; minds are developed from 'mind-stuff'.

This term 'mind-stuff' is due to Clifford, and to him we owe the most distinct statement of a mind-stuff theory. He uses the word 'feeling' for any sort of experience, whether belonging to a conscious individual or not. 'Elementary feeling co-exists with elementary brain-motion in the same way as consciousness co-exists with complex brain-

motion.'[1] But a feeling can exist by itself without forming
part of a consciousness. Of such feelings, *sentitur* is all that
can be said. Even elementary feelings are not the simplest
constituents of mind-stuff. There are 'remoter elements'
which cannot even be felt, but of which the simplest feeling
is built up. These ultimate elements are what Clifford calls
'Mind-stuff'. They and their combinations correspond to
motions of matter and are connected together in their sequence and co-existence by counterparts of the physical
laws of matter. 'A moving molecule of inorganic matter
does not possess mind or consciousness; but it possesses
a small piece of mind-stuff. When molecules are so combined together as to form the film on the underside of a
jelly-fish, the elements of mind-stuff which go along with
them are so combined as to form the faint beginnings of
Sentience. When the molecules are so combined as to
form the brain and nervous system of a vertebrate, the
corresponding elements of mind-stuff are so combined
as to form some kind of consciousness......When matter
takes the complex form of a living human brain, the corresponding mind-stuff takes the form of a human consciousness, having intelligence and volition.'[2]

Is any theory of this type defensible? No doubt it is
difficult to understand how a feeling can be felt, an experience experienced, in detachment from an individual subject. But it would be rash to pronounce this impossible.
The fatal weakness of the theory seems to lie in the assumption that from such mental occurrences, even if they exist,
the unity of an individual can be derived by any processes
of combination, interaction or modification. This will,
I hope, become plain when we examine the nature of
individual unity and the relation of the individual as knowing, feeling and willing subject to the universe of which he
is a part. This inquiry will lead us to reject decisively every

[1] W. K. Clifford, *Lectures and Essays*, vol. II, 'On the Nature of Things-
in-themselves', p. 83.
[2] *Ibid.* p. 85.

form of mind-stuff, and therefore to recognise as a fundamental principle that an individual mind can proceed only
from another individual mind which already exists.

There is an aspect of Clifford's theory which I have not
yet considered, though it raises a question of vital importance for us as well as for him. It concerns the ultimate
relation of mind and matter both in the individual and in the
universe. In the individual the relation is plainly twofold.
On the one hand, the individual subject knows material
objects in sense-perception and by inference and ideal construction based on the data of sense-perception; and he feels
and wills in relation to them. On the other hand, his conscious life is connected in a peculiar way with his bodily
organism and especially with his brain and nervous system.
These two relations seem at first sight to be essentially
distinct, so that neither can be explained by reference to the
other. But this is not Clifford's view. Starting from his
mind-stuff theory, he thinks that he can account for the
relation of body and mind in terms of the relation of mind as
percipient to matter as perceived. Matter as known to
common sense and science through sense-perception and
ideal construction from sensible data is, he urges, only
matter as it appears to us. Hence the question arises—
what is matter as it is in itself in distinction from matter as
phenomenon? From the point of view of the mind-stuff
theory, the answer, according to Clifford, lies ready to our
hands. Matter as it is in itself is mind, either in the form of
mere mind-stuff, or of unowned feelings or of psychical
individuals. The universal correlation of matter and mind
is really the relation of matter as represented in terms of our
sense-experience and matter as it actually is in itself apart
from our way of representing it. Thus what appears to us as
a 'moving molecule of inorganic matter' is in itself a 'small
piece of mind-stuff'; what appears to us as the film on the
underside of a jelly-fish is in itself mind-stuff so combined as
to form 'the faint beginnings of sentience'.[1] The relation

[1] *Ibid.* p. 85.

of a human mind to its body comes under the same general principle. What appears to us as a certain series of occurrences in a human brain is in itself the life-history of an individual consciousness. Now the general position that matter as it is in itself is really mental in its nature may be held, and has been held, by men who utterly reject the conception of mind-stuff. The hypothesis naturally suggests itself when once it is assumed that matter as known to us by way of sense-perception is an appearance to be distinguished from matter as it is in itself. If analysis of this distinction shows that the distinctive characteristics of what we know as matter are traceable to the mode in which we know it by way of sense, it would seem to follow that matter in itself is without them, that in its own intrinsic nature it is immaterial. Hence unless we are prepared to say that it is absolutely unknowable, we must regard it as partaking of the nature of mind. We thus reach by a new and independent line of thought the position that mind is universally correlated with matter. It is so correlated as being the reality of which matter is the appearance. The essential step in this argument is supplied by the proposition that the distinctive characteristics of matter, e.g. extension and motion in space, belong to it only as phenomenon, and are due to the way in which we know it through sense-perception and ideal construction from perceptual data. From our examination of the conditions of sense-perception we concluded that there is valid ground for a distinction between matter as it is in itself and matter as phenomenon.[1] But we saw reason to deny that what we know perceptually as matter is in itself not matter but mind. The proper distinction is rather between matter as incompletely known and as completely known. None the less our examination favoured Clifford's view that the relation of mind as percipient to matter as perceived object is essentially connected with and may be used to explain the relation of mind and body.

[1] See Chapter xi.

3. *The Monadism of Leibniz and Lotze*

If we reject any form of mind-stuff theory, we are bound to assert that individual mind is primary and without beginning or end; we are bound to assert that any individual which begins to be or ceases to be proceeds from some individual already pre-existing. But at this point there seems to be a choice of alternatives. Are we to postulate a single universal mind as the correlate of the material system as a whole? Or are we, either instead of this or besides this, to assume an indefinite multitude of finite individuals? Theories which people the universe through and through with psychical individuals play an important part in the history of philosophy. But it is noteworthy that no great philosopher has stopped short here. They have all seen reason for affirming the existence of one universal and eternal mind on whom the whole system of finite individuals depends.

There are two main forms of this theory, differing according to the view taken of the nature of matter.[1] If what we ordinarily call matter is regarded merely as a phenomenon; if, as it really exists apart from our sensuous knowledge, it is taken to be of the nature of mind; and if it is also held that all mind is individual, then a monadology, such as that of Leibniz or Lotze, is logically inevitable.[2] The material world must consist in a collection of individuals, each experiencing its own states and each having a unity and identity more or less analogous to that of the human mind, though they may indefinitely transcend or fall below human minds in the scale of existence. What we ordinarily call space and matter and the motion and interaction of the parts of matter are merely appearances to us. They are

---

[1] [The first form, which may be called a pure monadology, is represented by Leibniz and Lotze, and is treated in the present section; the second form is the theory of Fechner, treated in the next section.—Ed.]

[2] [Cf. *Mind and Matter*, pp. 170 ff. and especially pp. 209 ff. and 290 ff.—Ed.]

merely due to the way in which we sensuously apprehend the relations and changes of relation between the psychical units or monads that alone have being in and for themselves. There really is no material world such as is perceived and conceived by common sense and science. Yet everything within the experience of the monads—including human minds—proceeds just as if it did exist. This is so because, though it is a fiction, it is a fiction which is throughout founded on fact. The ultimate fact is the correspondence, in infinitely complex ways, of the course of experience in each monad to the course of experience in all the others. When, for instance, I have the experience of speaking, you have the experience of hearing. Some with equally good ears hear me less distinctly than others. Ordinarily we should say that this is because they are further away. But monadism inverts this view. Rather, being further away consists in hearing less distinctly. Similarly, when a stone impinges on a pane of glass, what really happens is roughly this. There is a set of monads which we may call the stone-group; and there is another which we may call the glass-group. When the members of the stone group pass through certain experienced states, then, in accordance with the general order of the universe, the members of the glass group pass through certain corresponding states. Correlations of this sort between psychical units, though not the intrinsic nature of the units themselves, are, so to speak, pictured by us in terms of sense-experience; and, so pictured, they appear as the physical event of the impact of a stone on glass. So, in general, the whole material world is a translation into the language of sense of an infinitely complex and intricate system of correlations between the inner experiences of the individuals which are the sole units really entering into its composition.

It is needless to say that theories of this kind are in sharp conflict with common sense. They are also stupendously difficult to work out, so that even the gigantic powers of Leibniz were overtaxed in grappling with the intricacies of the problem. Plainly, in the absence of cogent reasons to the contrary, it would be far simpler and easier to retain the conception of matter as a common field for the activity of psychical individuals and a common medium of communication between them. Indeed it is very hard to see how, if there were nothing in the universe but monads, they could be related in the way which the theory presupposes.

Having taken away space and matter as the common field of their action and the medium of communication between them, what possibility have we left of any real interconnexion? Individuality, as the theory conceives it, is merely a principle of unity and identity within the individual, and involves no communion with anything else. No two individuals can have common parts or common states or common boundaries. We seem to be left with a disjointed plurality of self-contained units, incapable of any relations corresponding to nearness and remoteness in space, to motion, to the combination and separation of the parts of matter or to the causal interaction of bodies. Why then should an event taking place in one monad make any difference to what takes place in others? Or if it does, why should it affect A in one manner and degree, and B in a quite different manner and degree? This difficulty was felt both by Leibniz and Lotze, and their solution is, in principle, the same. Both hold that the interconnexion of the monads is due to the agency of one universal mind, on which finite individuals depend. According to Leibniz, the same creative act which gives being to finite individuals so predetermines their nature and history that the changing states of each correspond in a systematic way to the changing states of all the others. This correspondence is what appears to our sensuous knowledge as the interaction of bodies. Strictly speaking there is no interaction between individuals; each is active only in its own self-development; they are connected with each other only by a pre-established · harmony. Of this pre-established harmony the relation of the mind of a man or animal to the group of monads which appears to sense-perception as the material phenomenon called his body is a special instance, and one of peculiar interest and importance. Lotze, in opposition to Leibniz, holds that monads do act on each other; but he maintains that this is possible only because they are limited modes or phases of one universal mind. Thus on the main question the two philosophers agree. For both of them, the connexion of finite individuals is due to a central all-embracing mind and is unintelligible on any other view. The individual, conceived as a monad, supplies no principle of unity except for its own inner being. A collection of monads therefore cannot constitute a world-system unless they have their common principle of unity in a central mind. *A fortiori*, it follows that a new monad cannot originate from pre-existing monads. If a human individual begins to exist for the first time at birth, it must owe its being to a special creative act of the universal mind. The only alternative is to suppose that the human mind does not begin to exist, for the first time, together with the development of the human body, but that it has always pre-existed, as a psychical unit of a lower order. What we take to be its origin will, on this view, be only a new phase in its life-history continued back into the endless past. As a matter of fact this is the doctrine of Leibniz. Yet even he is driven to account for the rational nature of man as due to a special act, or a kind of transcreation, by which God gives reason to each soul at the moment of birth.

4. *Fechner's Doctrine*

Pure monadism involves the view that what we call matter is merely an appearance within finite individual minds of what in itself is immaterial. It is otherwise with another type of theory, which has its chief representative in G. T. Fechner. For Fechner matter is ultimate and everywhere ultimately co-ordinate with mind; and he finds in the relation of human and animal minds to their bodies the key to the constitution of the universe as a whole and in all its parts. Everywhere there are psychical individuals each with its own bodily organisation; and, as the bodies are all parts of one material world, so the psychical individuals are included in one universal mind.

> All are but parts of one stupendous whole,
> Whose body nature is, and God the soul.

The principle on which Fechner proceeds is the unity and continuity of the universe. That order and correlation of processes which we call *life* cannot, he argues, be confined to the bodies of plants and animals and so exist in detachment from the rest of the material world. We cannot suppose that life emerges only here and there out of surrounding dead matter, like islets thrown up from the sea. On the contrary, vital process, as found in plants and animals, is only a partial phase of one continuous universal process, and has no separate existence of its own. Hence we must presuppose throughout the universe a teleological order akin to and including that of our own living bodies. Similarly, the connexion of human and animal organisms with conscious processes is an inexplicable anomaly if it is taken as an isolated occurrence. Here too, we must assume throughout nature specially organised and differentiated material systems, related to individual minds in a way fundamentally analogous to that in which our own minds are related to our own bodies. Nor is Fechner content with mere generalities. He argues in detail for the existence of individual consciousness in plants, though this may be as far below that of animals as the latter is below that of man. He also uses all his scientific knowledge, combined with the penetrative imagination of a poet, to show that our mother earth ought to be conceived as the living body of a Mind far transcending our own in range and power. The living beings which exist on the earth's surface ultimately proceed from it, and their life and organisation is a continuation of its life and organisation. There is a corresponding relation between the earth-soul and the conscious life in men and animals. Thus, unlike the pure monadists, Fechner holds that conscious individuals may be and are derived from and even included in other conscious individuals. But he fails to show, in any satisfactory way, how this can take place. He is in the main content to regard the origin of, let us say, a human mind as the counterpart of the process by which the human body comes into being. He never fairly faces the crucial question, why the result is a distinct individual, and not merely a new phase or mode of the one undivided earth-consciousness. The theory as a whole does not seem to follow necessarily from the general principles with which Fechner starts, and apart from these it has hardly sufficient support in the special evidence which he adduces. Granting, as we may, that an organisation continuous with and akin to that of living bodies pervades the universe, granting also that mind is primary and underived and everywhere correlated with matter, it does not therefore inevitably follow that every part of the material world must be either a living organism connected with a psychical individual, or a constituent of such an organism. At any rate this does not follow, if, as Fechner himself holds, there is one universal mind correlated with the material world as a whole. For it is open to us to account for the teleological order of nature and for the existence of finite minds as due to this universal mind. The special evidence by which Fechner tries, for example, to show that the earth has a soul, will scarcely be found convincing by any one who is not already fully prepared on general grounds to accept the conclusion. He does, I think, succeed in breaking down the initial prejudice which would reject offhand the hypo-thesis of an earth-soul as altogether wild and absurd. But he does not do much more than this. Neither his general grounds nor his special evidence show anything more than that his view is possible or, at the utmost, that it is not unlikely.

5. *The Transition to the Conception of a Universal Mind*

The same may be said of all theories which people the universe through and through with individual minds. The same general grounds on which they rely lead up to the belief in a Universal Mind; and given a Universal Mind they are not strictly necessary. Further, there is no special evidence sufficient to convince us of the existence of conscious individuals except as associated with human and other animal organisms. It by no means follows that there are no finite conscious beings except men and animals.

It may well be that some such theory as that of Fechner is true. If it were so, we could hardly expect to find empirical evidence for it differing much in kind and degree from that which Fechner adduces, unsatisfying as this is. But even if it is true, it can hardly be ultimate—at any rate if the universe is a unity and not an indefinite collection of items. If the universe is a unity, the ultimate fact can hardly be an indefinite plurality of dependent and derivative minds. The hypothesis of one underived and Universal Mind, even if it is not inevitable, is at least indicated as the most natural, and it will be confirmed when we approach the question from other points of view. It will be well, therefore, to attempt to define more precisely what we are to mean by it.

Chapter XIV

THE CONCEPTION OF
A UNIVERSAL MIND

1. *The Universal Mind as Supernatural and determining the Course of Nature*

It is plain that the conception of a Universal Mind raises problems fundamentally different from those which confront us in dealing with finite existences. We pass beyond the constitution and course of a nature to a Supernatural Being—I do not use the word God, because at this stage I want to avoid ethical and religious implications. The Universal Mind is supernatural inasmuch as it is a condition determining the whole course of nature—the whole course of events in space and time, and the whole system of their causal relations. For this reason it must in its own nature be without change or succession. It can have no beginning or end and it cannot become what it was not before, or cease to be what it was before.

Being an individual mind, it must be conceived by us, if we attempt to conceive it at all, as knowing and willing. But its knowledge cannot pass from less to more through successive stages involving the acquisition and sifting of fresh data, questioning, doubt and error. There cannot be any data which it does not possess or any implication of these data which is not completely transparent to it. Thus the Universal Mind must comprehend in its knowledge all that is past, present and future, all universal principles and all possibilities. Further, everything will be known to it in relation to everything else, as falling within the unity of a single whole. Its knowledge will be completely unified.

Similarly for will. We cannot intelligibly suppose the Eternal Individual to change its mind. We as finite beings have to find out by a gradual process of trial and failure what it is that we really want: in like manner we have by a gradual process to learn the means and to gain control over the means of attaining what we want. But in the Universal Mind there can be no such change or vicissitude. There can be for it no unconsidered alternatives which come to be preferred to others previously chosen. There can be no restriction through lack of means; for all means are through and through at its disposal. We may say that what it wills is the course of the world as a whole, including the existence and the life-history of individual minds. This implies complete unity of will, corresponding to complete unity of knowledge. We must not ascribe to the central and Eternal Mind anything analogous to a plurality of distinct volitions, but a single undivided purpose. Thus if we pick out this or that occurrence or group of occurrences, and say that this is separately willed, the statement is, strictly speaking, false. The Universal Mind, if there be one, can have no separate volitions, but only one undivided will.

2. *Limitations of our Knowledge of the Universal Mind*

Is anything more than we have laid down necessarily involved in the eternity or timelessness of the supreme individual ? In one sense, it is clear that far more is implied— far more than we can understand. We can proceed only from our point of view as finite beings; and from this point of view we cannot do more than indicate in general outline the way in which the Universal Mind, if there be one, must differ from our own. We cannot realise in thought or imagination what this difference positively means. Only an Eternal Being can know positively and directly what it is to be eternal. There is here a legitimate place for a critical and cautious agnosticism, such as I defended in Chapter II.

3. *To deny its Distinctness from Finite Existence is to deny the Reality of Change and Succession*

The account which I have given of the timeless being of the Universal Mind will seem to many crude and false. It will seem so to those who hold that all reality is a single individual, excluding from its eternal unity all real distinctness of parts or partial aspects, so that what common sense and science take for real multiplicity is apparent only, and due to our defective knowledge. On such a view there is no room for the Universal Mind as an individual really distinct from the world of finite existence. If it is real it must be the sole real being. But if it is the sole real being, then to say that it includes within it no change or succession is equivalent to saying that change and succession are not real. This again can only mean that change and succession do not exist—that in the universe there is no change anywhere and no succession anywhere.

4. *'Appearance' and 'Reality'*

It may be said, and has been said, that the denial of reality does not mean the denial of existence. What is unreal may none the less exist as an appearance. I do not see how this is possible in any natural or relevant sense of the words 'reality' and 'appearance'. What exists as mere appearance merely appears to exist, and does not really exist. But there is no difference between saying that something does not really exist and saying simply that it does not exist. We are therefore bound, on this view, to hold that it must be false to assert that a particular experience of thirst is followed by a particular experience of drinking. Thirst never really precedes the quenching of it; it cannot, because there really is no preceding or succeeding, because there really is no thirst and no quenching of it either in our experience or as physical fact. Such things merely appear to exist and are not real. The denial of the reality of time, vicissitude and finite existence cannot mean less than this, if the term 'real' is taken in any relevant sense—if it is taken in any sense which would warrant the denial that there can be a Universal Mind really distinct from the world of becoming and of finite individuals. But if all this is implied in the alleged unreality of change and succession and of finite existence in general, plainly we have a right to demand completely transparent and irresistibly cogent reasons before committing ourselves to such a position.

When we come to discuss the grounds for asserting the unity of the universe we shall see that these grounds in no way warrant us in assuming a unity incapable of including within itself real plurality and change. Here I would point out that such a theory is not internally coherent. Everything turns on strictly determining the sense in which the term 'appearance', and the opposition of appearance and reality, are to be understood. Now in the ordinary usage of language 'to appear' has two meanings, corresponding to the distinction between the verbal forms 'X appears to be Y' (or 'X appears as Y' or 'Y is an appearance of X'), and simply 'X appears'. It may mean not that something is an appearance of something else, but simply that it appears itself, that it is itself a direct apparition: we are immediately acquainted with it or immediately experience it. In this sense, what appears must be real in so far as it appears. Its reality and its appearance are coincident. In the other sense, we may say not that something appears, but that it appears to us to exist or to be qualified in a certain way. In this use of the word, I may say that what I see appears to me to be a crooked stick, though it may really be a straight stick dipped in water. In the other use, what appears is the direct visual apparition which actually is crooked and does not merely seem to be crooked. It is only in interpreting this as the appearance of a crooked stick that there is room for error.[1]

[1] [For other statements of the above distinction see the author's *Studies in Philosophy and Psychology*, Introd. p. VII and pp. 273–4 and 290; also *Mind and Matter*, pp. 208–9.—Ed.]

As in this instance, so always, 'appearing to be' ultimately presupposes direct appearance. Appearances which may or may not be real always presuppose appearances which must be real; and these last include an indefinite multiplicity of finite existences as such—the particular contents of sense-experience, in their change and succession, the alternation of pleasure and pain and of experienced success and failure. Or, if this is not so—if the changing and successive as such do not directly appear—then there must be some other direct appearance which we mistake for change and succession. But mistakes presuppose minds which make them—finite minds, which apprehend what is real in a broken and imperfect way and reach truth through trial and error. Now according to the theory, these finite individual minds are themselves mere appearances. But to what can they appear except to themselves? And how can they appear to themselves if they are themselves mere appearances? How can the imperfect apprehension which is to account for the distinction between what merely appears to be and what is real, be itself merely apparent?

There seems to be only one way of escape from this difficulty. It must be clearly and sharply recognised that the words 'to appear' and 'appearance' are here used in a sense quite different from that which attaches to them in ordinary language. They must be used in some sense which does not imply that what appears must appear to some mind. But no other sense is relevant to the present question. There is no other meaning of the words *real* and *unreal* which would warrant us in denying that there can be eternal being distinct from the world of becoming and finite existence. If we are to maintain this denial, we must say that change and succession as such do not exist, but merely seem to us to exist. If, none the less, an attempt is made to attach to the term 'appearance' some meaning which does not imply that what appears must appear to some mind, it will inevitably follow that what is thus called 'appearance' cannot consistently be accounted for as due to

the imperfection of our knowledge. The distinction between appearance and reality must on this view be a distinction which holds good for being itself, independently
of what any one thinks or perceives. It must be a difference
between one sort of being and another. But if so, wherein
can the difference consist? Are we to identify real being
with what is self-existent, and appearance with what is
dependent and derivative? If this is what is meant, why not
plainly say so? Why gratuitously substitute for the words
'dependent' and 'derivative' the ambiguous and misleading term 'appearance'? So far as the main issue is concerned, it is plain that what is derivative or dependent must
as such be distinct from that on which it depends or from
which it is derived; also that what has its source in real being
must itself be real. If it does not really exist it cannot really
be derived from what does really exist. If, for instance, the
successive and changing are really derived from a timeless
reality, then change and succession really are; they do not
merely seem to be.

Another alternative is to identify the relation of reality
and appearance with that of substantive and adjective. On
this view, there is only one individual and timeless substantive, which is called Reality, and all multiplicity and
change is merely adjectival, and is therefore called appearance. But we cannot change the nature of things by arbi-
trarily altering the use of words. Individual minds, such
as mine and yours, and this solid globe and even the particular contents of sense-experience cannot be transformed
into adjectives merely by calling them so. In any current
sense of the word these are known only as ultimate subjects
of adjectives, and if we try to think of them as adjectives of
anything else, we entirely fail. If these things are to be
named adjectives, the meaning of the term 'adjective' must
be radically changed. As a matter of fact, those who maintain that there is ultimately only one substantive do use the
term very loosely indeed. For them, anything included in
any kind of complex unity, so that it could not be what it is

apart from this whole, is an adjective of the whole. Hence, holding the universe to be a unity in this sense, they regard it as the ultimate substance of which everything else is an adjective. But this only means that everything is contained in the universe and could not otherwise be what it is. It by no means follows that the universe is the one and ultimate substance of which all else is an adjective.

5. *The Relation of the Universal Mind, as Knowing and Willing, to the finite World*

We have thus to regard the eternal being not as the absolute whole of being, but as ultimately distinct from and essentially connected with the universe of becoming and finite existence. Therefore in saying that the Universal Mind must be timeless, we mean only that it is timeless in its own nature as an individual. We do not mean that it is unrelated to the world of becoming. On the contrary, we have to conceive the world of becoming as known by it and willed by it. This implies that the temporal order, being real, is known and willed as what it really is. Succession and change are known and willed as succession and change.

Thus it must be wrong to say that the Eternal Mind is aware of what is past and what is future as if they were present. To be aware of the past or future as present would only be to make a blunder. It would be to take events as occurring before or after they actually occur. Similarly for will. What is willed by the Universal Mind is the time-order as a whole. From this point of view, we may say that the eternal purpose is eternally fulfilled. It is so because it includes in its indivisible unity what is, has been and is to be. But just because what is willed is a successive process, the eternal purpose can only be realised in successive stages, and the will to realise it is the will to realise it in successive stages. Thus we must not speak of it as being already fulfilled; for the word 'already' carries with it an exclusive reference to the past or present as distinguished from the future. Further, we have no right to exclude that distinction in the relative values of past, present and future which is implied in the conception of progressive development. On the contrary, as the successive progress advances, the single timeless process must be more and more fully realised in the sphere of becoming. If it is an evil purpose, the movement is towards evil; if it is a good purpose, the movement is towards good.

6. *Predestination, Foreknowledge and Free Will*

At present, it must be remembered, we are not concerned with ethical or purely religious questions. We are, however, within the domain of theology: and we may here say something about a vexed theological question which occupied the minds of Milton's devils—that of predestination, foreknowledge and free will. The problem arises out of a preconception of what is implied in freedom of choice. It is presupposed that when a man chooses freely, though he is, of course, limited to the alternatives before his mind at the time, yet the act of fixing on one of them rather than the others is in no sense determined by his nature or previous history, or by any other factors, natural or supernatural. The theological difficulty is this. The Universal Mind or, in theological language, the Divine Being, is omniscient. He knows everything. But how can He know a future event when it is not determined whether the event will occur or not? Now the plain and straightforward answer is that He cannot. He cannot, because to do so would be to make a mistake. If it is absolutely undetermined whether the event A or the event B will happen, it is not true that one of them, A, will happen to the exclusion of B. Otherwise, that would be certain which by hypothesis is neither certain nor probable but only possible. It is certain that the event A will either occur or not occur. But it is not certain that it will occur, and it is not certain that it will not. This is precisely what we mean by saying that it is undetermined.

There can therefore be no foreknowledge of what will take place. There can only be a baseless and arbitrary guess. To take for certain what is really not certain is merely to commit a blunder. But this is quite incompatible with the conception of omniscience. To be omniscient is to know whatever is true and not to know what is false or meaningless. To speak of knowing what is false or meaningless is a contradiction in terms.

The same holds for omnipotence. To be omnipotent is to be able to realise all possibilities. It cannot include the power to realise all impossibilities—to do what cannot be done. Thus if it is assumed to be possible that it shall be quite undetermined which of a number of alternative events shall happen, an Omnipotent Being must be able to produce this state of things. He must be able to make it undetermined which of the events shall happen. This would really be a power, and would therefore belong to an Allpowerful Being. But no being can both make the occurrence of an event indeterminate and also determine it. A being capable of this, far from being all-powerful, could not even exist at all.[1]

7. Implication of the View that the Relation of the Universal Mind to Matter is not that of Creator

So far, in developing what is implied in the conception of the Universal Mind, I have not discussed its ultimate relation to matter. I have regarded it as the ultimate source of finite minds, and hereafter I shall give further and weightier reasons for this view. But I have refrained from asserting that it is the ultimate source of matter. On the contrary, I have rather implied that matter is fundamen-

---

[1] Of course I have only been assuming the existence of undetermined events for the sake of argument: I do not mean to assert or suggest that there are such events, or that they are possible. All I say is that if there were such events, they could not be foreknown or predetermined either by a finite or by an infinite mind.

tally co-ordinate with mind; and this is in fact the position
which, with proper explanation, I shall maintain. What it
means will only become clear when we come to consider
the ultimate nature of matter and its relation to finite minds.
At present, I shall attempt to meet what seems to me to be
a theological prejudice. The traditional doctrine of the
theologians is that God, as Universal Mind, creates matter.
Now, supposing that this is so, yet matter must still be
distinct from, and in some way related to, its creator. For
us, the really important question concerns the nature of
this distinction and relation. The doctrine that matter is
created is important only so far as it may make a difference
in our answer to this question. What difference is it supposed to make? It excludes the possibility that the Universal Mind may be in any way restricted in its activity by
material conditions. What is created, being absolutely
dependent on its creator, cannot impose conditions on
his power. Hence, if God creates matter, its existence can
in no way impair His omnipotence. This we may grant.
The creator of matter must be all-powerful in relation to it.
But the converse does not follow, that a being all-powerful
in relation to matter must be its creator. We have to guard
ourselves against being misled by the analogy of finite
individuals who, owing to their finitude, can only have an
imperfect mastery of the material on which they have to
work. A human being can act on other parts of the material
world only through the medium of his own body, and even
over this his control is extremely partial and imperfect, and
gradually acquired. Matter is not only distinct from his
own being as a conscious individual, but almost entirely
separate and independent. But this does not hold good at
all for the Universal Mind. Though it does not create
matter, yet it may be all-powerful over matter. All that is
required for this is that the material world should be entirely transparent to it as an object of its knowledge, and entirely under its control as a field of its activity. There must
be no possibility within the sphere of material existence

which is hidden from it, or which it cannot realise. Distinctness must not be taken to imply independence or separate being. If these conditions are fulfilled the Universal Mind will be all-powerful in relation to matter, whether it creates matter or not. If it be said that in denying it this power we expressly limit its omnipotence, I reply that this objection begs the question. It presupposes that there is a power of creating matter. But if the existence of matter is primary and underived there is no such power. The ultimate constitution of the universe excludes it. If then there is no such power, it is in no way inconsistent with the omnipotence of the Universal Mind that it should not possess it—any more than it is inconsistent with its omniscience that it should not know what is false or meaningless.

Of course, on the view which I am here taking, it is owing to the Universal Mind that matter bears the character which it has for finite individuals, as conditioning and circumscribing their activity. But this is so, not because it creates matter, but because it creates finite minds.

Chapter XV

BODY AND MIND, AND THE DEPENDENCE OF FINITE INDIVIDUALS ON A UNIVERSAL MIND

1. *The Psychophysical Relation, as ordinarily interpreted, is also a Relation of Matter to Matter*

The key to the ultimate relation of mind and matter is to be found in the relation of the individual mind to its own sensa, and through these to the whole material world of which they are part. But side by side with this there is another distinct kind of connexion, between body and mind, and especially between brain-process and mental process. Does either of these two relations help us to understand the other? It is plain that if we start from the psychophysical relation as primary, the prospect is hopeless. To see this we have only to consider carefully what is meant by the so-called concomitance of mental process and brain-process. We then find that the facts are very inaccurately described. The so-called mental process is taken to include what is not properly mental at all. The sense-presentations of the individual are not properly mental, but rather material; yet in the psychophysical correlation they are regarded as mental occurrences and not as brain occurrences. The obvious reason is that the brain and its processes are considered merely as externally objective phenomena, and sense-presentations do not as such enter into the externally objective order at all.

The psychophysical concomitance is then not merely a relation of matter to mind. It is also a relation of matter to matter—of matter as content of sense-experience to matter as physical phenomenon.[1] We have then to seek

[1] Even if we agree to include sensa in what we call mind, the correlation and co-variation of brain occurrences and mental occurrences cannot of

some explanation of the psychophysical association of body and mind in terms of our general theory of the nature of matter and the way in which it is known to us. Any theory of the nature of matter which fails to give an intelligible account of the psychophysical relation is so far discredited, and is at a decisive disadvantage as compared with a theory which can satisfy the conditions. Let us apply this crucial test to our own view.

2. *The Connexion of Sensa with Brain-Process is a special instance of the Connexion between Matter as Phenomenon and as it is in itself*

On this view our own bodies, as phenomenally known, belong, like other bodies, to the physical order. But phenomenal knowledge is necessarily partial, abstract and schematic. This applies in particular to our knowledge of the brain-occurrences which are supposed to be directly associated with mental occurrences, including as mental the occurrence of sense-presentations. There must be qualities, and there may even be constituents, of the body as it is in itself, which escape us from the phenomenal point of view—the point of view of the biologist, anatomist, and physiologist. On the other hand, we have in our immediately experienced sensa a portion of matter known not as

---

itself yield the knowledge that there is such a thing as a brain: still less can it yield knowledge of any other physical object. The same holds good if we suppose the psychophysical correlation to extend to the material world in general. Mind, including its sensa, would then always accompany physical occurrences and vary concomitantly with them, and perhaps interact with them; but otherwise the two would fall apart, having nothing to do with each other. If this were all, mind would know nothing of matter and, this being so, it is hard to see how it could know anything else—even itself—or how it could exist at all. If then the two relations are to be brought together in any intelligible connexion within the unity of the universe, we must start from the relation of sense-presentations to the external world, and attempt from this point of view to account for the special relation of sense-presentations and processes taking place in the brain.

belonging to the physical order, but intuitively as it is in itself. Further, if we take sense-experience to include not only sense-impressions but their revivals as mental images and the like, there is no evidence for the correlation of mind and brain which is not, at the same time, evidence for the correlation of the content of sense-experience with brain. There is a twofold correspondence. Differences in feeling-attitude and in willing are matched by corresponding differences in the content of sense-experience: and sense-differences are matched by corresponding variations in brain-process. Hence the brain-process and the subjective life of knowledge, feeling and will must also vary together, begin together, and cease together.

3. *The Difficulty presented by the Difference in Nature between Brain-Process and Sensa*

If then we regard the connexion of sense-experience with physical process in the brain as a special instance of the general connexion between matter as phenomenally known and matter as it is in itself, we seem to be able to give a straightforward account of the relevant psychophysical facts. There is, however, what may at first sight appear a very serious difficulty, arising out of the unlikeness between the content of sense-experience and what we know of the brain. Phenomenal knowledge is such because it is only partial, abstract and schematic. We ought then to find only inadequacy in the phenomenal view, not a positive discrepancy of nature between matter as it is in itself and matter as belonging to the physical order. But there seems to be positive discrepancy between brain-process and the concomitant content of sense-experience. Our sensa, for instance, form a presentation-continuum. But we tend to regard the correlated occurrences in the brain as an interplay of discrete atoms and molecules. Such difficulties may appear formidable at first sight. They are, however, by no means insurmountable. We have to bear in mind that we are not concerned with the brain as a whole, but only with those processes which are most directly associated with sense-experience. But, if we inquire what precisely these are, we find ourselves even from the phenomenal point of view very much in the dark. Our knowledge is, indeed, little more than diluted ignorance. We have no right, for instance, to assume that the most direct physical concomitant of sense-experience consists in molecular processes, rather than in connected events going on in the ether, or whatever science may ultimately substitute for the conception of an etherial medium.

Above all, we must not lose sight of another possibility. As I have already pointed out, not only qualities but also partial constituents of matter as it is in itself may escape us in tracing the phenomenal order. This may be so, even though such constituents operate as factors determining the course of physical events. For they may belong to the unexplored background of conditions which we have constantly to take for granted, even though we cannot specify what they are. It seems on the whole the easier view that the content of sense-experience belongs to this unexplored background, and is therefore only indirectly represented in the phenomenal order. It follows that the individual subject as knowing, feeling and willing is still more indirectly represented. He is so only inasmuch as subjective life in its varying phases involves corresponding variations in sense-experience. The same is true if we consider the phenomenal world in general. This corresponds directly not to mind, but to matter as it is in itself. None the less, in certain small parts of the physical order, the phenomena are such as to enable us to recognise the presence of individual minds more or less akin to our own—those of other men and of animals. Finally, as I shall attempt hereafter to show, we have a more indefinite but essentially analogous knowledge of mind in nature generally.

4. *The Genesis of an Individual Subject and its Dependence on a Universal Mind*

If the view which I have expounded is right, it must be completely wrong to regard immediately experienced sensa as produced, so to speak, out of nothing by physical processes either in the brain or elsewhere. Your presentation-continuum or mine comes into being through the transformation of existing matter as it is in itself. It arises as a peculiarly differentiated and complex modification of this. The same process is known in the phenomenal order as the development of a living human brain, and especially as those processes in the brain, or connected with it, which are most directly associated with conscious life and sense-presentations.

The individual subject begins to exist when, and only when, a living body organised in a certain way comes into being. This means that it begins to exist when and only when an appropriate presentation-continuum arises as a special differentiation of the universal presentation-continuum which constitutes the whole material world as it is in itself. The specialised presentation-continuum does not, of course, of itself account for the emergence of the individual self. This presupposes the agency of pre-existing mind and ultimately of the Universal and Eternal Mind, which also, in another aspect of the same activity, controls absolutely the material process whereby the required presentation-continuum comes into being. In like manner we have to account for the continuance and development of the psychical individual, and for the vicissitudes of his life-history, so far as these are determined for him and not by him. Under this head we bring temporary interruptions of conscious life, such as occur more or less completely in sleep and under the action of drugs, and that apparent or real cessation which takes place at death.

5. *Psychophysical Dispositions*

We have to interpret from the same point of view the facts of retentiveness and reproduction and association, and all that is covered by that otherwise mysterious term 'psychophysical disposition'. What happens in the interval between the apparition of a presentation within our immediate experience and its subsequent revival? Dr Ward says that it is still present within the presentation-continuum of the individual, but becomes so faint and indistinct as to be no longer discernible. To me and most psychologists this view seems irreconcilable with the facts: and I cannot but regard it as an unfortunate legacy from the Leibnizian doctrine of the soul as an isolated monad[1]. Yet Leibniz and Ward are clearly right in seeking, if possible, some explanation which will preserve continuity of existence between the first occurrence of a presentation and its subsequent revival after an interval.

From our present point of view the explanation is obvious, and it covers the relevant psychophysical facts. When a presentation ceases to form part of our presentation-continuum, and is yet revivable, it still persists (in however modified a form), or at any rate the conditions of its recurrence persist, within that wider continuum which constitutes the whole world of matter as it is in itself. Further, they persist in that part of it which is the same as, or is intimately connected with, what we know phenomenally as a human brain. But retentiveness includes more than the persistence and possible reinstatement of presentations. It includes—though indeed in a different way—the possible recurrence of knowledge and interest previously acquired. Dispositions are cognitive, conative and affective as well as presentational. This is intelligible only if we take into account the universal correlation of mind and matter, as a duality in unity; the material occurrence is incomplete in

---

[1] [Ward comments: 'I have again and again disavowed the notion of isolated monads, and Leibniz himself did not hold to it consistently'.—Ed.]

itself without the psychical counterpart involved in its essential relation, if not to finite minds, at least to the Universal Mind. The same Eternal Mind, which is the ultimate source and sustainer of our mental life, in another inseparable aspect of its undivided activity penetrates and determines through and through the world of matter as it is in itself, investing it with characters which are otherwise inexplicable. Applying this to the special portion of matter which is known phenomenally as a human brain, we can see how a physiological disposition may be at the same time a psychical disposition. Our psychical being, at any moment of our existence, is in great part only potentially in our possession: it is, so to speak, held in trust for us by our Creator and Preserver. 'About us and around us are the everlasting arms.' The hope of immortality is the hope that, in some way which we need not waste time in guessing, the same support will be continued or renewed after death.[1]

6. *The Transmission Theory of William James*

It will be seen that this view has an essential affinity with the transmission theory of William James in his Ingersoll Lecture, which again meets us, more fully worked out, in the philosophy of Bergson. It may be fairly stated by reference to the lines of Shelley which James himself quotes:

> Life, like a dome of many-coloured glass,
> Stains the white radiance of eternity.

For James the dome of glass is the physical world, which is not distinguished by him from matter as it is in itself. The white radiance of eternity is the Eternal and Universal Mind. The white radiance tends to permeate the dome, and in so doing is variously refracted, and so stains the glass. In

---

[1] It is plain that the facts of mental heredity are capable of being interpreted in much the same way. But this is a topic on which I need not dwell, as I have nothing substantial to add to Dr Ward's most original and admirable treatment in the last chapter but one of his *Psychological Principles*.

like manner, the life of the Universal Mind tends to trans-
mit itself to the physical world, and in doing so gives rise
to those finite streams of consciousness, each with its own
body, known to us as our private selves. Such finite streams
of consciousness in men and animals correspond to the
stains on the glass. But the process of penetration is obstructed by the opaqueness of the medium, the resistance
offered by the material, which varies in different parts.
'Only at particular times and places would it seem that, as
a matter of fact, the veil of nature can grow thin and ruptur-
able enough for such effects to occur. But in those places . . .
glows of feeling, glimpses of insight, and streams of knowledge and perception float into our finite world.'[1] Thus 'the
life of souls as it is in its fulness will brea'. through our
several brains into this world in all sorts of restricted forms,
and with all the imperfections and queernesses that char-
acterize our finite individualities here below.'[2]

On the ultimate relation of the physical world to the
universal psychical life, James is obscure. He seems simply
to set them side by side as mutually foreign and exclusive
realms of being, so that it is hard to see how they can be
originally so connected that the one is capable of tending to
penetrate the other, and being obstructed by the other. But
I do not suppose that this is James's final view. He would
rather, I assume, accept something like Bergson's account
of physical existence as ultimately derivative. According to
Bergson the one absolute psychical life is primarily all that
is. But it consists in a process with two aspects, one by
which it attenuates itself, and takes the form of matter, the
other by which it concentrates itself as mind, yet without
losing its original unity. It is only within this original unity
that the antithesis of matter and mind has being. The
genesis of the finite individual is in principle explained by
him very much as James explains it.

How far does this transmission theory agree with the
result of our previous inquiry? I am, of course, at one with

[1] W. James, *Human Immortality*, 6th ed., p. 35.   [2] *Ibid.* pp. 36–7.

it in denying that brain-process or any material process produces or creates mind. I agree also that finite individuals arise wherever and whenever material conditions adapted to their existence come into being. Nor would I quarrel greatly with the statement that this is due to an influx from the Universal Mind[1]. Here, however, my agreement with James ends. I am bound to reject as a baseless fiction the conception of the Eternal Mind struggling to penetrate an alien and obstructive physical barrier and succeeding only here and there, where the resistance is comparatively feeble. This is quite untenable if we are to represent the relation of the Eternal Mind to the entire material system after the analogy of that of finite minds to their immediately experienced sensa. For, on this view, matter is eternally and completely controlled by mind, and cannot therefore offer obstruction to it. The same Eternal Mind, from which finite minds proceed also, in another aspect of the same individual activity moulds for them the presentation-continuum which they need for their existence and development.

7. *Extent and Limits of our Knowledge of the Universal Mind*

It will have puzzled and perhaps even shocked some of my readers that I have ascribed sense-experience to the Universal Mind, i.e. to God. If I am asked how this can be, I simply answer that I do not know, and that from the nature of the case neither I nor any finite being can know. But I should make the same answer if I were asked in what way the Universal Mind knows and wills. My position is that of the agnosticism of the great schoolmen which I attempted to define and defend in the second chapter. This does not imply that we do not know what is meant by

[1] The language is indeed metaphorical and inadequate: but no language can be found that is adequate, and metaphor is very difficult to avoid.

the words 'infinite' or 'self-complete'. So much we must understand. Otherwise we should not know what is meant by the words 'finite' or 'essentially incomplete'. Nor is it implied that we are debarred from ascribing positive features and characters to the self-complete Eternal Being as such. On the contrary, we must ascribe to it such features of finite beings as do not depend on their finitude. The principle is that limitation presupposes and therefore cannot constitute that which is limited. But it is just in the act of attributing these ultimate characters to the self-complete being, that the agnosticism of the schoolmen is unavoidable, if we are to escape a bottomless abyss of nonsense. For, being ourselves finite, we cannot positively realise in thought or imagination in what way the self-complete being possesses these characters. In the language of the schoolmen, God as He is in Himself is for us incomprehensible. Our knowledge, then, is in this respect essentially inadequate. But it need not therefore be essentially fallacious. It is fallacious only if and so far as we fail to recognise its inadequacy and treat it as if it were adequate. This, however, is not necessary. In attempting to realise, in thought or imagination, the positive nature of infinite being, we cannot avoid investing it with characters which can belong only to the finite as such. But we can also recognise, on critical reflexion, that if and so far as we do this, we think of it wrongly, and we are also clearly aware of the source, nature and direction of the error. It is thus possible to allow for and discount this natural 'fallacy' of finite thinking. By safeguarding ourselves in this way, we may reach a knowledge of the Infinite Being which, though profoundly inadequate, is not for our purpose essentially misleading. We may reach relatively valid ways of representing it from our own point of view. This is what Locke calls 'the extent of our tether'. As he puts it: 'If we can find out those measures whereby a rational creature, put in that state which man is in in this world, may and ought to govern his opinions, and actions depending thereon, we need not to be troubled that some other things escape our knowledge.'[1]

What I say then is that the relation of the Eternal Mind to matter may be validly represented from our finite point of view through the analogy of the relation of finite individuals to their own immediately experienced sensa. But the representation is valid only so far as we set aside whatever belongs to the limitations of sense-experience in ourselves. We must set aside as irrelevant and misleading the psychophysical relation of mind and body, and anything in the nature of an environment. Evidently, too, physical phenomena cannot exist for the Universal Mind except as they are known to exist for finite minds. Again, the material world as represented to the Eternal Individual Mind must have an internal unity and completeness, incomprehensible to us. Are we also to say that the Eternal Mind creates matter? Of course, in creating finite minds, it *ipso facto* creates their phenomenal point of view; and in this sense it may be said to create the physical world. But does it create matter as it is in itself? I certainly would not venture to deny that this is so. But I confess that I see no need for asserting it, and, as I have already argued,[2] it is not, so far as I can see, a demand of the religious consciousness. For religion it is sufficient that God should be complete master of matter—that He should not be in any way conditioned or restricted by it as a factor foreign or external to His own being. Granting this, it makes no essential difference whether He is supposed to create it or not.

We have now concluded our inquiry into the relation of mind and matter so far as this can be pursued by considering the nature of matter and the way in which we know it. We have to take up the same inquiry anew from another side, that of the nature of mind and the way in which we know it.

[1] *Essay Concerning Human Understanding*, Book 1, introduction, section 6.
[2] See Section 7 of the previous chapter.

BOOK FIVE

MIND AND OUR KNOWLEDGE OF IT

▼

Chapter XVI

OUR KNOWLEDGE OF OURSELVES, OTHER MINDS AND GOD[1]

1. *The Self's Awareness of itself*

I shall first briefly indicate my position on the question how the self is aware of itself. The self is known neither by acquaintance nor by inference. It is known in knowing subjective states as essentially incomplete. The being pleased with something, or desiring something, can neither be nor be known except as a phase in the life-history of a subject.

---

[1] [This chapter originally formed the last lecture of the Second Course. In transposing it to its present position I am guided in part by some anticipatory sentences which I have omitted from the end of the last chapter, in which the lecturer indicated to his audience what was to come. These show that the present lecture (or chapter) was not originally intended to come at the end. They are as follows: 'First I shall say something about the individual subject. Next I shall consider the nature and extent of the knowledge which the individual has of mind other than his own. This will lead to such topics as the teleological order of nature and the implications of moral and religious consciousness. Finally I shall briefly touch on the problems connected with the existence of evil and the destiny of the finite individual after the death of the body.' This programme did not work out, because the argument which begins with the discussion of cognitive unity in the next chapter developed itself in the writing in such a way as to lead without a break to the treatment of evil and immortality in the penultimate lecture, now the last chapter of this volume. The discussion of our knowledge of 'mind other than our own', including the divine mind, had therefore to be left to the last lecture; and this no doubt accounts for the very scanty treatment, at its beginning, of the self's knowledge of itself. I believe that if the lectures had been finally revised for publication this chapter would not have been left to the end, where it looks like an afterthought.—Ed.]

Subjective states themselves are known by acquaintance and memory in intimate and inseparable union. It has indeed been denied that we can know them by acquaintance, on the ground that they are not sense-presentations. Without stopping to discuss this view, it is sufficient to point out that at any rate they are not known by inference, and that the knowledge of them essentially depends on their being immediately experienced.

Awareness of the self and its states seems to be always present through the whole course of mental life. But it is nearly always more or less confused. It is only at an advanced stage of critical reflexion that we explicitly distinguish the self as subject from all that does not properly belong to its being. The awareness of feeling and conation is at first included without discrimination in the awareness of situations as agreeable or disagreeable, and of actions as successful or unsuccessful. Even when the self is distinguished as a unique existence from other things, it is not usually distinguished from its own body as inwardly apprehended through organic and motor sensa. At the perceptual level the embodied self is the whole body, as the instrument of perception and motor activity. As trains of ideas take the place of perceptions and arouse emotions and desires disconnected from the immediately present situation, the embodied self is withdrawn inward and is vaguely localised in the region of the midriff or heart. With conceptual thinking it comes to be identified with the head. Finally it is expressly distinguished as subject from its own body, as from all other bodies. In all these stages and phases, and not only in the last, we are, I hold, really aware of the self as a knowing, feeling and willing subject. The embodied self really is a self as well as embodied. And in knowing it we know the self as well as its embodiment, even though we do not recognise the distinction between them. I take it that Ferrier is right when he says that along with whatever else any subject knows it has some cognisance of self.

2. *Knowledge of other Minds is not reached by Inference but is involved in Self-awareness*[1]

Each individual knows himself only inasmuch as he immediately experiences his own subjective states and activities. In what way does he know minds other than his own, whose subjective states he does not immediately experience?

A common view is that the individual, knowing himself and his own bodily behaviour, comes to know others merely by inference from their bodily behaviour. Certain external bodies are more or less like his own and behave in distinctive ways as his own would have behaved under like circumstances. Hence he infers that they are actuated by a subjective life akin to his own. They are for him embodied selves even as he is an embodied self. I hear, for instance,

[1] [The later treatment in *Mind and Matter* (pp. 303–7) of the question how we come to know other minds may at first sight seem inconsistent with the argument of this chapter, but there is in fact no fundamental change of position. In *Mind and Matter* inference by analogy from bodily behaviour is rejected on the same general grounds as here. But the knowledge that one mind has of another is none the less explicitly said to be 'inferential, not immediate', the inference being based on responsive behaviour; whereas in the present chapter both kinds of inference are rejected as inadequate by themselves to account for this knowledge, and we read that: 'Whether emphasis is laid on responsiveness or on analogy, the fundamental position is logically the same.' The apparent inconsistency disappears when we realise that the treatment in *Mind and Matter* presupposes, as already established earlier in the book, the contention that 'the experiencing individual immediately knows external objects as continuous in existence with his own being, and therefore as fundamentally akin in their general nature to it, both in its bodily and in its mental aspect' (p. 306). Thus, to use the language of the present chapter, the individual making the inference is *not* 'initially cognisant merely of his own mental life, without any sort of reference, however vague and tentative, to any psychical existence beyond his own,' nor are the facts from which he draws it, 'as initially known, purely and entirely physical'. The existence of such psychical existence being taken as known, the part played by inference from responsive behaviour, taken in conjunction with the intersubjective intercourse to which it leads, is to establish that in special cases 'it takes the form of an individual mind, such as ours'.—Ed.]

a cry such as I myself might have uttered had I been in pain, and I infer that it comes from someone who is feeling a pain which I do not feel. Or, I perceive an external object resembling my own body turn pale and tremble, and I know by inference that it is the body of someone who is feeling afraid.

Again, the externally objective clues may on this view determine the inference, not so much by likeness to our own behaviour, as by what has been called responsiveness. This means that certain external objects move in a way which is distinctively and obtrusively relevant to our own life. I clasp a hand and the pressure is returned. The child is hungry, and the nurse feeds it; drops its rattle, and the nurse restores the rattle to its hand.

Whether emphasis is laid on responsiveness or on analogy, the fundamental position is logically the same. The individual is supposed to be initially cognisant merely of his own mental life, without any sort of reference, however vague and tentative, to any psychical existence, actual or possible, beyond his own. The existence and nature of other minds is supposed to be gathered by inference from certain facts which, as initially known, are purely and entirely physical. Further, these physical facts are known only by external perception, not at all as we know our own bodies internally, through motor and organic sensations. They lack, therefore, just those features through which our own bodies are most intimately connected with our own subjective life of emotion and active striving.

Now, even if this is supposed to be our original position, it is plainly not so now. On the contrary, it is now impossible to realise it in imagination. We are indeed constantly inferring the existence of other minds and their thoughts and feelings and emotions; and ultimately we can interpret these external clues only because we are ourselves knowing, willing and feeling minds. But in so proceeding we never start solely from knowledge of ourselves, without any kind of reference to psychical being other than our own. On the contrary, we constantly presuppose that there are other minds, and are thus prepared to look for and recognise signs and tokens of their presence. Our self-awareness is always awareness of the self in distinction from and relation to other selves. It is from self-awareness of this kind that we start, in inferring from external clues the existence of this or that mind other than our own.

Is this reference to minds other than our own due primarily to inferences through which we have previously discovered that other minds exist? Or, on the contrary, does self-awareness originally and essentially, just because it is self-awareness, involve reference to psychical existence other than the self, as the indispensable basis and presupposition of all detailed inferences by which we learn what special forms of psychical life are actually to be found in connexion with the special behaviour of special bodies? The second alternative seems to me to be clearly the right one. Just as the primary demand for causal connexion is founded on the essential incompleteness of temporal occurrences, which require to be supplemented by their causal conditions and consequences, so there is a primary demand for psychical existence beyond the self, founded on the essential incompleteness of the finite individual. And just as special causal connexions between this and that occurrence are inductively inferred from special clues, so it is by inference that we gain specific knowledge of this or that individual mind and of its states and activities.

3. *An Individual cognisant only of himself could not even think of Psychical Life other than his own*

My first ground for holding this view is this: if we suppose an individual who is cognisant only of himself, it is hard to see how even the thought of any psychical life other than his own could in the first instance occur to him. But if he has not even the thought, he cannot use it to interpret and explain the behaviour of external bodies. The question whether there is mind other than his own cannot be answered because it cannot be asked. To understand the point of this argument it is necessary to take quite rigorously the assumption that the individual begins by being cognisant only of his own psychical existence. We must not suppose him to be in any way aware that it is only himself that he knows. For the words 'only myself' already presuppose a reference to other selves. Again, we ought not to think of him as a solipsist. For a solipsist is one who doubts or denies the existence of others. But our supposed individual is as incapable of doubting or denying this as he is of asserting it.

What then must be his attitude towards the external phenomena which to us mean the presence of another mind? He could and would merely recognise the facts as he found them. Hearing a scream proceeding from a body which is not his, he would recognise that it is such as has been produced by his own body when pain was felt. He must also infer that if his own body were now producing it, there would be an accompanying pain. But as it is not his own body that is concerned, he has no reason to believe that any pain is felt. It will be said that this is an unnatural position. I agree. But it is so because the assumption we started with is unnatural—the assumption that the individual primarily knows only his own subjective life, as if this were after its kind self-existent and self-complete.

This argument, if it stood alone, might be too abstract and speculative to justify us in placing entire confidence in it. But it does not stand alone. It is supplemented and confirmed by all that we know about the actual development of knowledge in this direction. If there were no primary and universal ground and motive for presuming the presence of psychical life expressing itself in external phenomena; if, on the contrary, even the thought of minds other than our own were originally strange and alien, so that it had initially to be somehow obtruded on us by the exceptional behaviour of certain peculiar bodies—those of our fellow-men and of animals—if, I say, this were so, then initially only men and animals would appear as embodied selves. Further, if any attempt were made to extend by analogy a similar view to other parts of nature, it would be only tentative and provisional, and would soon break down when found to be useless for practical purposes.

4. *Primitive Animism*

Now if we turn to the facts, we find them to be quite otherwise. In primitive stages of culture we find the presence and operation of psychical agents, more or less definitely akin to human beings, recognised throughout nature. Rocks, mountains, trees, rivers, thunder and lightning, the sun, moon and stars are regarded as actuated by psychical individuals within them or behind them. For the savage, the world is mostly worked by personal or quasi-personal beings, with an inner nature or character analogous to his own, acting on impulses and motives like his own, and liable like himself to be moved by appeals to their pity, their fears and their hopes. In general, wherever the primitive man finds his own subjective being stirred and quickened by the presence of external objects, so that they are for him distinct centres of interest and emotion, he invests them with an individual psychical life answering to his own.

This primitive view of nature has indeed been profoundly modified—in part restricted and in part transformed—by the subsequent development of knowledge. But the primary tendency to find in the world in general a psychical life in some way answering to our own has never been in principle eradicated. We do not indeed personify things so as to attribute to them feelings and desires, such as we experience. None the less, we do not in ordinary life perceive and imagine them merely as parcels of matter, distinguished by us from the rest merely for our own convenience. On the contrary, we apprehend them as having a distinctive individual unity of their own, analogous to that of our own embodied selves. This propensity to individualise even inanimate objects is strongest and most definite where our interests are most strongly concentrated on them. Thus the sailor's attitude towards his ship approximates to actual personification; the same may be said of the golfer who in a moment of excitement calls to his golf ball to stop when it is going too far. But these are only extreme instances of our proneness to ascribe to material things an individual being which does not belong to them considered merely as bits of matter. In thus individualising things we also inevitably treat them as active and passive in a way fundamentally akin to that in which we, as embodied selves, are active and passive. We refer their external behaviour to active tendencies belonging to their inner nature. This is implied in the ordinary use of active verbs: the waves dash themselves against the rocks; the mine explodes and spreads havoc; the wind uproots trees and drives the clouds before it.

5. Animism in Philosophy and Science

This view of nature is not confined to pre-scientific and unscientific thought. It is also conspicuous in the history of philosophy and science. Why does an unsupported stone fall to the ground? Aristotle says that the natural place of the stone is the centre of the material universe, and that therefore it actually tends to seek the centre. When we lift it from the ground we are doing violence to its inner nature, a violence against which it struggles. If we turn from Aristotle to Newton, we are told that the earth exerts a force whereby it attracts the stone to it. This view is still plainly anthropomorphic. The action of the earth is conceived on the analogy of our own activity in pulling or drawing things towards us. Coming down to our own times, we find men of science making a deliberate effort to banish all traces of anthropomorphism from their conception of natural processes, and to regard them as merely material. Whatever the justification for this position, I would here remark only: (1) that the very protest against anthropomorphism presupposes a natural propensity towards it; and (2) that any man of science, when actually confronted with such an event as a tree's being blown down by a violent gale, would, like other people, perceive it as a conflict of opposing forces.

6. *The 'Primary Demand' points to Psychical Life beyond the range of Human and Animal Organisms*

I have stated two arguments, but they must not be taken apart from each other. The second, and others like it which I have not time to bring forward, must be regarded merely as supplementing the first. According to the first, no external clues or indications would lead the individual even to think of psychical life beyond his own, were he not primarily prepared to seek it by the essential incompleteness of his own. The second argument, and others of the same type, merely furnish empirical confirmation of this position by showing that the actual course of the development of the knowledge of other minds is such as we have a right to expect if it is valid.

We start then with the thesis that just as our knowledge of a physical world is primarily grounded in the essential incompleteness of the immediate content of sense-experience, and just as our knowledge of causal relations is primarily grounded in the essential incompleteness of temporal occurrence, so all our knowledge of subjective life beyond our own is primarily grounded in the essential incompleteness of our own subjective being, which requires to be supplemented by a psychical life other than itself.

From this principle two important corollaries flow. In the first place, the primary demand is in no way invalidated by errors of detail in the attempt to satisfy its requirements. It is no more invalidated than the primary demand for causal order is invalidated by the countless blunders which have been made and will be made concerning special causal relations between special occurrences. In the second place, it is only the primary demand itself that can ultimately determine what clues and indications shall be taken as evidence of the presence of the psychical life, or what relative value they shall have. It is therefore arbitrary to prescribe in advance of experience what clues will or ought to appeal to us. In particular, we have no right in this way to limit the range of psychical life in the universe so as to connect it only with bodies presenting special analogies in their structure and behaviour to our own—with human and animal organisms. Such specific analogies are no doubt required to justify the inference to the existence of minds which in their specific nature, conditions and limitations are like our own. The natural precipitancy of savage thought fails to take account of this logical condition, and so falls into the fallacies of a crude anthropomorphism, personifying rocks, streams, trees, etc.—fallacies which advancing knowledge gradually arrests, but never wholly eradicates. But it by no means follows that the primary tendency to posit psychical life in the universe beyond the range of human and animal organisms is fundamentally misleading. Stripped of anthropomorphic fallacy, and so logically corrected, it may still be valid.

7. Aesthetic Animism

Let us consider it in the two forms in which it has maintained itself even in the most advanced stages of human thought. These are involved in the aesthetic and in the religious attitude to nature. Aesthetic appreciation and enjoyment, and the general view of the world which pervades them and makes them possible, are, if not logically incompatible with the abstractly scientific way of thinking, at least sentimentally opposed to it. The antagonism finds typical expression in Wordsworth's line: 'I need not proud philosophy to tell me what thou art.' The poet, confronting nature in its concrete fullness, finds his own subjective life stirred and quickened in a way which requires as the counterpart of his own emotional attitude a corresponding psychical life within or actuating natural objects and processes. Hence he cannot have or maintain his own aesthetic feeling without apprehending them as animated by some analogue of his own subjective life. This is not confined to poetry. The same principle is involved in the aesthetic feeling for the spring or sweep of a curve, or the grace and ease with which a column supports a superincumbent weight.

It will be said that this aesthetic attitude cannot ultimately be taken seriously. It is merely a make-believe, a play of imagination. Tennyson does not really believe that his brook is an embodied self. He only thinks of it as if it were so. Now I fully admit that in detail the aesthetic interpretation of nature as animated by mind is in the main a play of imagination. But I cannot admit, and it would be suicidal for the poet or artist himself to admit, that it is *mere* play. The aesthetic imagination cannot sustain itself, and cannot maintain its claim to be a fundamentally important form of human activity, unless it presupposes its fiction to be rooted and grounded in the real being of things. It is rooted and grounded on the assumption that matter is not merely matter, but is in some way, however mysterious, correlated with what essentially partakes of the nature of mind. This underlying assumption becomes explicit in the philosophical poets, who approach from the aesthetic point of view the problem of the constitution of the universe as a whole. When Wordsworth speaks of

> ...something far more deeply interfused,
> Whose dwelling is the light of setting suns,
> And the round ocean and the living air,

he is expressing an intense and profound conviction, having its source in direct insight, inseparable from his aesthetic feelings. He is not merely indulging in a play of imagination.

8. *Philosophy and Religious Experience*

At this stage the poet ceases to be merely a poet and stands on the threshold of religious experience, if he has not already crossed it. Religious experience is an emotional and conative attitude towards the whole of being, which is groundless and irrational unless a psychical life answering to it, as its appropriate object, really pervades and controls the universe, including the individual who feels it. Such an attitude differs profoundly from the merely aesthetic, inasmuch as in its full development it involves the entire nature of man, aesthetic, theoretic and practical—his entire outlook on the whole of which he is a member. Now those who have this religious experience find it a ground for believing in the reality of its object; a ground which cannot be stated in any formal argument, and cannot therefore be communicated to one who does not sufficiently share in the experience itself which is its source. The belief thus arising may indeed be disturbed and even, it may be, upset by difficulties and objections. But apart from such counter-motives, the religious experience carries conviction in proportion as it is intense, comprehensive and persistent. In it is to be sought the most important ground which has actually led mankind to believe in God.

What has the philosopher to say concerning the validity of this ground? Let us be clear on one point from the outset. We cannot translate the evidence of the religious experience into any formal argument without missing precisely what gives it its distinctive cogency. We cannot, for instance, argue that because men feel in a certain way therefore there is a God. If the religious experience is really cogent, its peculiar cogency can be appreciated only in actually experiencing it, not in any external description or definition of it.

On the other hand, there is a question which the philosopher can and ought to regard as falling within his own province—the question whether, on critical reflexion, we can find good reasons for regarding this sort of evidence as fallacious. If there are no such reasons—if, on the contrary, we find reason for regarding it as a sort of evidence which may be or ought to be cogent—then it is unchallenged, and there is no ground for rejecting it as invalid.

Now, all that is urged on the negative side seems to involve a misunderstanding of the conditions of the problem. The main contention is that we are here dealing with a survival of the primitive anthropomorphism which has been already discredited by advancing knowledge. We have seen that wherever the anthropomorphic fallacy is found it arises from a natural precipitancy, which leads us to infer the existence of minds resembling our own in connexion with bodies which are not sufficiently similar in their structure and behaviour to justify the supposed mental likeness. A fallacy of this kind has, of course, played a large part in determining the special forms of religious belief, and even now perhaps it is difficult to free ourselves from it entirely. But it has also played a large part in human development generally, and even in the history of science. Even the man of science, in dealing with such conditions as that of force, thinks it necessary to protest against anthropomorphism. But, just as crude anthropomorphism is irreconcilable with fully developed science, so it is irreconcilable with the highest forms of religious experience. The highest forms of religious experience include a boundless awe and reverence, and a sense of unfathomable mystery, which demand for their object a Being entirely transcending the conditions and limitations of any conceivable finite individual.

What ground then can be found in religious experience for regarding this Being as a mind at all? There can be none which is not absurdly inadequate, if we regard the ultimate ground as merely an inference from a supposed analogy between the constitution and behaviour of our own embodied selves and the constitution and course of nature. But, as I have tried to show, inference of this type cannot, in the long run, adequately account for the knowledge of any psychical existence beyond our own. It can only serve to determine how far we are justified in assuming other minds to be like our own in their specific nature, conditions and limitations. Apart from such special questions, the ultimate ground for our knowledge of other minds is not to be found in any inference. It lies in the essential incompleteness of our existence. If this be so, the primary demand arising from the incompleteness of the self can alone prescribe what is required to satisfy it. It does so in religious experience.

It is also possible to state a formal argument. The demand for psychical life beyond our own is founded on the essential incompleteness of the finite individual as such. It cannot therefore be met by positing the existence of any finite individual or group of finite selves. For however far we go in this direction the essential incompleteness still remains. We can rest only in the conception of a Universal and Eternal Mind. Granting the principle that all knowledge of minds beyond our own is grounded on the essential incompleteness of the self, this reasoning seems to be valid. The main reason for distrusting it is that it is too abstract and speculative to carry practical conviction. But its value is greatly enhanced if we consider its bearing on religious experience. The question will then be whether critical analysis supplies reasons for regarding the belief which has its source in religious experience as fallacious or as valid. I have already pointed out that the reasons for which it is often condemned as misleading will not bear examination. It is not, as is hastily supposed, an obstinate survival of primitive anthropomorphism. To this I have now to add that the formal argument I have just stated enables us to see both how the belief based on religious experience may be valid, and why on abstract grounds it ought to be valid. The formal argument is, if you like, dry bones; but clothed in the flesh and blood of concrete religious experience these dry bones live.

9. *Restatement of the Argument from Design*

It is from the same point of view, the essential incompleteness of the individual self as such, that we have to consider
what used to be called the argument for the existence of
a God from the evidence of a design in nature. In its traditional form this argument is conceived as based on the
analogy between the artificial products of human contrivance and certain natural phenomena—e.g. between a tele-
scope and the human eye, or between a watch and the solar
system. So regarded the reasoning is open to the charge
of crude anthropomorphism. The question is whether it
can be otherwise stated, so as to exclude fallacy of this
sort.

Now it is at any rate plain that there is found in nature
a certain peculiar order, which for want of a better word we
must call teleological. What is the distinctive nature of this
order? We may be tempted to answer that it is such as to
suggest mind as its source. But it will clear the ground for
further discussion if, at the outset, we can find some distinctive description of it which does not include a reference
to psychical life. Negatively, we may say that the teleological order does not consist merely in conformity to general
laws of causation. All nature is equally conformable to
causal law, shot rubbish as much as the living brain of
a man. But teleological order is found in very varying degrees of complexity and perfection—in a very high degree
in the living brain, hardly at all in the shot rubbish. Positively, we may say that the teleological order is a systematic
order of and in the concrete complexity of particular things
and processes. There is teleological order in a watch, not
merely because its parts interact in accordance with the laws
of mechanics, but especially and distinctively because these
parts are combined, shaped, and coadjusted in a systematic arrangement, so as to make the hands on the dial
move in a certain uniform and systematic way. Every
effect, it is true, is traceable to a complex of conditions

grouped in a certain manner. But there is a teleological order only if and so far as there is system in the grouping.

Between a piece of mechanism such as a watch and a living body there is an immense difference. To name only one, we can hardly conceive a living body to be externally put together and taken to pieces. None the less, the general nature of teleological order is, in principle, the same for both. Whatever the laws to which vital phenomena conform, whether or not these are merely physical or chemical, at any rate the teleological constitution of living matter does not consist in mere conformity to general laws. It consists in a concrete complexity of partial factors and processes so interdependent, co-ordinated and intermingled as to keep going the whole process of life within each organism and from generation to generation. Coming to so-called inorganic matter, we find here also the same sort of systematic order, though in less complexity. We find for instance the beautifully teleological order of chemical combinations and reactions, reaching its culmination in the chemistry of carbon compounds.

Note next that it is in general a mistake to regard any given teleological complex as existing in self-contained isolation, rather than as part of a more comprehensive system. The life of an organism, for instance, is not something independently going on within the organism itself. Rather it is an immensely complex and systematic transaction perpetually taking place between the living body and its environment. Hence it must be conceived as only part of a concrete teleological arrangement, essentially including the system of surrounding conditions within which it has its being and which alone make it possible.

This applies also to the regress in time to the antecedent conditions on which the genesis of teleological systems depends. If we inquire into the origin of the living body of a man, we trace it back to the living bodies of other human beings. If we ask how human bodies first arose, we are referred to earlier forms of organic life, through a long

series of transitions, until we reach forms which are regarded as primordial. But even primordial types of life consist
in an immensely complex system of correlated factors and
processes. Indeed Professor Bateson has been led by experimental evidence seriously to raise the question whether
primordial forms of protoplasm are really more simple than
the developed forms, or whether, on the contrary, they
have not a complex constitution exceeding that of the most
advanced product of evolution.

If we press the question of origin further and inquire how
living matter came into being, there are two possible
answers. One is that there has always been living matter,
and that life has always been derived from pre-existing life
—a very difficult position to maintain. The other is that life
has its beginning in inanimate matter. But if we adopt this
last alternative, we are bound to assume that the antecedent
conditions formed a complex system of factors and processes, such and so coadjusted as to account for the systematic complexity of the living matter derived from them.
We have a hint of the sort of prearrangement required in
the structure and behaviour of colloid substances. However far we go back, the same principle seems to hold good.
Existing teleological arrangements presuppose prior teleological arrangements adapted to account for them.

Having explained what I mean by the teleological order
of nature, I have next to consider its relation to mind.
There is an original tendency to regard it as evidence of the
presence of psychical life in nature. Is this tendency essentially misleading? For reasons already given, we must not
attempt to justify it by any supposed special analogies
between the external products of human intelligence and
will and certain natural phenomena. But there is another
line of argument which seems to me sound. Let us begin
by asking why the behaviour of our bodies, as actuated by
our minds, and the external products of human will and
intelligence have, as such, a teleological order at all. There
can be but one answer to this question; the external ex-

pressions of human will and intelligence have, as such, a teleological order only because of prior teleological order in the mind itself. The systematic coadjustment of the parts of a watch is traceable to a corresponding order in the mental processes of the watch-maker who understands the plan of it, and who in making it guides himself in accordance with the plan. The same holds of the contrivance of means to ends on the part of the inventor of watches. Similarly, the teleological order of a printed copy of Newton's *Principia* or Shakespeare's *Sonnets* presupposes a teleological order in the working of the minds of Shakespeare and Newton. In general, the unity of the individual mind-complex is constituted by unity of interest and knowledge, and wherever such unity is present in any degree, in that degree there is teleological order. This is the first step in my argument.

The second is that the individual mind as a teleological complex cannot exist in isolation; it has its being only as part of a wider teleological system. This includes, first of all, the immensely complex organism of the living body, which makes possible the mental life of men and animals. It includes also the whole antecedent series of concrete pre-arrangements through which the living body came into being, stretching backward to the primordial forms of life, and beyond these to the systematic complex of conditions required for their origin, and so on indefinitely. Thus if we are asked to account for the teleological order of a watch, in referring to the mind of the watch-maker we are only assigning one partial factor, which can neither exist nor operate except in teleological union with an immensely complex and extensive group of conditions, traceable backward in time to a period before there was life on the earth, and even before the earth or solar system came into being. This system is a whole, and we are bound to treat it as such. We must not account on one principle for teleological order in mind and the external results of mental activity as such, and on another radically different principle for teleological order in the material world in general. Approaching the question in this way, there are two and only two alternatives. One is to follow our natural and original tendency to treat teleological order in general as evidence of the special presence of mind. The other is to regard teleological order as belonging primarily to matter, and only derivatively to mind. This second view presupposes that individual minds are somehow generated by merely material conditions, and that it is to the systematic correlation and co-adjustment of these conditions that such correlation and co-adjustment as we find in mental life, e.g. in your thought and mine at this moment, are entirely due.

Now I have argued in [*Mind and Matter*][1] that mind cannot be the outcome of merely material conditions or of anything that is not already mind. But this belongs to another distinct line of reasoning. The point I now wish to emphasise is this: that teleological order belongs to mind by its own intrinsic nature, and that it does not belong to mere matter by its own intrinsic nature. The psychical life of the feeling, striving and knowing individual essentially involves some degree of unity of knowledge and interest, and an intrinsic tendency to the further development of such unity. But where there is unity of knowledge and interest there is already teleological order. On the other hand, the constituent particles of the material world might conceivably have been grouped in an endless multiplicity of alternative ways without presenting such teleological order as we find—i.e. a teleological order which includes and makes possible the psychical life of human beings, their intercourse with each other and the products of their activity such as pictures, poems, churches and telephones. It is accidental to the nature of matter as such, however completely it may obey causal law, that its parts should be combined and interrelated in this way; and as a mere question of chance the odds are immeasurably against it. There is, therefore, at least a strong presumption in favour of the

[1] [Typescript: 'my previous course of lectures.'—Ed.]

first alternative, that the teleological order of nature in general has its source in mind.

The presumption is at least strong enough to give some importance to this line of argument as a relatively independent contribution to the manifold grounds for assuming a Universal Mind, which by their convergence mutually support each other, and which have a concrete focus in the higher forms of religious experience.

Chapter XVII

COGNITIVE UNITY AS IMPLYING THE UNITY OF THE UNIVERSE

1. *The Unity of the Mind-Complex*

A material thing contains parts which are themselves material things in the same sense as the whole to which they belong, and as such retain their identity when separated from the whole. The fragments of a broken cup, for instance, pre-existed as parts of the unbroken cup, and continue to exist as distinct parcels of matter when the cup has been shivered. But mind does not contain other minds as its parts. It has therefore a peculiar unity which does not and cannot belong to matter. Just in so far as a mind has this peculiar unity, it is what we call an individual self. It is not divisible into other units of the same sort.[1]

What is implied in this unity? It is clear that whatever else it implies, it at least involves the interconnexion of different cognitions, feelings and conations with each other as entering into a complex unity of an altogether unique kind. But it may also be held, and is very frequently taken for granted, that as the indispensable condition of this complex unity there must also be a simple being, distinct from it and all its various cognitions, feelings and conations, which serves to connect them with each other. This simple being itself is known only through a 'that-which' definition. It is 'that which' owns, and in owning connects, the various modes and phases of knowledge and interest. So conceived, it is called the 'pure subject' or 'transcendental self', and is contrasted with the empirical or historical self—the more

---

[1] In what is known as the dissociation of the personality, relatively new and distinct individuals do indeed emerge; but they do not pre-exist as parts of the original personality. Properly speaking, it is only psychophysical dispositions which are so dissociated from each other. (See Chapter xx.)

or less unified complex which passes through various vicis-situdes in the life of the individual. A distinction of this sort is not due merely to the subtlety of metaphysicians, but is found in a vague form in our ordinary uncritical thought. We naturally tend to represent the mind as if it were a circle or sphere, the circumference corresponding to the objects minded by it, the radii to its various ways of mind-ing them, and the punctual simplicity of the centre to the pure subject. Some such diagrammatic representation is for the practical purposes of ordinary daily life highly con-venient, and for these purposes not seriously misleading. But we must not precipitately translate it into a hard and fast metaphysical theory.

Whether there is a pure subject or not, at any rate there is a complex mental life—a mind-complex; and we are justi-fied in asserting the existence of a pure subject only if the complex unity of the mental life can be shown to presuppose it as an indispensable condition. We must then analyse the mind-complex, so as to determine wherein its unity con-sists, and also what is and is not included in the unity of the manifold.

We have first to note that there are two sides to our mental life, distinct though inseparable, which are broadly distinguishable as (1) knowledge of objects, and (2) in-terest in them. In discussing the unity of the mind-complex, it is necessary for the sake of clearness to deal first with cognitive unity and then with unity of interest. (For reasons which will appear as we proceed, it would be impossible to reverse this order.)

2. *Cognitive Unity and its Objective Correlate*

What is unity of knowledge? If we consider this question just as it stands, and do not mix it with others arising out of it, the answer is simple and direct. Unity of knowledge is identical with knowledge of unity. It is actually or poten-tially present if and so far as items in any way diverse are or can be known or thought of as in any way connected or related, or as partial features or aspects of any kind of whole. Suppose that a sound is perceived and then another sound after it; if the second is apprehended as succeeding the first, or louder than the first, or different from the first, or otherwise related to it, to this extent both are known in one undivided knowledge. If such relations are not actually known or thought of, yet, in so far as it is possible that they may be so, the cognitive unity is potential. On the other hand, where distinct items are severally apprehended but without any cognisance, actual or potential, of relation between them, there is no cognitive unity. This happens, for instance, when of two successive sounds, one is known only to A and the other only to B. When this is so, there cannot be any known relation between them either in the mind of A or in that of B. It is just discontinuities of this sort which constitute A and B distinct cognitive individuals.

Assuming that this analysis is correct as far as it goes, it is yet in one respect fundamentally inadequate. It fails to account for cognitive unity, actual or potential, as coextensive with the unity of the individual 'I' or 'self'. For anything we have hitherto said, it might occur, so to speak, in patches isolated from each other, according as objects happened to present themselves each with an internal unity of its own, but self-complete in detachment from the others. We have, then, still to account for cognitive unity as necessarily pervading and connecting, potentially or actually, all stages and phases in the life-history of an individual mind. In other words, we have to account for the motive which has led, rightly or wrongly, to the theory of a pure subject.

We can do this only in one way. There must be for the knowing individual one all-inclusive object, comprehending all other objects—whether particular or universal, actual, possible or impossible—as its partial and essentially incomplete features and aspects. This means that the unity of the cognitive self, if it is not an illusion, implies as its indispensable correlate the unity of the universe.

It follows that whatever else the individual knows he must in some measure and degree, however rudimentary, be cognisant of the universe in its unity. But how? In very different ways and degrees, varying with the special conditions of individual existence and stages of mental development: different for us, at the level of the present philosophical discussion, and for the cat watching a mouse-hole. Yet the cat's knowledge, just as much as ours, presupposes [1] the unity of the universe: otherwise it could never go beyond the content of its own immediate experience, and could not even know this. What we require is a general view applying to all stages of mental development—to animals as well as to human beings.

3. *Cognitive Unity includes Ignorance*

The first and most important step is to recognise that cognitive unity includes not only what is commonly called knowledge, but also what is commonly called ignorance. This would be impossible if the ignorance consisted in the absolute absence of all cognitive relation between the mind and what it is ignorant of. But this is not so. We may indeed, by straining the use of language, say that a stone is absolutely ignorant in this sense. It is so because it is also incapable of knowledge. The stone does not know what is happening at the centre of the earth; neither do I. But the stone's ignorance, if we may use the word at all, is essentially different from mine. What I say that I am ignorant of, I at least know as being unknown to me, and as connected with what I do know. In this sense my ignorance has an object, and the stone's has none. In this sense it is equally true to say that the stone is ignorant of everything, and that it is ignorant of nothing. But if I said that I was ignorant of nothing, I could only mean that I knew everything.

Now we have seen that the cognitive unity of the individual, as pervading, potentially or actually, all phases of his life-history, implies the unity of the universe as the form

[1] [Ward pertinently asks: 'For whom? Surely not for the cat?'—Ed.]

of all his knowledge. But if this be so, all ignorance on the part of an individual knower must be of the relative type, and not at all comparable with the nescience of a stone. He must at least refer to what he is ignorant of as belonging to the domain of the unknown, and as connected with what he otherwise knows. Thus his cognitive unity will include both his knowledge and his ignorance.

This is plain enough when we consider the mental attitude of questioning or inquiring, of seeking to know what we do not know already. When we raise a question, we do not, indeed, know what the answer is. None the less, in the very act of questioning, we define what it is that we are ignorant of. We define it as related in a more or less determinate way to what is presupposed in the question itself. What is thus presupposed is apprehended as essentially incomplete, and the answer is apprehended as what is required to complete it. But if knowledge of the unknown, as such, is implied in the ignorance which takes shape in actual questions, it must also be implied in the ignorance which does not. It is implied in the mere possibility of asking questions, so far as this depends on the nature of the object, and not on subjective interest or other special conditions of individual existence. There must be a field for inquiry offered to the cognitive subject—a field apprehended as unknown, an object therefore of relative and not absolute ignorance. But what we know and what, in this relative sense, we do not know, constitute together one universe of being, which is the correlate and counterpart of the unity of knowledge.

4. *Degrees of Cognitive Unity*

This unity of knowledge is essential to the unity and identity of every cognitive individual. Each, as Leibniz said, represents the universe from his own point of view. In different individuals the unity is present in very different ways and degrees, according to the diverse conditions and circumstances of their finite existence. It may be complete, though in a manner incomprehensible to us, in the Universal Mind. In finite individuals it is variously restricted by the limitations of their immediate experience, by the special constitution of their bodies and the environment in which they are placed, and by their limited power of forming mental dispositions through which preacquired knowledge is retained and reproduced as the basis of subsequent developments.

Of these conditions, the limitations of interest and retentiveness are most fundamental. We may illustrate the way in which they operate by considering in broad outline the typical contrast between the mental life of man and that of animals. Human beings are capable of a progressive development which is impossible under the conditions of animal life. They penetrate the region of the unknown by a process in which the answers to previous questions open out new lines of inquiry, and in which the answers to different questions are made to throw light on each other. Knowledge thus becomes at once wider in range and more completely unified. This of course holds in very varying degrees for different men and different groups of men. But, in the main, capacity for such development marks off distinctively human reason from animal intelligence. Its highest stage is reached when the unity of the universe, which even in animals is the logical form of knowledge, becomes itself more or less clearly and explicitly an object of thought and inquiry. I occupy this position myself in the present volume; but it is also equally occupied by the sceptics, such as Mr Russell, who doubt or deny that the universe is a unity. For if it were not a unity, I do not see how the question whether it is so or not could even be raised at all.

5. Cognitive Unity in Animals

This progressive development, which culminates in the system of the sciences, in the higher forms of religion, and in philosophy, is arrested in its initial stages by the conditions of animal as distinct from human existence. One fundamental reason is the specific limitation of the range of animal interests. If a potential question is also to be an actual questioning, the individual must feel a need which requires the question to be answered. In human beings the progressive opening out of relatively novel fields for inquiry is in a large measure accompanied by the emergence of relatively new directions of interest and attention. In an animal, on the contrary, interest is circumscribed by what we call animal needs, and consists mainly in instincts, impulses and emotions, more or less modified and specialised by experience. These are concerned primarily with the search for food, self-protection against danger, sexual relations, the care for offspring and the like. Even in these directions they are circumscribed in a peculiar way. They are mainly such that they can be satisfied by immediate bodily action in relation to sensibly present situations as these arise, and do not require the working out of plans in advance of the occasion for putting them into execution. This is made possible in the first instance because the animal has not only congenital interests, excitable under appropriate circumstances, but also another sort of congenital equipment. Its neuro-muscular system is congenitally so organised that in the presence of the appropriate situation which conditions impulse and emotion, it finds itself performing complex movements, useful in the satisfaction of its needs, which it does not have to learn by experience. Thus nature does for the animal what human beings have to learn to do for themselves. When animals are not thus engaged in meeting the practical exigencies of a present situation, they either tend to sink into somnolence, or to gratify in the form of play the same primitive impulses as occupy them in the serious business of their lives. The kitten practises with the fallen leaves the movements of a cat with a mouse.

Besides this limitation of interest, and closely connected with it, there is a limitation on the side of retentiveness and reproduction. Animals do indeed learn by experience. They retain knowledge previously acquired in their practical dealings with previous situations, so as to bring it to bear on new situations more or less similar. What is wanting to them, or present only in a comparatively slight degree, is the power of free ideal revival. By this I mean such revival as is involved in occupying the mind more or less persistently with what is not connected with circumstances present to the senses at the time.[1]

Under trains of free ideas we have to include not only ideal anticipation of the future, but also series of reminiscences of what has happened in the past. A dog may miss his master acutely. But there is no reason to believe that he sits down and calls to mind in successive order past scenes and incidents in which they both shared. Or, to take a less sentimental example from Dr Ward, one can hardly imagine a retrospective dog 'regretting, like one of *Punch's* heroes, that he did not have another slice of that mutton'.[2]

This contrast between the human and animal mind illustrates in a conspicuous example the way in which cognitive unity may vary with the conditions of individual existence. But however it may vary in detail, its fundamental nature remains the same. It consists throughout in apprehension of relation and connexion, it embraces the field of what we call ignorance, and it is essentially correlated with the unity of the universe.

[1] A cat which has failed after strenuous and repeated efforts to escape from a cage, by pulling a lock or pressing a button, will also fail to learn to do the trick by watching another cat succeed under the same circumstances. It will not even notice the other cat except in a transitory and perfunctory way. There is a lack of interest. But lack of interest is a quite insufficient explanation. Why does the animal fail to be interested in what touches it so nearly? It is difficult to suggest any reason except that the animal fails to recall its own previous experience in similar situations, because of an incapacity for free ideal revival. This may serve as an example of a multitude of relevant facts all pointing to the same conclusion, that trains of free ideas, even if present at all, play but little part in the ordinary mental life of the higher animals.

[2] *Psychological Principles*, p. 189.

6. *Is there an Act or State of Knowing?*

Must we add that it presupposes a pure subject, distinct from it, on which it depends? The usual argument of those who hold this view is as follows: If A is to be known as related to B, the same being who knows A must also know B. There must therefore be a cognitive subject distinct from both A and B, and equally present to both of them. But this reasoning plainly moves in a vicious circle. It is true that if A can only be known by a pure subject, and if again B can only be known by a pure subject, it must be the same pure subject which knows the relation between them. If, however, neither the knowledge of A nor that of B, taken by itself, presupposes a pure subject, there is no reason why such a subject should be required to account for knowledge of a relation between them. What has to be shown is that, quite apart from reference to cognitive unity, knowledge as such includes (1) a pure subject, set over against an object, (2) a distinct relation of a peculiar kind between the cognitive subject and the object.

This analysis raises the further question how we are to conceive the relation between knower and known. The most natural suggestion is that, following the apparent analogy of such processes as desire and will, we should regard knowing as an act or state of the subject, and what is known as the object of this act. Now I entirely deny that there is any subjective act or state which can properly and strictly be called cognitive. Here I come into violent collision with the neo-realists and especially with Mr Moore, for whom the fundamental and flagrant fallacy of idealism consists in an alleged confusion between what is known and the supposed act of knowing it.

At the outset I have to notice a very important ambiguity. What, strictly speaking, are we to regard as the object of the supposed cognitive act? Is it only what is already being known, or is it also and as well what is as yet unknown? Does the cognitive act bring within our ken what we were previously ignorant of, or does it only begin to exist when ignorance has given place to knowledge? Is there no difference between the knowing of things and the process which makes them known? The question, once definitely raised, seems to answer itself. There must be a difference. Yet those who maintain the theory of cognitive acts do not appear to recognise a distinction. For them knowing is not merely knowing, but also a process whereby things with a being and nature independent of the mind are in the first instance brought into cognitive relation to it. It follows inevitably from this tacit assumption that the mind can only be externally related to its objects, and thus there can be no standing-ground for idealism. The cognitive act is supposed in the first instance to be 'directed upon' something quite distinct and separate from the mind whose act it is. This being so, the same mutual externality and independence must remain, when the thing has actually become known. For the act is taken to be the same, whether it is the act of making known what is unknown or the act of knowing it when it is known. It thus becomes impossible to regard what is known as being in the mind or belonging to the mind-complex. To say this would be like saying that when a stone breaks glass, the glass becomes part of the stone which breaks it. Those who regard knowledge as an external relation do, in fact, picture it to themselves as if it were a relation between bodies external to each other in space. Consciously or unconsciously, they confuse it with the relation of the percipient's body to the thing which he sees and touches. Just as, in looking at a table, the body confronts the table with the eyes turned towards it, so in knowing, the mind is pictured as confronting what it knows, and turning towards this in a cognitive act. From this point of view it is just as great nonsense to say that what is known, just because it is known, is in the mind which knows it, as it is to say that the table seen, just because it is seen, is in the eye used in seeing it. I have no doubt that Professor Alexander's use of the words 'contemplate' and 'contemplation' tends to ensnare him in this metaphor. What the words inevitably suggest is the picture of some one gazing at something with his bodily eyes. This bodily attitude being ascribed confusedly to the mind also, the mind is imagined as confronting or standing over against what it knows.

It follows from this discussion that we have a twofold question to deal with. (1) Is knowing itself an act? (2) Is it a cognitive act of essentially the same kind as that by which we penetrate the region of ignorance, asking questions and getting answers and, in general, making known what was previously unknown? I am prepared to maintain, first, that knowing itself is not an act and, secondly, that the process by which we come to know what we did not know before does involve an activity, but that this activity is not itself knowledge.

7. *Getting to know, or attending, is a Mental Activity*

There is indeed a mental activity which brings, or tends to bring, within the sphere of positive knowledge what was previously outside it. But this always consists in some form of subjective interest, and some phase of conation, with its inseparable feeling, agreeable or disagreeable. The interest is such that it requires for its fulfilment fuller knowledge of what is already known imperfectly. It includes all questioning, inquiry, seeking, searching, watching, waiting, taking notice, being on the alert, grappling with a problem, following the thread of an argument, concentration on a topic, etc. We may conveniently comprehend all its various modes and phases under a common term—*Attention*. Attention always presupposes knowledge, and tends to give rise to further knowledge. But in itself it is a form of interest and not a cognitive act. There is therefore no subjective act having this function which can be strictly and properly called an act of knowing.

8. *Is Judgment or Assertion a Cognitive Act?*

Let us now examine actual knowledge as distinct from the processes which give rise to it. From this point of view it may seem that there is at least one cognitive act, that of judging or mentally asserting. What is this if it is not cognitive? I answer that in so far as it is an act, it is not mere cognition. The word *judgment* is ambiguous. In its widest application, it covers all knowledge about anything; there is judgment in this sense wherever anything is known as being such and such, or so and so related, or even as existing at all. It is thus coextensive with knowledge in general. But in this sense it by no means implies anything that can be called a mental act of asserting or believing. When we look at a page of print, we apprehend the black letters as being letters and black, and as contrasted with the white paper. But we do not usually go through the act of mentally affirming that there are letters, that they are black, and that as such they are contrasted with the surrounding white. Similarly, when I meet a man in the street, I know him for a man, but I do not usually say to myself 'this is a man', or go through any process akin to the act of judging which would be expressed in this verbal statement. It is no exaggeration to say that by far the greater part of what we know or believe is thus taken for granted, without any acts of asserting or believing. Even what we do assert is picked out from a complex background which is not asserted but merely known. If I say 'The sun has dark spots on it', this presupposes that there is a sun with all the qualities and relations which give the word 'sun' meaning and significance for me; yet I am not asserting that there is a sun, and I am not asserting anything of it except that it has dark spots. The distinction is well illustrated by that between the merely attributive and the predicative use of adjectives. In the statement that 'The white horse is lame', whiteness is not affirmed of the horse as lameness is, yet the horse is known or believed to be white.

The act of asserting or believing arises only when the thought of alternatives is in some way suggested. When I see a man plainly, I take him for a man without mentally affirming that he is so. But if I see something dimly in the distance, and want to know what it is, then, if on approaching it my curiosity is satisfied, I mentally make the judgment which would be expressed in the words 'it's a man' or 'it's a tree'. Though for the most part I simply see the sun as shining without asserting that it shines, yet if I happen to think of yesterday's rain and this suggests the thought that it might have been raining now, I acknowledge, with or without words, that 'the sun is shining to-day'. In general, the act of judging is always preconditioned by an interrogative attitude of mind. Alternatives are suggested, so that the question arises: Which is realised? The answer may follow so close on the heels of the question, that the question is, so to speak, suppressed at its birth. I say to a man, 'Are you sober?' and he replies at once, 'Of course I am'. In his mind, if not in mine, the question is answered as soon as asked. It would never have occurred to him if I had not thrust it upon him.

In what then does the act of judgment consist? It consists in concentrating on one alternative as if there were no others. If the discarded alternatives are before the mind at all, they are not so in the same sense. They may be present as alternative answers to the question 'What might be or might have been?', not to the question 'What is or may be?'.

There is a close analogy between the act of judging and that of voluntary decision. The difference lies in the nature of the initial question, which is not 'What alternative is in fact real?', but 'What alternative shall I make real?'. The act of deciding, like that of judging, consists in fixing the attention on one alternative and withdrawing it from others. When the thought of something to be done occupies attention to the exclusion of conflicting suggestion, bodily action follows of itself, so far as it is otherwise in our power.

9. *Knowledge, being a Condition of all Subjective Acts, cannot itself be a Subjective Act*

We conclude then that acts of judging and supposing, as well as acts of questioning, doubting, inquiring, though they essentially imply cognition as their precondition, are not themselves cognitive. The decision between alternatives in an act of judgment is, like an act of voluntary choice, a phase of conative process; it presupposes knowledge, but the character on account of which we call it an act is conative, not cognitive. When we consider knowledge in abstraction from all such states and processes, it is impossible to detect in it any act of knowing distinct from its object, as, for instance, desire is distinct from what is desired. There can be no subjective act or state of this sort without an object to which is is directed. But the object is an object for a subject only if and so far as it is already known or thought of. Knowledge, then, is a logical precondition of all subjective acts or states, and therefore cannot itself be a subjective act or state.[1] To be an object for me, it is not enough that a thing should have being apart from me. As known or thought of it must be, to use the phrase of ordinary language, 'in the mind'. Whether I assert or deny, doubt or suppose that pigs have wings, or inquire whether they have them, or desire that they should have them, or am pleased that they do have them, I must already know what is meant by 'pigs' having wings'.

If this analysis is correct, there is no distinction between knowing and being known at all analogous to that between striking and being struck, or even to that of being above and being below. The difference is only in the point of view from which the same fact is regarded. When I say 'I know something' I emphasise the relation which it thereby acquires with my mind-complex as a whole. It is connected

---

[1] Of course I do not mean that the object may be first known and afterwards attended to. The knowledge and the attention must be coincident, though distinct.

with other things known within my cognitive unity. It is an actual or possible object of my subjective states or processes, such as desire and aversion. On the other hand, when I say 'This is known to me', though all these relations to my mental complex as a whole are implied, they are not especially emphasised. Knowledge is rather considered from the point of view of the thing, and stress is laid on the distinction between being known and being unknown.

10. 'Knownness' is not a Passing State of what is known but a Unique Fact

What account are we to give of this distinction? Plainly 'knownness', if we may be allowed the word, has no separate existence as a distinct particular by the side of what is known. Knownness is only abstractly distinguishable from what is known. Are we then to regard it as a passing state of what is known, so that the transition from being unknown to being known is like that from water solid to water fluid? The suggested analogy breaks down in essential respects. (1) In the first place, seeing that the same being may be simultaneously known to many distinct individuals, we should have to ascribe to it as many numerically distinct states indistinguishable in kind, existing together. It is as if we were to attribute to the same water several distinct fluidities at once. (2) In the second place, the supposed state of being known involves no change or difference in the qualities and relations which belong to the thing as unknown. There cannot be any alteration in these. Otherwise it would not be what was previously unknown that became known, but something different. We must not, then, treat the passage from ignorance to knowledge as, in any ordinary sense, a change in what is previously unknown. It is not a passage from one positive state to another incompatible with it, which ceases to exist in the transition. Being unknown is not such a positive state. It is only the absence of knownness. (3) Clearly connected with this is another essential distinction. Knownness is not merely one character among others. It has the unique peculiarity of qualifying all the other characters, at least potentially. When we say that a piece of water is fluid, it is not implied that its transparency, or specific gravity, or bulk or shape is fluid. It is meaningless to assert that its fluidity is itself fluid, or that its previously solid state is fluid, or that the change from this to the fluid state is fluid. Yet all this is capable of being known. Even the character of being known, and the difference between being known and being unknown, and the passage from being known to being unknown are facts of which we are cognisant. As we have seen, even in ignorance, and more definitely in inquiry, we at least know the unknown as such.

For these reasons, we must refuse to regard knownness either as a state of what is known or as a relation, whether external or internal, to anything else.[1] It is a unique and ultimate fact for which all analogies break down when they are pushed too far. But since we must refer to it in some language, we have to select terms for the purpose. The usage of the schoolmen, though not satisfactory, seems on the whole best to supply what is required. The difference between being known and being unknown to this or that individual was described by them as a difference between two ways of being, two manners of existing. The being which belongs to things even when they are unknown is called by them 'formal' being. The way of being which

---

[1] [There does not seem to be any argument, in either this or the preceding section, to prove that 'knownness' is not a relation. At the end of the previous section it is pointed out that what I know 'thereby acquires a relation with my mind-complex', in being 'connected with other things known within my cognitive unity'. There is clearly no contradiction between this and the statement that 'knownness' is not itself a relation. But the assertion in this section that it is not a relation stands unsupported. The whole passage in this section from (3) in the preceding paragraph down to the end of the second sentence of this paragraph has a line against it in the typescript which suggests that the author regarded it as in some way unsatisfactory.—Ed.]

consists in being known, is called 'objective' being, because through it things are objects for a mind. They are also said to have 'intentional' being, inasmuch as the mind is intended or directed towards them. The word 'intentional' implies an act, and for the schoolmen it implied that knowing itself is an act. But we may interpret it as meaning that form of being which is necessary in order that anything may be the object of a subjective state or activity. Whatever is to be the object of attention or desire or hope or fear, must first be an object, i.e. it must be known or thought of.

This account of knowledge is in no way inconsistent with what is fundamentally true in neo-realism, the position that knowing in no way alters the being of what is known. On the contrary, nothing can be or become known except in so far as it has formal being. There is no being which merely consists in being perceived or thought of. The formal being need not, of course, be actual particular existence. It includes what belongs to universal and logical possibilities or impossibilities. But even impossibilities could not be known as such if they did not exist as such.

Chapter XVIII

IDEALISM AND THE UNIVERSAL MIND

1. *The Idealist Doctrine that there can be no Unknown Being*

Before turning to unity of interest, there is a problem with which we are now in a position to deal, of central significance in its bearing on the ultimate nature of the whole universe of being. In what precedes I have taken for granted that 'formal being' is quite independent of being known within the unity of this or that individual mind-complex. This would only be denied by a solipsist who took himself for the sole self-complete being. But it is another question whether anything can have being which is unknown to any mind. This is the vital issue between idealists and their opponents. The idealist contends that unknown being is an impossible abstraction. When he attempts to realise in thought being separate from knowing, he finds the same sort of difficulty as he does in attempting to conceive knowing without anything known. It appears evident to him that absolutely unknown being is an abstraction which cannot subsist by itself. If this is not clear to others, he has ways and means of making them see it. He asks them to consider such entities as universals, possibilities, relations and forms of unity, the past as such and the future as such. Can these, he asks, be supposed to have being apart from any mind which conceives them? From the plain man and from everybody except the modern school of neo-realists he will get the answer which he expects. They will acknowledge that such entities, at least, are nothing apart from thinking minds. Only actual particulars, they will say, can have being without being known or thought of. Many philosophers, the nominalists and conceptualists, would add that only actual particulars can have a being which does not consist in being thought of. Only these have formal reality. Universals and possibilities are, in Locke's language, 'the work of the understanding'. They are, so to speak, merely devices framed by the mind in order to enable it to deal with particulars.

At this point the idealist steps in and, as I should state his case, argues as follows: It is impossible to regard universals, relations and possibilities as superadded by the knowing mind to an independent reality which in itself is complete without them. On the contrary, the merely particular and actual is an impossible abstraction which cannot have being by itself. It cannot merely exist, it must have a nature. It must have 'whatness' as well as 'thatness'. But if particulars have a nature, they must share a general nature. The only reason why we cannot know them except as belonging to sorts and kinds and classes, is that they cannot exist except as belonging to sorts and kinds and classes. It is true that our appreciation of the general nature of things is limited by the limitation of the knowledge and interest due to the conditions of our finite existence. But the apprehension of particulars is limited in the same way. Attention may select certain general aspects and certain particular existences rather than others. But to select is not to create. The same holds for possibilities. These are founded in the general nature of things. The universal has possible as well as actual instances. It holds still more obviously for relations. How could the knowing mind superinduce relations on an initial multiplicity of unrelated particulars? In order to do so, it is a logical precondition that it should first know them in their isolation, and then, so to speak, weave a web of relations between them. But it is impossible to see how the relating process could begin. In knowing the absolutely disjointed items, knowledge would itself be split up into as many disjointed cognitions. There could be no unity of knowledge. For this consists of knowledge of unity, and cannot therefore exist where there is no unity to know.

2. *Two Forms of the Idealist View of the Relation between Knowing and Being, and the Neo-Realist's Case against both*

It follows that universals and their possible instances and relations belong to the constitution of the universe, just as truly as actually existing particulars, and form an inseparable unity with them. They must therefore be treated on the same footing as regards their dependence on knowledge or independence of it. Now the idealist takes it as an undeniable fact that universals, possibilities and relations owe their being to thought, or at least presuppose it. Hence he maintains that all being depends on a knowing mind, or at least presupposes it. Here there are two alternatives. The connexion may be treated as essential correlation or interdependence, so that neither can be without the other. Or, again, it may be taken as one-sided dependence, so that the mind is regarded as creating its objects. Many, if not most, idealists seem to favour the second view. I cannot follow them; and if idealism means this, I am not an idealist. T. H. Green, for instance, does not question Locke's position that universals and ideas of relation, and the possibilities which Locke calls 'modes', are the work of the understanding. What he insists on is that, if this be so, the same must be true of all being. But as the universe is plainly not the creation of a finite individual, it must ultimately be due to a universal mind. Hence Green infers that there must be an absolute spiritual principle of unity, which not only unites differences but creates them by its own self-differentiation. Fichte and (at least according to some of his interpreters) Hegel too, teach a similar doctrine.

Let us now consider the position of the opponents and critics of both forms of the idealist view. We may take as its most adequate representative the modern school of neo-realists, or at least those of them who show a general understanding of the point at issue. These agree with the idealists that in relation to knowledge all forms of being are to be treated as on the same footing. But instead of holding that they are all equally inseparable from knowledge, they maintain the exact opposite. They maintain that, if there were no cognitive minds in existence, all forms of being might subsist unaltered, except of course the minds themselves, and facts about them. With this reservation they hold that it is quite indifferent to the being of universals and relations, as well as to that of particulars, whether they are known to anyone or not. They say the same for possibilities and probabilities, unless indeed they quite unjustifiably regard them as due merely to the imperfection of our knowledge.

The neo-realist's position is ultimately founded on the principle which we have already recognised as true, the principle that knowing cannot make or modify what is known. This excludes the possibility that the knowing mind in any way generates or produces its own objects. But it does not necessarily follow that anything can have being without being known. For that a further assumption is needed, which does indeed imply the general principle, but is not implied by it. This assumption is contained in the peculiar neo-realist theory of knowledge as an external relation between mutually exclusive entities—on the one side, the mind with its cognitive acts; on the other, what is known to it. On this view it is as absurd to say that nothing can exist unknown to any mind, as it would be to say that a pen cannot exist except when someone is holding it, or that an inkpot cannot exist except when it is placed on some desk. But I have already examined this theory at length, and found it untenable.

If idealism is taken to mean that knowledge as such produces or generates what is known, I agree with the neo-realist in rejecting it. But I cannot accept his view that, knowledge being an external relation, it is ultimately accidental to being that it should be known. On the contrary, I am so far an idealist that for me knowing and being are inseparably united as ultimate and coessential aspects of the universe as a whole. Idealism, as thus defined, seems to be a necessary corollary of that view of the nature of knowledge which I reached in my last chapter. It follows from this position, as well as from that of the neo-realist, that knowledge does not produce or alter what is known.[1]

3. There must always have been Knowing Minds or a Knowing Mind

If we set aside as untenable the external relation theory, it remains for us to consider how the ultimate question between idealism and neo-realism is affected by the general principle that knowledge cannot make or modify its objects. This principle, so far from affording support to neo-realism, seems to constitute the strongest ground for rejecting it, and for accepting instead the inseparable unity of knowing and being in the ultimate constitution of the universe. When a finite individual comes to know what he did not know before, what he comes to know is not altered in any of the characters or relations which belong to it as unknown. If any of these characters or relations were transformed in the process, he could not be said to know what he previously did not know, but something else instead. It follows that if knowledge does not pre-exist, there is no possible change or transformation of what does pre-exist by which it can become known. No modification in the qualities of pre-existing beings in their relations or interactions, or the forms of unity in which they are combined, will give the required result. In a universe of absolutely unknown being, nothing could change into a known being. It follows that since there are knowing minds now, there must always have been knowing minds, or at least one knowing mind.

[1] [The above paragraph was handwritten by the author on a separate sheet inserted among the typewritten pages at about this point, without any indication of where it was to go, or what passage, if any, it was to replace. It fits here a little awkwardly, but I have preferred to leave it as part of the text, for which it was intended, rather than to relegate it to a footnote.—Ed.]

Here we are confronted by the old alternatives. Are we bound to assume one eternal and universal mind, or is it enough to suppose an endless succession of finite individuals each generated by others? The second view must be rejected for reasons which I have already partly referred to.[1] A new mind arises with the development of the germ-cell into a new body. Are we then to say that all germ-cells are connected with rudimentary minds, and that one of them is generated by another, or by the fusion of two others? Again, if we trace back the origin of the parent organism itself to its ancestors, we shall be compelled to posit minds correlated with the simplest forms of animal life, and ultimately with inorganic matter. It may be that some such theory is true. If it were, I do not see how it could be either established or refuted by empirical evidence. In spite of the huge assumption it makes, it might still be regarded at least as one alternative hypothesis, among others, if it really offered a satisfactory explanation. But whether any such theory is tenable or not, it ultimately fails to solve our problem. For if each individual owes his existence to another, we cannot ultimately account for any one of them unless we account for all of them; and we cannot do this simply by multiplying their number. The difficulty is logically the same whether there is an infinite number of them or only two.

4. *The Argument from the Correlation between the Unity of Knowledge and the Unity of the Universe to the existence of a Universal Mind*

To this argument may be added another that is more important. This is based on the unity of knowledge as essentially correlated with the unity of the universe. The finite individual knows the universe; but he knows it only from his own limited point of view. He knows it only in apprehending its partial features and aspects as essentially

[1] Cf. Chapter XIII, Section 3.

incomplete, and therefore included in a whole which transcends and includes them. Further, for each individual the partial being which he ultimately starts with, as in the proper sense the source and support of all other knowledge, is the content of his own immediate experience. But in experiencing this he experiences nothing beyond it. It is experienced in isolation from all else in the universe. Yet it cannot be known without the knowledge of more than itself. How is this possible? I have so far confined myself to insisting that it must be possible, because otherwise the existence and development of knowledge would be impossible, and knowledge is once for all an ultimate fact which we cannot set aside. If we reject knowing we have no longer any right to assume being; but if we take knowledge for granted we must also assert whatever it implies. Now, as I have tried to show, everything short of the whole of being, beginning with the content of immediate experience, is known as essentially incomplete, and could not otherwise be known at all. How, I again ask, is this possible? The mere fact that something is essentially incomplete does not of itself explain how it can be known as such. For the thought of the part as such presupposes the thought of the whole, just as much as the thought of the whole presupposes that of the part. Now for finite beings what is initially given to be known is only that part which is existentially present in their immediate experience. How then can they ever know more than this? And if they can know no more than this, how can they know even this? How can the unity of the universe be for them the form of all knowledge, and itself become, as mental development advances, an explicit object of knowledge?

There is, I submit, only one way of meeting the difficulty. It disappears if finite minds have their source, not in finite conditions, but in a Universal Mind. The Universal Mind communicates to its finite creatures its own omniscience, so far as this is compatible with their finitude. Their knowledge is limited inasmuch as only part of the whole is initially given to their immediate experience, and this means that they can only know from a finite point of view. The only way, then, in which they can partake in the omniscience of the Universal Mind is by knowing the universe as we have found that they actually do know it— that is, by apprehending the part as essentially incomplete and continued beyond itself within a more comprehensive being.

This is the way in which we are led to idealism through analysis of knowledge and the unity of knowledge. There is another convergent path, starting with the inquiry whether anything can actually exist without being actually experienced. This we have already followed, in considering the nature of matter as it is in itself.

There yet remains another converging line of inquiry so significant and important for the purpose of this book that the others may be regarded only as necessary preparation for it. This starts from subjective interest and the unity of interest, and leads up to the view of the unity of the universe as including the unity of values in an ultimate good.

Chapter XIX

UNITY OF INTEREST AS IMPLYING THE UNITY OF THE UNIVERSE[1]

1. *The Nature of Conative and of Affective Interest*

In order that anything should be an object of interest, it is a logical, though not a temporal, precondition that it should be, however indefinitely, an object of knowledge. Interest is present so far as we are not totally indifferent to what we know or think of. It has two main forms or aspects, the conative and the affective. There is conation in so far as we want or require something in connexion with what we know or think of. We may want it more fully known without being otherwise altered: or, negatively, we may merely want to dismiss it from our thought. This direction of conation may be brought under the general head of *Attention*, including the refusal to attend. Again, we may want the thing itself altered in its formal being. This is the practical direction of conation, and it also has two phases, positive and negative. We may want something or some situation to continue and develop in accordance with its distinctive nature, or we may want it destroyed or removed. We may want a young plant to grow and bear fruit, or we may want it uprooted and thrown on a rubbish heap. The positive direction of conation may be called appetite; the negative, aversion. Hobbes distinguished them as 'endeavour toward' and 'endeavour fromward'.

Affective interest consists in being pleased or displeased with something, and also in feeling various sorts of specific emotion towards it, such as fear or anger. In general,

[1] [This title serves to mark the relation of the present chapter to chapter XVII ('Cognitive Unity as implying the Unity of the Universe'), but the promise implied in it is only finally fulfilled in chapter XXI, after the digression on mental conflict in the next chapter.—Ed.]

affection and conation do not occur separately, but are distinguishable as aspects of one interest; even in aesthetic enjoyment the felt pleasure is blended with a felt tendency to keep and develop the object in consciousness as fully and distinctly as possible. Pleasure and displeasure correspond to appetition and aversion—endeavour toward and endeavour fromward. So far as conative tendency is not arrested by obstacles in the development towards its fulfilment, there is appetition and pleasure. If it is obstructed in such a way that it cannot progress towards its goal without actually getting rid of the obstacle, or at least mentally ignoring it, there is aversion and pain.

We have seen that all forms and phases of interest imply some cognisance of what we are interested in. It is equally true that knowledge implies interest. Otherwise it could not develop or begin to develop. For the mental life is a process of which cognition is only one side. The driving power without which the process cannot proceed is interest. There is, for instance, no questioning or inquiry unless an answer is wanted, however slightly and transiently.

Interest on its conative side is a subjective activity, on its affective side it is a subjective state. The activity may, of course, be in varying degrees successful or unsuccessful. But wherever there is a felt tendency, however completely the circumstances may deny it fulfilment, there is subjective activity. It is present, for instance, and may be intensely present, in the futile longing to undo the past, in the desire that we had not done what it now makes us blush to recall.

When we analyse what is implied in being interested, we find that it is a complex unity in which there are three distinguishable constituents. On the one hand, there is an object known or thought of, concerning which the interest is felt. On the other hand, there is a certain sort of immediate experience which gives the interest its distinctive character. This immediate experience we may call feeling. There is a difference in the nature of the feeling which distinguishes being pleased from being pained, appetition from aversion, anger from fear. In the third place, there is a unique sort of relation between the feeling on the one side and what therefore we call its object on the other. This relation is what is described as feeling interested in this or that. Through this relation what would otherwise be merely agreeable or disagreeable feeling is a feeling-attitude towards an object—a feeling pleased or pained with it or about it. What would otherwise be blind restlessness is a desire for something. Note that the relation is altogether unique in its nature. When I am pained about something, this does not, for instance, merely mean that the something is a causal condition of my pain. I may be uncomfortable owing to the fact that I have taken poisonous food. Yet I cannot be displeased about this unless I know or believe that I have done so. I may instead be displeased with the merely supposed fact that I have some disease which I have not.

Besides this peculiar complex unity including object, feeling and the relation between them, is it also necessary to assume a pure subject? So far this seems superfluous. The analysis of what is implied in being interested is complete without it. The same 'I' is interested in different ways and at different times in different objects. Does this involve a simple being as a principle of unity? Whether there is such a distinct simple being or not, it is at any rate clear that, on the side of interest, as on the side of knowledge, the mind has the unity of a complex. But given this sort of unity, there does not seem to be any cogent reason for assuming a simple being as its condition. The analysis seems complete if we take into account unity of interest as well as unity of knowledge.

2. *Unity of Interest is Interest in Unity*

Unity of knowledge is knowledge of unity. Similarly, unity of interest is interest in unity. In the process by which conation passes or fails to pass to its fulfilment, however varied this may be in detail throughout its successive phases, the conation remains the same, so far as its object is recognisably the same. The object may be and perhaps always is more completely and accurately defined as the process advances. But there is no break in the continuity of interest; for what was before vaguely and perhaps erroneously apprehended is identified with what is now more distinctly and accurately apprehended. Nor is the continuity destroyed by temporal interruption. It persists in so far as the interest in the one object is spontaneously renewed after the interruption is over. Take, for instance, the endeavour to solve a problem, theoretical or practical. What we are aiming at is the solution; but we do not know definitely what this is, otherwise the problem would be already solved. Nor do we know what questions and difficulties will emerge as we proceed, or what alternatives will have to be rejected. All this we can only find out by trial. Yet there is unity of interest from the beginning to the moment of final success or failure.

In general this sort of unity is present if and so far as we are interested in anything as in any way connected with or related to anything else, or as a partial feature or aspect of anything else. It may be theoretical, practical or aesthetic, according as it is concerned, let us say, with the bringing of particular facts under a general law, the control of conduct by principles and ideals, or the artistic unity of a play or poem or of a piece of music. It is present in some way or degree at all stages of mental development, from the cat's pursuit of a bird to Einstein's pursuit of the connexion between the laws of motion and the law of gravitation.

3. *Degrees of Unity of Interest*

Unity of interest is present at all levels, but in very variable modes and degrees, for different individuals and different classes of individuals. Unless it is present actually or potentially, there is no individual at all, no identical self. But as from the point of view of knowledge, so from that of interest, the one self may be more or less imperfectly unified, and its unity may be more developed in some directions than others. The animal passes from one relatively detached impulse and emotion to another, as its external circumstances and its own organic sensations vary.

In a less degree, this is true also of the young child whose attention flits and wanders as it happens to be caught in turn by this or that feature of its immediate environment. But as knowledge advances in range and organisation, there arise, partly conditioned by this development and partly conditioning it, more permanently general and comprehensive tendencies, which may pervade and dominate the whole mental life. Such are love of money in the miser, ambition in some politicians, patriotism or philanthropy in others, selfishness in the man who is always seeking his own private advantage, art for art's sake in some artists. The sentiments I have named, though they cover a wide range, are none the less one-sided, inasmuch as many aspects of the world and of human life which the individual may have to deal with remain outside them. Hence the unity which depends on them is incomplete and precarious. The most comprehensive and permanent synthesis is supplied by the higher forms of religious and moral sentiment which are concerned with the universe as a whole and man's place in it. Wordsworth's 'happy warrior' may be taken as a type of this highest unity pervading the whole life-history of the individual.[1]

[1] [The preceding argument is summarised as follows in the author's printed synopsis of the Second Course of Gifford Lectures: 'Unity of interest is interest in unity. It is present if and so far as we are interested in anything not merely for its own sake, but as a partial feature or aspect of a whole which transcends and includes it. Without some degree of such unity there is no individual identity of the self as feeling and willing; but, as from the point of view of knowledge, so from that of interest, the one self may be more or less imperfectly unified. Indeed, it would seem that the unity never can be complete. The fullest unity of which the individual as such is capable is never actually attained, but always something to be sought after. It belongs to a potential or ideal self of which the actual self, past or present, is only a partial phase. The nature of this ideal unity may be illustrated by mental conflict resulting in mental dissociation.'

There has so far been no explicit reference in the text to the distinction and relation between the 'ideal' and the 'actual' self, but the excursion into the psychology of mental dissociation, which occupies the next chapter, is excused on the ground that 'it brings to light in a peculiarly impressive way the distinction between the actual temporary self and the ideal self'; and in the succeeding chapter the distinction is taken as already established and its philosophical implications are examined.—Ed.]

Chapter XX

MENTAL CONFLICT AND MENTAL DISSOCIATION

1. *Conflict of Interests as aroused by Theoretical Contradiction*

In what way may unity of interest fail or be broken? There is first of all the mere irrelevance or mutual detachment of different conative processes, such as is illustrated by a child's chasing a butterfly, as contrasted with the same child's playing at horses or learning to read, or entering on his course as a new boy at school.[1]

A second form of disunion arises from the competition of irrelevant interests aroused at the same time. This may be called distraction. A simple instance is that of a child in a shop simultaneously attracted by different toys.

The third and last form of disunion consists in positive antagonism or conflict of interests. Its counterpart on the side of knowledge is logical contradiction; and contradiction may also give rise to it, so far as contradiction is an obstacle in the search for truth. The varied course which a conflict of interests is capable of under varying conditions may be fully illustrated by such instances. The contradic-

---

[1] This kind of disunion constitutes a serious objection to the definition of happiness as a sum of pleasures unmixed with pains, or a balance of pleasure over pain. For the pleasure may be due to the satisfaction of transient and disconnected tendencies. But what we distinctly mean by happiness is the satisfaction of the self as a whole. It exists, therefore, only in so far as that partial interest and satisfaction is a step towards, or at least subordinate to, the satisfaction of wider and more permanent interests. Mere amount of pleasure cannot therefore constitute it. It also depends on the variable degree in which the self enjoying the pleasures is one and the same self. Wordsworth's 'happy warrior' is peculiarly happy in this respect; and the man of pleasure, or rather of pleasures, is likely to be peculiarly unhappy.

tion, inasmuch as it disturbs positive interest in the development of thought and the answering of questions, is an object of aversion. Now there are, as I said before, two ways in which the mind tends to deal with what it dislikes. There is the tendency to turn away from it to something else; and there is the tendency to remove or alter it. Both these tendencies show themselves in face of a theoretical contradiction. If the positive interest which urges us to further inquiry is feeble, we may give up the problem as soon as it confronts us. If the positive interest is sufficiently strong, it will lead to a more or less prolonged and intense attempt to solve the apparent contradiction, by gaining a comprehensive view of the relevant conditions enabling us to detect the error or confusion which occasioned the difficulty. If in this struggle we fail to make encouraging progress, and if we become tired, aversion may become relatively stronger, and we may refuse to attend to the problem any longer, and occupy ourselves with other topics. Yet in so far as a positive interest is still unsatisfied, the mental disposition left behind by the conscious process will tend spontaneously to come into action. There will be a tendency to recur to the baffling problem at intervals; more especially when the mind is only weakly interested in other and disconnected pursuits. We are, for instance, apt to recur to the question when we awake from sleep through the night, and it may influence our dreams. Even when there is no actual recurrence of a distinct effort to deal with the difficulty, yet the conative disposition—i.e. the disposition left behind by the unsatisfied striving—may influence conscious life by giving rise to vague trouble or uneasiness. There is a burden on the mind. On the other hand, just as dispositions spontaneously tend to be re-excited inasmuch as they are formed by positive conative process, so they tend to be kept in abeyance so far as they result from felt aversion. The course of conscious process will be determined by the relative strength of the opposing tendencies, and these will vary with varying special conditions. A group of dispositions may, for a longer or shorter time, fail to be revived. Yet they will always be, so to speak, lying in wait, to reassert themselves so far as circumstances permit.

2. *The Influence of Practical Needs*

Even in the pursuit of knowledge practical needs play a part as well as theoretical curiosity, and in most minds they are of predominant importance. They may not only prompt inquiry, but may in large measure determine which of two contradictory courses is to be accepted. A man of science who is thoroughly committed to a certain theory, so that it is taken for granted as a matter of course in his scientific work, and so that for him his own personal reputation and the sense of his own importance are bound up with it, will find it a hard struggle to deal impartially with the evidence and arguments for an opposing view. He dwells on whatever seems to favour his own position, and ignores or misrepresents both to himself and to others what seems incompatible with it. If his love of truth is strong, he will have an uneasy conscience and recurrent misgiving. He will tend to treat his opponents as personal enemies and resent being reminded by others of unwelcome facts. Perhaps this uneasiness may grow and become more definite until at last he shakes himself free from prejudice and accepts the repugnant alternative. On the other hand, he may end in confirming himself more fully in his old way of thinking and in barring out whatever would trouble it.

In such instances as these the conflict arises in the first instance in connexion with theoretical interest. But for the most part the mental struggle is primarily practical. Such are the struggle between fear and the motives which lead a man to confront danger; the opposition between philanthropy or any desire or impulse to relieve distress and the shrinking from the sight or thought of pain; between the repugnance to writing letters, felt so strongly by some persons, and the practical need for getting them written;

between the love for an unworthy object and the aversion arising from a sense of his unworthiness. Under the same head comes all conflict between duty and inclination.

Mental struggles of this sort always involve aversion as well as appetition. Even when two contending interests are both in themselves positive, so that their objects are attractive, yet the object of each is an object of aversion, inasmuch as it stands in the way of the satisfaction of the other. Now where there is aversion there is a tendency to ignore—to refuse to attend to—what is disliked when it is present—a tendency which takes effect so far as it is not counteracted by other motives. Further, the same tendency is a tendency to forget the repugnant object and to exclude it from influence on conscious life. Thus a man who, shrinking from letter-writing, turns his attention to more congenial pursuits is likely to forget all about the neglected duty until he is unpleasantly reminded of it by disagreeable consequences. He will then plead that it has quite slipped from his mind. On the other hand, if his sense of duty is strong, he will feel vaguely uneasy at intervals, or even persistently, and the suppressed tendency to get the letters written will come back of itself, and may issue in a sudden burst of impatient energy which clears off a heap of arrears at once.

3. *Mental Dissociation*. (*a*) *Dissociated Dispositions*

Broadly speaking, there are two ways out of mental conflict. The one is by facing unwelcome facts, and striving persistently to alter them, or to readjust our attitude towards them. The other is by ignoring and forgetting them. Of these the positive way leads in general to a higher and more comprehensive unity of interest and of the mental life in general. The negative way leads, for the most part, to disintegration and decay. This principle is illustrated in a startling manner by pathological cases of mental dissociation, which in its extreme form may give rise to what is called multiple

298 MIND AND OUR KNOWLEDGE OF IT

personality. Suppose that repugnance to letter-writing has
not only led a man to forget all about the letters which he
ought to have written, but has gone so far that he cannot
call them to mind when someone reminds him of them, and
when he himself tries to recollect them. This would amount
to mental dissociation. The failure of memory need not
imply that the corresponding mental dispositions are without influence on his conscious life. They may work under-
ground, so to speak, in indirect and circuitous ways. Thus
the man who cannot remember his neglected correspondence might feel otherwise inexplicable antipathies. He
might, without knowing why, hate the sight of a postman
or a postage stamp. He might also have fits of nervous
anxiety without obvious reason. His dream-life might also
be affected. He might have disagreeable dreams, for
example of swimming in a sea of ink. Such experiences
would represent a sort of compromise between prevailing
interests which bar the re-excitement of the relevant dispositions, and their own tendency to enter consciousness.
The conditions which I have described are all found at least
in certain forms of mental dissociation, which consist primarily in a more or less complete exclusion of a group of
mental dispositions from the conscious life in which they
were originally formed.

The example I have given is a fanciful one. The mental
conflict connected with letter-writing can hardly be so
intense and deep-rooted as to occasion a split of the kind
I have described. It is otherwise with suppressed sexual
tendencies and those connected with self-preservation, such
as fear and the struggle to master fear. Sexual examples are
given in abundance and with much curious detail in the
works of Freud and his followers. Examples connected
with the struggle against danger have become familiar
through the Great War of 1914–18 under the name of
shell-shock. A man who has been buried in a dug-out may
be unable to recall the occurrence or connected circumstances. Yet the disposition left behind by it may still

operate to determine his conscious life in various indirect ways. He may, for instance, have a horror of all enclosed spaces. Or a man who has broken down under the stress of anxiety lest he should fail in his duty through fear, may still be subject to nervous distress of the same kind, which he cannot trace to its source. I have heard of one instance in which the horror of the war, apart from participation in actual fighting, led to a somewhat similar result. A man was so affected by this that, through his shrinking from the idea of it, he came to deny that there was really any war. According to him, people were only pretending when they talked and behaved as if there were one.

In all cases of this type, the method of cure which has been found to give the most thorough and permanent results, proceeds on the principle followed by the psycho-analyst. The dissociated dispositions must cease to be dissociated. They must be restored to their normal connexion with the mental life. The patient must be brought to face the repugnant facts and ideas which the very intensity of his aversion had placed beyond his power to recall in any ordinary way. He must face them and readjust his mental attitude to them by regarding them in a new light and from a higher and more comprehensive point of view. The disease is a breach in unity of interest, and the cure is to restore unity of interest. To effect this is difficult. The means on which the psychoanalyst mainly relies consist in inducing the patient to recall his dreams. The dissociated dispositions constantly operate, though in a curiously disguised and indirect way, to determine dream-life. Thus if, under skilled guidance, the patient can be brought to remember his dreams with sufficient fullness and distinctness, and to follow the trains of ideas suggested in recalling them, he is placed on the track of his forgotten experiences, and is enabled to understand the source of his trouble and to deal with it intelligently.

4. *Mental Dissociation.* (*b*) *Dissociated Streams of Consciousness and 'Multiple Personality'*

So far I have spoken only of dissociated dispositions, not of dissociated consciousness. But if the split-off group of dispositions and the processes which go on in it are sufficiently complex, we have good evidence that they may be connected with a distinct stream of mental life—with what is, at least relatively and temporarily, a distinct individual. It is hard to determine under what precise conditions this new departure begins. There is no good reason for assuming that anything of the sort takes place in our normal life. When the mathematician is not thinking at all about mathematics, but playing cricket instead, we can hardly suppose this to mean that his mathematical knowledge still exists for him as a split-off stream of conscious process. If we proceeded on this principle, we should be faced by absurd consequences. We should have to suppose that the entire range of the man's acquired mathematical knowledge in all its details is present to another finite consciousness, or to a series of them, in so far as it is not present to his own.[1]

---

[1] [At this point the following passage was marked for deletion, perhaps because the author thought that it unnecessarily interrupted the main stream of the argument: 'Nor is the hypothesis of co-consciousness required even when dispositions change and interact. A man, for instance, makes a more or less strenuous effort to recall a name and fails. But after a lapse of time, during which his mind has been occupied with disconnected topics, the name suddenly occurs to him. Here it is enough to say that a dispositional process is initiated by the effort to recollect, and that this continues and leads to the desired result, even after relevant conscious activity has ceased. Such interactions of dispositions, initiated by conscious activity and subserving the interests of conscious life, are constantly going on and are often very complex. But it is only where there is pathological dissociation that we find good evidence of distinct streams of consciousness, each connected with a separate system of dispositions. Even under these conditions the hypothesis has no solid support, except in a special class of cases. It does not seem to be warranted by the ordinary symptoms of the patient treated by the psychoanalyst. He has indeed to assume dissociated and dispositional processes of much complexity. But his ground for doing so is

Perhaps the only convincing evidence of the existence of dissociated streams of consciousness arising from dissociated dispositions is to be found in communication with them in the way of social intercourse. This exists in cases of what are called multiple personality. It would seem that this arises mostly, and perhaps always, through a conflict of interests, when the antagonism is so deep-seated that the detached groups of dispositions are sufficiently extensive, organised and complex to be capable of subserving a separate stream of conscious process. The doubling may, it would seem, occur simultaneously. But the evidence is clearest and fullest for what is called alternating personality, in which each system of dispositions takes its turn to the exclusion of the others. The several systems must of course have certain fundamental constituents in common. But these are neutral in the original conflict which gave rise to dissociation: they are those involved in the use of language, in the recognition of ordinary objects, and the like. On the other hand, personal memories connected with the period of conflict belong ordinarily to one of the personalities, and not to the other. Further, as might be expected from the conditions of their origin, the divided personalities present a marked contrast in character and sentiment.

A girl has a passionate affection for a lover. She discovers him to be unworthy, and the whole complex of sentiments connected with morality, religion, decency and

their indirect influence on the normal conscious life, and especially on the dreams, of the patient. He has no direct evidence that they are connected with a distinct conscious life. He is indeed prone to talk of them as if this were so, as if indeed they involved distinct trains of thought and reasoning. But this procedure seems due to a fallacy of confusion—a confusion between the process which the psychoanalyst is analysing and describing and that which takes place in his own mind when he analyses and describes it. In any case it is plain from his own account of them that the hypothetical trains of thought are, for the most part, of a very strange kind, with an altogether peculiar 'logic' of their own. They are such as could not occur in any conscious mind otherwise known to us, and a close examination makes it very difficult to see how they could occur at all'.—Ed.]

respectability is revolted by his unworthiness. Hence she is torn asunder or, more accurately, she tends to be torn asunder, by conflicting interests. There are two ways in which she may deal with the situation—either by facing the facts or by evading them. If she faces the facts she may, while keeping in view her lover's unworthiness, and the powerful motives which prompt her to reject him, none the less make up her mind to cling to him, whatever the consequences. Or again she may, while keeping in view the thought of her lover and what makes or made him attractive, none the less make up her mind to reject him and live without him. Neither of these courses leads to disintegration, and if the more universal and comprehensive interest prevails, the result, at the cost of much suffering, will be a higher unity of the mental life as a whole. Mental dissociation arises from ignoring and evading what is repugnant, instead of confronting it and coming to a decision about it. Each of the antagonistic interests, as it becomes dominant, makes a way to its own satisfaction by excluding the thought and barring the recall of whatever obstructs it. When in our example this proceeds so far that there are two distinct and alternating streams of conscious process, for one of which all personal memories of the lover, and of whatever is connected with him and of the period of life in which he played a part, are gone and cannot by any ordinary means be recovered, whereas for the other, while all this remains, the relevant moral and prudential considerations have fallen into abeyance—when this takes place, we have what is known as a double personality, with a marked contrast of character. One of the relatively distinct individuals will be impulsive, irresponsible, and frivolous. The other will be sedate, sober and respectable.

5. *Even in Cases of 'Multiple Personality' there is ultimately only one Self*

What is the significance of a mental disruption of this kind? Does it mean that there are two ultimate individuals? Or are they to be regarded as, in principle, provisional and passing phases in the life-history of one individual? Are they really different persons, or impersonations of one and the same person? Even for normal human beings, the unity of the self as a whole is never completely present in any one stage, phase or period of their actual history. It includes not only the actual past and future, but potential developments without which it is essentially incomplete. This holds for interest as well as for knowledge. It is from this point of view that a man may disown and repudiate his past conduct, however inevitably it may have flowed from the motives which swayed him at the moment. He feels that if he had been more fully himself he would have acted otherwise. Even in the moment of choice between alternatives, he may feel that for the self as a whole there is always a possibility of deciding otherwise than he actually decides. In this way we may partly at least account for that consciousness of free will which so stubbornly maintains itself against the arguments of the determinist.

It is with reference to this ideal self that we now raise the question whether in multiple personality there are so many ultimately distinct individuals, or only provisionally severed phases of one individual which transcends and includes them. It seems clear that there is ultimately only one self. In the first place, the divided streams of conscious life so far overlap that they share in common dispositions formed before the cleavage took place. They thus branch from a common stock. There is nothing corresponding to this in the relation of what, in ordinary social intercourse, we recognise as different individuals. In the second place, each of the so-called personalities leads a troubled, thwarted and essentially incomplete existence, due to its severance from the others. One dissociated system of dispositions does not remain inert when the other becomes dominant, but re-asserts itself in all the indirect ways familiar in the simpler cases of suppressed desire with which the psychoanalyst deals. The storm and stress and the dramatic struggles which thus arise have been vividly described in the well-known book by Morton Prince.[1]

Sometimes the evidence strongly suggests that both the warring personalities are simultaneously conscious. What-ever form the conflict may assume, it is a civil strife rather than a war between foreign powers. Each of the parties to it strives to regain its position in the community from which it has been exiled. It is true that it does so blindly by banishing and suppressing its rival. But the end cannot be attained in this way, which leads only to a succession of revolutions and counter-revolutions. The development of each personality is arrested by its dissociation from the other, and the only way to remove the obstruction is to reunite them in a higher synthesis. This is precisely what the mental pathologist, with some measure of success, attempts to do, either by hypnosis or suggestion, or by the more thorough methods of psychoanalysis. For the mental pathologist, dissociation is a disease, and the cure for it is to heal the breach by restoring the unity of interest. But this implies that the relatively distinct personalities are only phases of the one ideal self.

[1] *The Dissociation of a Personality.*

Chapter XXI

GOOD, EVIL AND GOD

1. *No Finite Good can give Final Satisfaction*

My excuse for the excursion into psychology of the last chapter is that it brings to light in a peculiarly impressive way the distinction between the actual temporary self and the ideal self. We have now to examine generally what is involved in this conception from a philosophical point of view. The grand question is whether ideal unity of interest, like ideal unity of knowledge, has its objective correlate in the unity of the universe.

For finite beings all objects of knowledge are essentially incomplete, and presuppose a unity which transcends and includes them. Does the same hold within the sphere of interest? Are the objects which satisfy will and desire in like manner essentially incomplete, presupposing one ideal good which comprehends them all within its unity? This would mean that for the ideal self there could be no secure and final satisfaction in the attainment of any finite good, small or great. To rest in such finite ends as if they were self-complete must, on this view, lead in the long run to painful disillusion. Just as in the sphere of knowledge to take any truth as the whole of truth is an immense error and leads to further error, so to treat any special good as the whole would be an immense evil leading to greater evils.

I say 'would be'. But in one respect at any rate I am simply describing human life as it is. Whether the explanation I suggest is true or not, at any rate there can be no doubt that finite and temporary objects of desire and will give no final satisfaction. Without dwelling on a hackneyed topic I need only appeal to all that has been said and written

on the vanity of human wishes, from the author of Eccles-
iastes to the most modern pessimist. 'What profit hath
a man of all his labour which he takes under the sun?' says
the preacher. 'There is indeed one element in human
destiny', R. L. Stevenson writes, 'that not blindness itself
can controvert: whatever else we are intended to do, we
are not intended to succeed; failure is the fate allotted.'[1] It
may be said that some individuals may with luck succeed in
their special aims and rejoice in their success. But this is
merely what Professor James calls 'happy-go-lucky contentment'. Even the most favoured individual is at the
mercy of circumstances and under the shadow of death.

But we have not to consider merely this or that individual. We have to take account of all conscious life and
of all communities of conscious lives in the boundless course
of time. From this point of view there is no actual achievement which can be regarded as in itself finally satisfactory.
There is none which may not carry within it the seeds of
evils which outweigh it. All are at the mercy of what Byron
calls 'circumstance, that unspiritual God and miscreator'.
This holds not only for low, narrow and selfish aims, but for
those which are noble, comprehensive and benevolent, if
they are directed to a result to be attained in a finite time and
under finite conditions. Let the philanthropist succeed in
bringing about the millennium he aspires after: yet he cannot command the future. His work may, in its ultimate
issue, produce more evil than good. In general, the power
of nature, as Spinoza said, infinitely exceeds the power of
man. No finite individual or group of individuals can count
on shaping circumstances in accordance with their special
desires and aspirations.

There is another equally fundamental way in which
finite goods are ultimately unsatisfactory. This may be
expressed in the saying of Hobbes that there is no contentment except in proceeding. Every specific and limited
conation ceases when it is completely fulfilled, and unless it

---

[1] *A Christmas Sermon* (Ethical Studies, Tusitala Ed., vol. 26).

opens out further interests and activities ends in the dissatisfaction of satiety. Thus in the pursuit of knowledge, the
questions which have been completely answered cease to
have interest except in so far as they give rise to further
questions or help to answer them. So with all the limited
and transitory objects of human striving.

2. *Ideal Good and Finite Goods*

It follows that if human life is to be ultimately and in principle worth living—if it is to be a good life—it can be so
only through the pursuit of an ideal good, exempt from
temporal vicissitudes and inexhaustible, so that it can never
give rise to satiety. If there be such a good, it cannot have
its being in isolation from finite values, any more than the
whole of truth can have its being in isolation from special
truths. Rather it must include and complete whatever is
good in finite goods. Any of these, taken as final and sufficient by itself, may be on the whole evil rather than good, so
that it cannot be truly said that we ought to pursue it. But
taken as a step or stage in the realisation of the ideal it
cannot lead to satiety, or be at the mercy of uncontrollable
circumstances, and we can say of it that we ought, as far as
in us lies, to realise it. The ideal good must be such as to
make worth while our finite striving and effort, with all the
painful struggles and disappointments they involve.

But are we justified in asserting that the universal good
so conceived is anything but a figment of our imagination?
Does it really belong to the nature of the universe as
a whole? Is it really implied in the essential incompleteness
of finite values? May it not be that all finite aims are in fact
ultimately doomed, without escape of any sort, to disillusion
and disappointment, so that 'Vanity of vanities' is the last
word? Is there any other reason for denying this position
except that we do not like it? Are we not in danger of merely
assuming something to be true simply because we want it to
be true?

This objection would be fatal if goodness, worth or value consisted simply in being desired or in satisfying desire. Consider the parallel case of the unity of knowledge as correlated with the unity of the universe. This conception would be nonsense if truth simply consisted in being believed. For if this were so, truth would be merely a shifting accident of finite minds. It would vary from individual to individual, and for the same individual at different moments. There could not be even so much unity as is involved in error, contradiction, or questioning. All that could be meant by the essential incompleteness of limited truth would be that beliefs are unstable, giving place to each other in turn. In other words, there would not be any truth or error at all. Knowledge in finite beings presupposes a reality which is predetermined independently of their judgments about it. A belief can be true or erroneous only if it is concerned with what belongs to the constitution of the universe, and not merely to that of the individual as such. Hence the essential incompleteness of the objects of finite knowledge implies the unity of the universe, and not merely instability in the state of the knowing subject.

Now the same holds within the sphere of interest. What we call goodness, worth and value are not such because they satisfy actual desires. Rather, they are what ought to be desired, whether they are so or not. Otherwise they would shift and vary with the variable desires of different individuals and social groups, and also for the same individual or group at different times. There would be no other condition to determine them. The drunkard's craving for drink would be in principle on the same level as the philanthropist's benevolent enthusiasm to redeem him from his drunkenness. If the philanthropist were himself to become a drunkard absorbed in the gratification of his appetite, there would merely be a shifting of values, no transition from higher to lower, or from good to evil. On this view 'pushpin would be as good as poetry and the pig on a level with Socrates'. But to assume this is to take away all that we distinctively mean by goodness, worth and value. Worth or value is something which subsists independently of its being appreciated by you or me. It can be appreciated wrongly as well as rightly. We come to appreciate it, so far as we do so at all, through a gradual development involving trial and failure, strictly analogous to the development of knowledge, involving in like manner trial and failure.

Value then is objective. It belongs to the constitution of the universe, and not merely to that of the individual who appreciates it or fails to appreciate it, or appreciates it wrongly. Hence the incompleteness of finite values is essential incompleteness. It means that finite good cannot be what it is—cannot be good at all—unless it belongs to the self-complete unity of a universal good. We ought to realise what is good; but it cannot be truly said of any end that it ought to be pursued if its achievement may lead, in the long run, to evil rather than good. Yet this is true of all finite goods, if they are taken as ultimate and self-complete. The finite good can be really good, only if it is a partial expression of the one absolute good, which cannot lead to satiety, or be for ever at the mercy of alien circumstances. But if the self-complete good is not to be at the mercy of alien circumstances, it cannot be a mere 'ought to be', making impotent demands on actual existence. On the contrary, its power must be in some way commensurate with its authority. It must have might as it has right. It must be the controlling and all-pervasive scheme of the universe as a whole, including all finite beings, all temporal process, past, present and future.

3. *The Ideal Good is the Implicit and Potential Object of all striving, but our Actual Will and Purpose is often opposed to it*

The unity of the universe has thus two aspects. In one it is the correlate of the unity of knowledge and the logical form of its development in finite beings, and it also emerges, at a certain stage, as itself a more or less explicit object of thought and inquiry. In the other, it is the correlate of unity of interest and the logical form of its development, and also itself emerges, at a certain stage, as an object of will and emotion. It is the only ultimately satisfactory object of desire and will. This cannot, of course, mean that it gratifies all desires which finite beings may happen to feel. It is continually crucifying these, so far as they are not in accordance with it. So far as we seek our good apart from it, we are doomed to failure and disappointment. On the other hand, if we seek our good in it and as part of it, we are ultimately secure. Hence we may say that our activity is always directed towards it implicitly and potentially, however far our actual will and purpose may stray from it and be opposed to it. In this sense it is, in the language of Socrates: 'that good which every soul pursues as the end of all its actions, dimly divining that it is something, but unable to apprehend adequately its nature'. We may express this by saying that the absolute good is that to which the development of the ideal self ultimately tends. The development of the ideal self is cut short by death, and marred and obstructed by the accidents of finite life. But the belief in the absolute good means for us that these obstacles are not final—that, from a more comprehensive point of view, they would be seen to be worth while. This, you may say, is impossible if death ends all for the finite individual. I admit that in that case it is impossible (though there are some who would deny this). But I shall return to this point later.[1]

It is sometimes argued that in assuming the ideal good, we are simply believing something because we wish it to be true. Do we in fact wish it to be true? It is of course obvious that in so far as we desire the ideal good, we desire that it should not be an illusion. But how far does the natural man consistently and predominantly desire the ideal and universal good, and all else only as included in this? Does he

[1] See sections 10 and 11, pp. 321–3.

not continually substitute for it the gratification of his finite
desires, so that if these are denied him, he cries out that life
is a fraud? Men no doubt desire the continuance or renewal
of their lives after death. But they do so in the special and
limited way which happens to appeal to their imagination.
Tell them that the manner of it is incomprehensible to us
and they feel baffled and disappointed. To desire the absolute good we must already have faith in it, but we do not
desire it merely because we have faith in it. In general, the
way which leads in the direction of the good is not the prim-
rose path of dalliance. Many a sinner feels as if he would
rather take the chance of hell than accept the hazards and
hardships of the pursuit of the highest good. Yet in the long
run he must follow the path that leads to it. For in a universe where the absolute good reigns all other ways are
blind alleys.

4. *The Ideal Good as the Scheme of the Universe*

The Good, thus conceived, can be no mere possibility idly
confronting actual existence. It must rather belong to the
constitution of the whole universe in its indivisible unity.
It must be the all-embracing scheme of the whole. We may
express this by saying that in its own way it is eternally real.
But we must be careful how we choose our words and
phrases. It is misleading to assert that it is already realised,
or even that it is eternally realised. For the word 'already'
and the past participle 'realised' inevitably suggest a temporal reference which is entirely out of place. We can never
say of the self-complete good in its completeness: 'Lo, it is
here!' or 'Lo, it is there!'. It is not something which
actually exists at this or that moment of time, still less at all
moments. It is not even 'a far-off divine event to which the
whole creation moves'. It is neither an event nor far off. It
is rather the unity of plan of the whole course of events,
past, present and future. In believing in it, therefore, we do
not commit ourselves to the position that whatever is

is right, but the contrary. What is can never more than partially coincide with what ought to be. It includes much that ought not to be.

5. *Finite Knowledge and Enjoyment of the Good*

We here touch upon the problem of evil. But before directly dealing with it, we must first consider in what way finite minds are capable of knowing or enjoying the absolute good. Plainly there is here a place for what I have called legitimate agnosticism. The finite individual can have no direct insight into the nature of the eternal and infinite good in its self-complete unity. He can only know it as involved in the essential incompleteness of finite values. Otherwise it is incomprehensible to him. But he can understand why and how it is incomprehensible, and in what direction his knowledge necessarily falls short of it. In distinguishing degrees of incompleteness, he sees that he represents it less inadequately and less incorrectly in terms of the comparatively higher than in terms of the lower good. But he can obtain in this way only relatively valid ways of representing it from his own limited point of view, and if he takes these as ultimate and adequate, he inevitably falls into error and meets with insuperable difficulties.

Similarly, the finite individual cannot possess or enjoy the good in its completeness. He can only have his share in it, the share which comes to him in playing his distinctive part within the whole scheme. On the other hand, the good would not be self-complete if each finite individual did not have his distinctive share in it, eternally secured to him and not at the mercy of alien circumstances.

6. *Evil and the Good*

I have said that we are relatively right in representing the absolute good in terms of what to us are higher goods rather than lower, and that this need not lead us astray if we

remember that any finite representation is, as such, necessarily inadequate. But there is one way of representing it
which is not only relatively but absolutely false. It is absolutely false to represent it as evil. For evil and good are
mutually contrary. The good as such cannot be evil, nor the
evil as such good. Yet the complete good, though its goodness can never be evil, must in some way include the evil
which we actually find in the universe. The good must be
essentially incomplete without the evil, and the evil must be
essentially incomplete without it.

It is easy to see how the second part of this statement is
true. Evil has no separate and independent being apart
from what is good. It is parasitic on good and presupposes
it, as error presupposes truth. As it is only truth concerning
which we can make a mistake, so evil is the perversion or
obstruction of what is in itself good. Disease is bad only
inasmuch as the life which struggles to maintain itself
against dissolution is good. Wickedness can be bad only
because the moral order is good. There is, as Dr Ward says,
no independent and positive principle of evil. Imagine
a devil as black as he can be painted, and you will succeed
only by making him a fallen angel or a fallen god. You must
endow him with vast knowledge and insight and energy
and consistency of purpose, and all this is good in itself.
You will end by reverencing him for his burning throne.
Why then is he so bad? Because the worst is the corruption
of the best.

This does not imply that evil is mere negation or privation. On the contrary, inasmuch as good is positive, evil
must be correspondingly positive, just as the strongest man
dies hardest.

Evil then is essentially incomplete, and is incapable of
existing apart from good. It is not so plain that the good is
essentially incomplete without evil. Yet here, too, we have
a significant clue in our own experience. What is good,
or at any rate what is best, for finite beings has no separate
being for them apart from their pursuit of it. It must be

made their own through their own efforts in striving and struggling towards it; and an essential condition of this is that there should be obstacles to strive and struggle against; in other words, there must be evil. Place a man in circumstances such that his every wish and impulse is fulfilled as soon as formed; instead of the highest good the results are moral stagnation and decay and the unrest of satiety. Good could come to such a man only if he set himself to fight against these evils and overcome them.

Note that evil can fulfil this function only if it be really evil and treated as such. If the struggle against it is good, it cannot itself be good. It must be uncompromisingly opposed and hated, never tolerated or welcomed. Fighting a cholera epidemic may bring out all that is best in a man. But it would not do so if he himself caused it or permitted it to occur in order to use it as a means to his own moral development.

7. *Can this Position be maintained in the face of overwhelming Evils?*

We have then a clue in our own experience which enables us to understand in some degree, from our finite point of view, how in principle the complete good may include, or at least might include, evil as an essential condition of its completeness. This position would, I think, have been generally accepted as a matter of course were it not for what is naturally felt as a stupendous difficulty. The clue seems to fail us in a most bewildering way when we fully confront the facts. It fails us in the face of the nature of some of the special evils with which we are actually confronted in experience, and of their appalling and crushing immensity. The academic philosopher or 'mealy-mouthed moralist', in the comparative comfort of his sheltered life, may be blind or may pretend to be blind to all this. But come to grips with reality and his way of talking seems to be ridiculously inadequate and irrelevant.

Let me first say a word on a point which concerns me personally—the position of the academic philosopher. It is not only such as he who put their trust explicitly or implicitly in absolute good as including and transcending evil. It is also the saints and martyrs and men of religious genius—including for this purpose the Crucified One himself. Under this head I rank all who, amid great tribulation and in the teeth of disheartening circumstances, practically pursue ideal good, convinced that the pursuit is not ultimately in vain. I include all those who under such conditions abide by the 'everlasting yea' of Carlyle rather than by the 'everlasting no'. If what is required is practical inspiration and support, it is to such as these that we must look, and not to the philosopher as such, and certainly not to the 'mealy-mouthed moralist'. The philosopher has a different and a vastly humbler task. He has to examine in the dry light of reason the logical presuppositions of the practical attitude which I have described, and to inquire whether these presuppositions are logically tenable or the reverse. But his work is not needless even from a practical point of view. As Bishop Butler said, even speculative difficulties are a trial, and to some the chief trial.

This being understood, let us go back to the original difficulty, treating it, as within our limits we are bound to do, merely as a logical and not as a practical difficulty. The question we are concerned with is whether the nature and the magnitude of the evil we find in the world is logically compatible with the belief in the ultimate goodness of the universe. So far as I can see, however natural and inevitable it may be that this difficulty should be keenly felt, it is, none the less, logically baseless.[1] If evil is a necessary ingredient

---

[1] [The rest of this paragraph as it originally stood is deleted, and a transition rather doubtfully indicated to a point near the beginning of the next paragraph. The deletion may perhaps be due to Ward's marginal note: 'All this will, I fear, strike the reader as very formal and academic.' I have tried to interpret and carry out the intention of the author, but the reader may feel that the argument now left in the text to solve the 'logical difficulty'

in the universal good, then, just as complete good is to us incomprehensible, so the evil must be incomprehensible both in nature and degree, except in so far as we see it to be an indispensable condition of our own development towards good. We can even see that if evil were comprehensible to us in detail, it could not fulfil its function in our own moral development. If it were, so to speak, visibly served out in measured doses, like a wholesome but nasty medicine administered by a wise and just judge, should we not come to make light of it and treat it as a matter of course? Should we not be tempted to treat it as if it were a sort of good, and even

needs further support, and may wish to judge for himself how far the omitted passage, printed below, supplies this: 'Whatever consequences follow from a proposition, and are found to agree with facts, do not refute but corroborate the truth of the proposition. But this is just the position which now confronts us. The eternal and complete good, if it has being at all, cannot, from the nature of the case, be known in its completeness to finite beings. All that they can assert of it unconditionally is what is involved in the very conception of it as the absolute good—that it makes the struggle and the evil of finite lives worth while. All that we can do beyond this is to frame for ourselves, from our limited point of view, comparatively valid ways of representing it. But the modes of representing it, though relatively valid, must always fall immeasurably short of the whole truth, and if we fail to remember how and why and in what direction they are inadequate, they are bound to mislead us. Now if evil is a necessary ingredient in the universal good, then, just as complete good is to us incomprehensible, so the evil must be incomprehensible both in nature and degree. We have indeed in our own experience a valid way of representing to ourselves how in principle the ideal good is essentially incomplete without evil. But more than this we cannot, from the nature of the case, look for. It is absurd to expect in this way to understand, even partially, more than a relatively small part of the evils which we actually confront, so as to be able to see their place and function within the universal scheme. If we start with any such claim, we ought to find ourselves defeated by the staggering immensity of the evil which we vainly seek to comprehend. But what we ought logically to expect agrees with the facts as we find them. There is then, I submit, no logical difficulty. There is indeed an enormous practical difficulty. But with this only practical religion and not philosophy can pretend to deal.

'Evil, then, both in its amount and distribution, and the special ways in which it occurs, is unintelligible to us except in so far as we see it to be an indispensable condition of our own development towards good.'—Ed.]

ourselves do evil that good might come? But under these conditions its function in our own development would disappear. It fulfils this function only inasmuch as it awakes in us unbounded horror and loathing and arouses us to uncompromising antagonism. But this it could never do if it were arranged and distributed and measured out, as we might arrange, distribute and measure if we were planning a universe according to our own puny ideas of justice.

I have not been preaching smooth things. If optimism consists in attempting to make light of evil or to explain it away, then certainly I am no optimist, but rather a pessimist. But in another and deeper sense, the view I have been expounding is the most thoroughgoing optimism conceivable. For on this view evil is nothing separate from and independent of good. It has being only in the development of the good as a struggle against it. It is thus included and transcended by the complete good, which is eternally opposed to it and eternally victorious over it. Hence the vastness of evil, indefinitely surpassing the utmost efforts of finite beings to express in words, or to match in imagination, is an indication of the incomprehensible immensity of the good which transcends and includes it and makes it all worth while.

8. *Good and God*

So far I have spoken only of the absolute good and not of God. But it is hardly necessary to point out that without a God all that I have said is nonsense. The complete good, if indeed it is to be complete, must not be ultimately at the mercy of alien circumstances. It cannot subsist as a mere 'ought to be', making idle demands of a reality which is indifferent to it. There is therefore an actual agency not indifferent to it, which eternally secures its eternal fulfilment within the universe as a whole. 'Not indifferent to it', therefore a mind; 'which secures its fulfilment', therefore a mind which effectively wills it; 'which secures its fulfilment eternally within the universe as a whole', therefore not any finite mind, or collection of finite minds, but a mind which belongs to the fundamental constitution of the universe in its unity—a universal and eternal mind—God, in fact—the God of theism, not of pantheism.

This seems to me to be the most satisfactory form in which to put what has been called the moral argument for the existence of God. Like other arguments, and more than the others, it must not be taken apart from religious experience. It is in actual religious experience that the force of it is felt, even though it may not be explicitly formulated, or may be very imperfectly formulated. What the philosopher can do is to supply, as far as is possible, an abstract account of the nature of the grounds which vaguely underlie human belief in God, so that we may be able to judge whether they are logically defensible.

Starting from the being of the complete good, we may infer the existence of a Universal Mind who wills it as the eternal plan of the universe. It is equally open to us to reverse this process. Quite apart from any reference to good and evil, we have already found many reasons for holding that there is a Universal Mind. But if this be so, it must will the absolute good, and nothing short of this or other than this. For the absolute good is, as Socrates says, 'that which every soul seeks, dimly divining its nature'. It is what the ideal self wills potentially and implicitly. So far as it actually wills what is evil rather than what is good, what is wrong rather than what is right, this can only be due to the conditions of finite existence under which the actual self continually falls short of, and more or less diverges from, the ideal self. But where the ideal self is completely achieved, as it must be in a mind free from finite conditions and the vicissitudes of temporal processes, the distinction between it and the actual self disappears. Thus the universal and eternal mind must will the complete good, just as it must know the complete truth.

9. *God and Evil*

Now that we have introduced the conception of God, it may be expected that we should go back again to the problem of evil and consider the vexed question how the existence of evil is reconcilable with the divine goodness. But this demand is unjustifiable. No new question arises at this stage. In principle we have already dealt with the topic in considering the absolute good without any reference to the divine mind. God is absolutely good only because he wills the absolute good. There is nothing greater or better than this that the utmost stretch of omniscience could realise. But the absolute good essentially involves struggle against evil, evil corresponding to the incomprehensible immensity of the complete good. God must will a good which includes evil as something not to be tolerated, but hated, opposed and destroyed. If we suppose Him to will some imaginary good other than this, then, assuming His omnipotence, we should be ascribing to Him not infinite benevolence but infinite self-indulgence. Either He would not be all-powerful, or He would not be supremely good.

If this seems too bold a statement, it is at least better founded than the familiar thesis that if God were both good and all-powerful, there would be no evil. This contention owes its apparent cogency to a crude anthropomorphism, which takes too literally our human ways of representing the Infinite and Eternal Being as it is in its own positive nature. From our finite point of view we inevitably tend to represent God as using means to an end which are not included in the end itself. Now a man proceeding in this way may reach his end through various alternative means, some simple, direct and harmless, others relatively clumsy and difficult, and involving more or less physical and even moral evil. But the better the man the more reluctant will he be to use means in themselves bad, unless the end is sufficiently good to justify them, and unless alternative courses are not open to him. Indeed, if the only path to his goal is through moral wrongdoing, the good man as such will refuse to commit it for the sake of any end, however attractive. For this would be what is called doing evil that good may come. On the other hand, the more wise and powerful the man is, the more able he will be to reach his end by comparatively direct and easy means, and to avoid including in these what is in itself repugnant to him. Now (the argument goes) suppose him to be perfectly good and at the same time all-powerful: are we not bound to assert that, being perfectly good, he would not pursue an end by means in any way bad, if it could be otherwise attained; and that, being all-powerful, he would be able to attain it otherwise? He would indeed be able to attain it without the use of any means at all; for the relation of means and ends conditions the practical activity only of finite beings. God then, if there were a God, would immediately produce the highest possible good without any admixture of evil.

This would be a sound argument if the underlying assumption were true, that evil can condition good only as a means to a good end. It would then follow irresistibly that, since an Omniscient Being has no need of such means, or indeed of any means, if He were also perfectly good there would be no evil in the universe. Now in fact there is colossal evil; does it not follow on this assumption that there is no Being who is at once omnipotent and perfectly good?

But the underlying assumption is utterly false. It is false that the only way in which evil can condition good is as a means to a good end. We can see this in our own finite experience. The surgeon curing a disease by a painful operation does indeed use means in themselves bad. But he does not use the disease itself as a means to its own cure. Yet, unless the disease existed, he could not accomplish the good work of curing it. Or, to revert to a previous illustration, fighting a cholera epidemic may bring out what is best in a man. But it does so only if and so far as he does not himself will the cholera as a means to his own moral improvement. Yet he could not fight the cholera if there were no cholera to fight. Of these two ways in which evil can condition good, that of means to an end and that of inclusion in good as something to be hated and abolished, it seems to be very frequently taken for granted that the latter is confined to finite individuals, and that for an Infinite Being evil, if it exists at all, can only be a means to an end. Now my whole contention is that this view is preposterous; it exactly reverses the truth. God cannot need evil as a means to good. But if He wills the highest good, He wills a good which is essentially incomplete without the struggle against evil, and is therefore essentially incomplete without evil as something to be hated and overcome. Thus evil for Him is not a means to an end, but is included in the end itself, as belonging to its intrinsic nature.

It is easy and futile to play upon the word omnipotence; if the word is to have any intelligible meaning, it must mean the power to realise all possibilities, but not impossibilities. For instance, it does not include the ability to have the good which presupposes struggle against evil without the struggle, or to have the struggle without evil to fight. Such power is not omnipotence. The proper name for it is nonsense—not divine nonsense, but our own nonsense.

10. *Finite Individuals must enjoy a Personal Share of the Absolute Good*

The terms *end* and *means* cannot properly be used except as correlatives. In the strict use of language, therefore, we ought not to speak of the absolute good as an *end* of the Divine activity. For this inevitably suggests that it is pursued by means which are not included in it. When we have fully grasped this, we are in a position to deal with a most mischievous fallacy. It is sometimes held or suggested that the share of finite individuals in the absolute good cannot belong to the finite individuals themselves as such, but is only a result to which their striving and struggling and pain and failure are merely tributary—a result enjoyed not by them, but by the Infinite Mind. I admit that some who may appear to teach this doctrine do not really mean it. I do not suppose, for instance, that Dr Bosanquet really means it. But if and so far as this may be seriously intended, it introduces the finite distinction of means and end, where there is no place for it. It makes the lives of finite individuals, with all their tribulations and failures, a means to the absolute good as an end, instead of including them in it. But the absolute good cannot be itself the complete good, unless it completes the good for *them*. To call them 'mere appearances' makes no difference. They are, at any rate, appearances which strive and struggle, enjoy and suffer, aspire and are disappointed. This being so, to treat their sufferings and tribulations merely as means to an end is what is condemned as 'doing evil that good may come'.

Good can include evil only by overcoming and transcending it. But under what conditions can evil be said to be overcome? It is not enough that it should lead in some way or other to a greater good behind it. We do not overcome the evil of disease in one patient by learning from it how to cure the like disease in other patients. We do not overcome the evil of robbery by using the ill-gotten gains to found a hospital. Evil is the perversion or obstruction of what is otherwise good. It cannot, in any relevant sense, be overcome except in the victorious development of the very good which it infects and mars. Hence evil, so far as it affects a finite individual, must be overcome, if at all, in and for the very individual who suffers and sins.[1]

---

[1] [The following sentences, relevant to the above section, are perhaps worth rescuing from an earlier passage in this chapter, which was deleted by the author: 'I cannot see how the good can be self-complete if any individual misses his share in it, so that for him evil rather than good is ultimate. I cannot understand how one individual can be substituted for others. Each has his own unique development, and cannot be treated as merely a counter in the game of another, even though this other is eternal and infinite'.—Ed.]

11. *Immortality*

This demand constitutes all that is essential in the doctrine of immortality, and the demand itself must not, for a moment, be confused with our feeble and ignorant fancies concerning the way in which it may be met. These may turn out intrinsically unsatisfactory, or they may be seen to conflict with facts. The general position is not, on that account, affected in the smallest degree. There is, however, one point on which I feel bound to insist. To speak of immortality is to cheat ourselves with words unless the demand is really met, without subterfuge or evasion. It is, for instance, futile to say that it is already eternally fulfilled, except in the sense that the eternal nature of the universe requires its fulfilment. It is, if anything, more futile to talk of 'living on in the memory of posterity'. On the other hand, some who appear to deny or doubt immortality, and even say that they do so, may none the less believe all that is essential to it. They may, for instance, hold that the destiny of the individual soul is to be absorbed or incorporated in the Eternal Mind. The vital question then arises whether, in being so absorbed or incorporated, the finite individual loses his individual identity—loses conscious unity with his own past—or, on the contrary, possesses this in the fullest possible way. If identity is lost, there can be no immortality. If it is retained, we have not a denial of the general principle, but a special form of it.[1]

12. *The Meaning of God's Hatred of Evil*

It follows from all that I have said that the complete good includes evil only as something to be hated and abolished.

[1] It is a form which baffles our imagination and may therefore seem unsatisfactory and even repugnant to many of us. None the less, I do not see how anyone can be justified in denying the possibility of it, or in denying that in this way the strivings and struggles of finite existence would find complete fulfilment. Certainly if we are to pin ourselves to one special view, this has in many respects great advantages. It is akin to the teaching of Dean Inge, and I am not sure that Dr Bosanquet really intends to reject it.

The Universal Mind must therefore hate it in a degree which to us is incomprehensibly great. How are we to represent this to ourselves from our finite point of view? We can do so only in terms of our own experience. But we learn to hate evil, as we ought to hate it, in suffering from it, and by the struggle against it in ourselves and in others. Are we then to think of the Eternal Mind as suffering in this way? Are we to ascribe to it sentiments and emotions such as we feel ourselves? Clearly the truth must be widely removed from this. The Eternal Mind is above the ebb and flow of things; it is 'rest at the heart of endless agitation'.

Yet if we try to escape altogether this sort of anthropomorphism we inevitably fall into another which is incomparably more false and mischievous. We tend to think of the Eternal Mind as enjoying an Epicurean calm, aloof from the struggle and evil in which finite individuals are immersed. We regard it as a spectator of the battlefield, but not as itself involved in the strife. But this way of correcting anthropomorphism takes a fundamentally false direction. It is just as if we were to represent the divine knowledge as ignorance, merely because all analogies drawn from knowledge in finite beings are essentially inadequate to convey positive insight into the nature of an Infinite and Eternal Being as such. Divine knowledge differs from ours in being more than we can understand, not in being less than we can understand. Similarly, when we say that God hates evil, the word 'hate' is misleading in so far as we are unable in imagination to divest hatred of the forms which it assumes in finite beings. But let us make no mistake about the nature and direction of the error. We err not because the Divine antagonism to evil is less than we can figure to ourselves through finite analogies, but because it is incomprehensibly greater. 'The Lord God is a consuming fire' and 'Man of War'. He is so because He is Love, and His tender mercies are over all His works.

The same holds good for suffering in finite beings. This must, I venture to think, have its incomprehensible counterpart in the Divine nature. This may appear a hazardous position. But I cannot think that it is too bold, when I consider the appeal made to the religious consciousness by the Christian doctrine of a crucified God. It is significant also that the Christian creed corrects what might otherwise be too anthropomorphic in its teaching by holding that it is God the Son and not God the Father who suffers. In one aspect of His nature He is truly represented as participating in the misery of finite being. In another He is eternally triumphant and enjoys eternal blessedness.

INDEX

330 INDEX

Eternal Being. *See* Mind, Universal

Evil, of conflict between theoretical and practical interest, 16; and finite individuals, 31; and the Universal Mind, 31, 229; compatible with the goodness of the finite world, 35; ch. XXI *passim*; essential to good, 312–17, but not as a means to it, 320–1; dependent on good, but not a mere negation, 313

EWING, A. C., xxiv

Experience, immediate, not itself knowledge, but a precondition of a way of knowing, 68; of subjective processes as well as of sensa, but not of the past, 69–70, yet essential to memory, 137; of particulars, not of universals, 140; ultimate source of all knowledge, 140–1, 287. *See also* (1) Incompleteness, of what is immediately experienced; (2) Knowledge by acquaintance; (3) Sensa

Extension, visual and tactual, 127–31, 147, 149, 170–2. *See also* (1) Shape and size, awareness of; (2) Touch

FECHNER, G. T., his form of monadism, 218–21

FERRIER, J. F. on self-awareness, 245

FICHTE believes in a self-differentiating spiritual principle, 283

FINDLAY, J. N., xli n.

FLÜGEL, J. C., xxxvi

FOCH, Marshal, his term 'assurance', 12

Force, recognised in sense-perception, but has no counterpart in the content of immediate experience, 177–8; conception of, defended against the charge of anthropomorphism, 251–2

Foreknowledge, 229–30

'Formal' and 'objective' being, 279–80, 281–2

Free will, 229–30, 303

FREUD, xxxv, xxxviii; on sexual examples of mental conflict, 298

GAUTAMA as representing the claims of the religious consciousness, 20

Gestalt psychology, xxxix–xl *and* n.

Getting to know, interest in, 273–4, 289–91

GIFFORD LECTURES, xix–xxiv, xxvii, xxxii, xxxiii; 1–2, 17, 77 n., 293 n.

GOD, difficulty of being 'ethically neutral' about, 6–9; indifferent to belief in His own existence, 18; as revealed in religious experience, 19–20; limitations of our knowledge of His nature, 27–34, 223, 241–3; does not create possibilities and cannot do the impossible, 97, 230, or have foreknowledge of an undetermined future, 229–30; not necessarily the Creator of matter, 230–2, 243; argument from design for the existence of, 317–18; does not use means to ends, 319–21; as suffering, 324–5; in Berkeley's philosophy, 123–6, 124 n.; in Leibniz's philosophy, does not create the eternal truths, 97; gives reason to each soul at birth, 218. *See also* Mind, Universal

Good, ideal (absolute, self-complete, universal), ch. XXI *passim*; and finite goods, 307–9; objectivity of, 308–9; the object of all striving, 309–11; as the scheme of the Universe, 311–12; finite knowledge of and enjoyment of, 312, 321–2 *and* n.; incomplete without evil, 312–17, 322; and God, 317–18. *See also* Evil

Goods, finite, do not give final satisfaction, 305–7; and ideal good, 307–9; objectivity of, 308–9

Hallucinations, 143–4

HAMILTON, W., xxxviii

332
INDEX

Inference, involved in seeing and feeling, 117, 118; physical objects not known by, 132–4, nor are universals, 134; implies universals, 134, 141–2; relation between premises and conclusion in, 138–9, 141; self-evidence a limiting case of, 139–40; its secondary role in knowledge of other selves, 246 n., 246–50. *See also* Induction

Infinite series, possible but not as self-complete, 50–2

INGE, W. R., on immortality, 323 n.

INQUISITION, SPANISH, involves practical postulates inseparable from intolerance, 17

Interaction, simultaneous relation of, 175

Interest, theoretical and practical, 11–16, 18, 296–7; implies knowledge, 289, and is implied by it, 290; has positive and negative aspects, 289–90, and affective and conative aspects, 289–90; involves object, feeling and a relation between them, 290–1. *See also* (1) Attention; (2) Interest, unity of

Interest, unity of, together with unity of knowledge constitutes unity of the mind-complex, 261, 265; ch. XIX *passim*; is interest in unity, 291–2, 293 n.; degrees of, 292–3 *and* n.; ideal, 305. *See also* (1) Conflict, mental; (2) Dissociation, mental; (3) Good, ideal

JAMES, W., on religious experience, 22; on a system of cutaneous equivalences, 189; his 'transmission' theory of the relation between the Universal Mind and the physical world, 239–41; on 'happy-go-lucky contentment', 306

JOSEPH, H. W. B., xli

Judgment not a cognitive act, 275–6

KANT, xxxv; on the relation of particulars to universals, 106; on the place of sense-perception in knowledge of the external world, 114, 140–1; on the productive imagination, 149; on matter as phenomenon and as it is in itself, 199; and Russell, 106; and Hume, 109

KER, ELLA, xxx

KNIGHT, R., xxv n.

Knowing, not a state or an act, 203, 272–8, but a condition of all subjective states or acts, 277–8; and being, inseparable, 281–5; does not change or create its object, 283–5

Knowledge and opinion, 89–91

Knowledge by acquaintance and knowledge about, Russell's theory of, 54–8, 65–76, 120, 133–5, 140. *See also* (1) Experience, immediate; (2) Sensa

Knowledge by description, Russell's theory of, 59–66; as asserting probability, not necessary connexion, criticised, 82–4

Knowledge of matter. *See* Matter, knowledge of

Knowledge, theory of, xl–xliv

Knowledge, unity of. *See* Unity, cognitive

Knownness, a unique fact, 278–80

KOFFKA, K., xxxix, xl *and* n.

LAZARUS, M., xxix

LEIBNIZ, denies that God created the eternal truths, 97; on our knowledge of the external world, 114; his monadism, 215–18, 238; on the individual's knowledge of the universe, 268; and Kant, 109; and Ward, 238 *and* n.

Light as a medium of perception, 172

Living matter, genesis of, 259–60

Local signs, 156, 162–3, 168–71

LOCKE, xxviii, xxxvii, xxxviii; on substance, 73; on active and passive powers, 94, 183; on sense as the channel of the ideas of external things, 112, 146; on the limits of knowledge, 242–3; on universals and possibilities as 'the work of the understanding', 282–3

Logic, Hegel's, 44

Logic, symbolic, and pure mathematics, concerned with universal relations between universals, 58, and with their possible as well as actual instances, 91–2, 93, 106; their subject-matter discovered, not created, by our thinking, 89–90

Logically primary, as distinct from psychologically primitive, 142–3

LOTZE, his monadism, 215–18

LUCRETIUS not ethically neutral, 8

MCDOUGALL, W., xxxviii *and* n., xl

MACE, C. A., xxv n., xxxiii, xl n., xli, xlix

MACKIE, J., xxiv, 86 n.

MCTAGGART, J. M. E., xxx

Manual of Psychology, A, the author's, xx, xxx–xxxi, xxxviii, xl

Materialism, xix, xx, xxi; means the dependence of mind on the finitude of finite things, 31; already rejected in *Mind and Matter*, 31, 110, 209, 210 *and* n., 262

Mathematics, pure. *See* Logic, symbolic

Matter, common-sense presuppositions about, 111–13; as including sensa, 196–9; as phenomenon and as it is in itself, 199–201, 209, 234–6

Matter, knowledge of, Book III *passim*; common-sense presuppositions about, 112–13; the philosophical problem about, 113–16; through primary sense-knowledge, 116–19, 142–6; the part played by sensa in, 119–34, 142–9, 199–201; as a causal system, ch. IX *passim*, 185–6; in its quantitative relations, ch. X *passim*; through measurement by superposition, 186–91. *See also* (1) Perception, external and internal; (2) Qualities, primary and secondary; (3) Sensa

'Mechanical and Teleological Causality', the author's contribution to symposium on, xlv–xlvi

MEINONG, xli n.

Memory, xlii; is aware of its own inadequacy, 75; a primary way of knowing, 75, 117–18; develops from the incompleteness of present experience, 132 n., 135–7; Russell's view that there is acquaintance by, criticised, 57, 69–70, 75. *See also* Retentiveness

Metaphysics, constructive, excluded if there is no universe, 23–4; its purpose and method, 107–9; Russell's rejection of, 53

MILL, J. S., on permanent possibilities of sensation, 95, 124, criticised, 125–7; holds that we primarily perceive only our own sensa, 119, 122–3, and that sensa exist only as perceived, 123; the relation between the physical object and 'its' sensa in terms of his theory, 128–9; on inference, 141–2, 179; and Berkeley and Russell, 62 n., 95, 119, 122–32

Mind, xxi, xliii, xlv–xlvii; fundamental in the nature of the universe, 22, 26, 110, Book IV *passim*; and body, 110, Book IV *passim* (esp. ch. XV); and matter, Book IV *passim*; finite, dependent on other mind, 210–11, 237. *See also* (1) Mind, Universal; (2) Self

336 INDEX

Psychoanalysis and dissociated dispositions, 299, 304

Psychologically primitive as distinct from logically primary, 142–3. *See also* Sense-knowledge, primary

Qualities, are not universals, 77–9; primary and secondary, 116, 191–7, 200–1; Russell on, 77–8

Questioning, implies knowledge of a field of inquiry, 268–9; a form of interest or attention, 274, 290; implies cognition, but not itself cognitive, 275–7; presupposed by the act of judging, 276

'Real Being and Being for Thought', the author's article on, 91 n., 104 n.

Reality, as relative to (*a*) possibility, (*b*) appearance, 99, 107, 227–8. *See also* (1) Appearance; (2) Possibilities

REID, T., on sense-knowledge, 119

Relatedness as distinguished from intrinsic characters, 54–5, 58, 67–8, 73, 76. *See also* knowledge by acquaintance and knowledge about

Relations, as particular as what they relate, 77–8; idealist theory of their mind-dependence, 281–3, rejected by neo-realists, 283–5; regarded by Russell as universals, 77

Relativity, theory of, 191

Religious (*a*) beliefs, 3–4, 6–10, 18–22; (*b*) consciousness, 20, 108; (*c*) experience, 19–22, 255–7; (*d*) emotion, 24–5

Repetition, constant, 181–3

'Reply to Mr Joseph', the author's article entitled, xxxi, xlii

Resistance, effort against, 157–9, 166, 172, 186

Retentiveness, 238. *See also* Memory

ROBERTSON, CROOM, xxviii

RUSSELL, BERTRAND, xxiii, xxxiii; on theoretical and practical interest, 4–5; his pluralism, 10–11, 36–7, 39–40, 43, 46–7, 53, 58, 269, criticised, 66–8; on the possibility of infinite collections, 50; his theory of knowledge, ch. IV *passim*; and constructive metaphysics, 53, 66, 109; on knowledge by acquaintance and knowledge about, 54–8, 65–76, 133; on sense-data, 56–7, 61–2 *and* n., 70–4, 115 n., 119, 122, 127; on knowledge of universals, 57–8; on memory-knowledge, 57, 69–70, 75; on knowledge by description, 59–66, 71, 82–6; on induction, 62 n., 86–8 *and* n.; on universals and particulars, 77–8, 80–1, 89–91, 106; on probability and necessity, 82–4, 86–8; on permanent possibilities of sensation, 95, 127; on error, 104; on Hegelianism, 39–40 *and* n., 43, 46–7; and Berkeley and Mill, 62 n., 95, 119, 122, 127; and Hume, 109; and Kant, 106

ST ANDREWS, UNIVERSITY OF, xxxii, xxxiii, xxxvi

ST FRANCIS, as representing the claims of the religious consciousness, 24

ST JOHN'S COLLEGE, CAMBRIDGE, xix, xxv, xxvi, xxix, xxxiii

SCHILLER, F. C. S., his pragmatism, 4

SCHOPENHAUER, his pessimism, 31

Scepticism does not imply 'ethical neutrality', 89

Science, physical, deals with possible instances, 91, 93–5; its presuppositions about matter, 111–13; and philosophy, 113–15, 119; and common sense, 115–16; method of, 180–1; its view of primary and secondary qualities, 191–3, criticised, 193–5; and mind-stuff theories, 211. *See also* Construction, ideal

INDEX

337

Scotus, Duns, his agnosticism, 24

Self, xlv, xlvi–xlviii; embodied, 245; unity of the, 261, 264–6, 289–93; empirical, 264–5; pure, 264–5, 272, 291; actual and ideal, 293 n., 303, 305, 318; Russell on knowledge of, 57. *See also* (1) Conflict, mental; (2) Interest, unity of; (3) Unity, cognitive

Self-awareness, 244–5, 248; Russell on, 57; Ferrier on, 245

Self-completeness, 46–7, 50–1, 58, 60, 102. *See also* Incompleteness

Self-contradiction, 42–7, 50

Self-evidence, 47–54, 139–40

Selves, knowledge of other, ch. XVI *passim*; not reached through inference starting solely from self-knowledge, 246–50, but involves original reference to other psychical being, 248–50, though existence of particular selves is inferred, 246 n., 247–8; animistic basis of, 250–4

Sensa (sense-data, data of experience, contents of immediate experience, sense-appearances, sense-impressions, contents of sense-experience, presentations), xli–xliv; like mental states, known by immediate experience, 70, but themselves material, not mental, 120, 197, 200, 208, 233, nor physical, 122, 197–9; incompleteness of, 81–2, 112–13, 132 n., 133–4, 141, 144–6, 198–9; their function in our knowledge of matter, Book III *passim*; partial extracts from a material continuum, 112, 190, 198, 208–9, 234–5; only exist as experienced by a mind, 204–8, but not necessarily a finite mind, 120; visual, different from other sensa, 203–7; and subjective states, 203–4, 207–8; and mental images, 208; in internal perception, ch. VIII *passim*; order of presentation of, how distinguished from the external order, 150–3, 157–9; subjective control of, 151, 153–8; organic, 155–7; Russell on, 56–7, 61–2 *and* n., 70–4, 115 n., 119, 122, 127. *See also* (1) Extension, visual and tactual; (2) Touch

Sensation, permanent possibilities of, 95, 124–31, 152–3

Sense-knowledge, primary, 112, 116–20, ch. VII *passim*; not inferential, 132–3; depends on incompleteness of what is immediately experienced, 133–4; its data, 142–4; internal perception a survival of, 156–7; correlation begins in, 167–8, as does apprehension of causal relations, 173–4; the logical basis of our knowledge of matter, 190. *See also* Sensa

Sense-perception. *See* Sensa

Sensory-continuum, xliii

Sentience, organic, 206 *and* n.

Series, infinite, can exist, but not as self-complete, 50–2. *See also* Beginning, absolute

Shakespeare, his *Hamlet* an example of the development of the possible in imagination, 97–8; his *Sonnets* an example of teleological order, 261

Shand, A. F., xxxiii, xxxvii

Shelley, his atheism, 10; and James's 'transmission' theory, 239

Shell-shock, 298–9

Sidgwick, H., xxvi

Sight and touch. *See* (1) Extension, visual and tactual; (2) Touch

Sin, 7. *See also* Evil

Socrates, on error in the *Theaetetus*, 104; on pursuit of the Good, 310, 318

Solipsism, 249

'Some Fundamental Points in the Theory of Knowledge', the author's article on, xlii n.

Spearman, C., xxx, xxxviii

on their relation to induction, 86–8 *and* n.; Russell's theory of their independent existence criticised, 89–91, 106. *See also* Possibilities

Universe, unity of, xxii, xlviii–xlix; assumed by common sense, but denied by some philosophers, 1–2, 107–8; a presupposition of the religious consciousness, 22, 108, and of all metaphysical construction, 22–3, 108, and of agnosticism, 23–4; chs. III and IV *passim*; as a universal form of knowledge, 167–8; causal unity one aspect of, 176; implied by cognitive unity, 265–7, 271, 309–10; contributes to proof of the existence of a Universal Mind, 286–8; implied by unity of interest, 309–12; and the ideal Good, 311–12; Russell's rejection of, 10–11, 36–7, 53, 58, 269, criticised, 66–8, 107; Hegelian doctrine of, 37–50; Fechner on, 219–20. *See also* (1) Agnosticism; (2) Incompleteness; (3) Pluralism

Variation, concomitant, 180–1, 183

VOLTAIRE, his character Zadig as typifying scientific method, 180

Voluntary decision, 96–7, 276–7. *See also* Activity, voluntary

WAITZ, T., xxix

WARD, J., xxiii–xxiv, xxvi, xxxiv, xxxv, xxxviii, xl, xliii; on the effect of belief in God, 7–8; his term 'presentation-continuum', 147; on reinstatement of former sensations, 149, 238; on variations in size and shape of cutaneous sensa, 168–9; says that shape is not a sensum, 169 n.; on sensa as differentiations of a homogeneous presentation-continuum, 205; on general and organic sentience, 206 n.; disavows isolated monads, 238 n.; referred to, on interpretation of mental heredity, 239 n.; on the author's view that the cat's knowledge presupposes the unity of the universe, 267 n.; on animals' lack of free ideas, 271; denies a positive principle of evil, 313; on the author's treatment of evil, 315 n.

Whole, knowledge of, through part, 74–5, 287. *See also* Incompleteness

Wilde Readership in Mental Philosophy, xxix

Will. *See* (1) Activity, voluntary; (2) Voluntary decision

WILSON, J. COOK, xxxi

WISDOM, JOHN, xl

Wishes, vanity of human, 306–7

WORDSWORTH, as representing the claims of the religious consciousness, 20; quoted, on 'proud philosophy', 254; his *Lines Written near Tintern Abbey* quoted, 254; his 'happy warrior' as typifying the highest degree of unity of interest, 293

WRIGHT, J. N., xxv n.

WUNDT on pain, 208

Zadig, Voltaire's character, as typifying scientific method, 180